GEORGE DIGBY:
HERO AND VILLAIN.

By Roy Digby Thomas.

authorHOUSE™

1663 LIBERTY DRIVE, SUITE 200
BLOOMINGTON, INDIANA 47403
(800) 839-8640
WWW.AUTHORHOUSE.COM

© *2005 Roy Digby Thomas. All Rights Reserved.*

No part of this book may be reproduced, stored in a retrieval system, or transmitted by any means without the written permission of the author.

First published by AuthorHouse 09/08/05

ISBN: 1-4208-6776-8 (sc)

Library of Congress Control Number: 2005905719

Printed in the United States of America
Bloomington, Indiana

This book is printed on acid-free paper.

Painting of George Digby by Van Dyck on the cover reproduced by kind permission of the trustees of Dulwich Picture Gallery

Acknowledgements.

This book has taken four years to research, write and prepare for publication. Over that period, I have received help and support from a number of quarters, and it is fair to say that the book would not have been published without this help.
    I owe a particular debt of gratitude to Dr Stephen Wright, an historian specialising on the seventeenth century, who guided me across the many minefields facing an unwary amateur, and who provided invaluable input into the content of the book. He pointed me in the right direction several times, and revealed new sources from which I gained additional data on George Digby. Moreover, he worked tirelessly and constructively to help me complete the task.
    Early drafts of the book were in a form quite unlike the finished article. To my son, Warren, my wife, Eileen, and my friend, Jim Chaffey, thank you for the hours you put in identifying errors and suggesting improvements.
    Finally, to the many reference libraries I turned for research, thank you for your readiness to help, your prompt response to my requests, and guidance through the jungle.

Roy Digby Thomas.

Contents.

Acknowledgements.	v
Introduction.	ix
Chapter 1. Childhood.	1
Chapter 2. Home In England.	14
Chapter 3. The Parliamentarian.	25
Chapter 4. Strafford.	41
Chapter 5. Driven Into Exile.	54
Chapter 6. Parting Of The Ways.	68
Chapter 7. Exile.	77
Chapter 8. Civil War.	91
Chapter 9. The King's Chief Adviser.	114
Chapter 10. Things Fall Apart.	133
Chapter 11. Endgame.	143
Chapter 12. Defeat.	166
Chapter 13. Ireland.	184
Chapter 14. Exile In France.	203
Chapter 15. Attempts To Regain The Throne.	220
Chapter 16. Restoration.	245
Chapter 17. Final Days.	271
Epilogue.	279
Appendix.	285
Reference Sources.	288
Bibliography.	290
Notes.	294
Index.	309

Introduction.

The subject of this book, George Digby, has been described as one of the most brilliant minds of his time, a man at the heart of momentous events in the seventeenth century. He played a prominent part in politics, in the Royalist army during the Civil Wars in England, as a member of King Charles II's entourage in exile and as a courtier after the Restoration. Yet he was a man of extraordinary contrasts. Walpole summed up George's life as follows: "A singular person, whose life was one contradiction...... With great parts, he always hurt himself and his friends; with romantic bravery, he was always an unsuccessful commander."[1]

Charming, witty, intelligent, daring and brave, he attracted crowned monarchs, statesmen and great soldiers, who all bestowed patronage upon him. He made and then squandered a fortune several times over. At the same time he managed to infuriate colleagues and enemies alike. Close to the throne, with the persuasive powers to make his influence felt, he achieved much less than many of his contemporaries who were in less fortunate positions. A one-time close friend of one of the intellectual giants of the age, Edward Hyde, Earl of Clarendon, George was ultimately the chief architect of that great man's downfall and exile. Always fascinating, he was seldom still, forever dreaming up bright ideas, then dropping them as suddenly as he had thought of them.

History has been unkind to George Digby. Edward Hyde, who had been a close friend in his youth, became his bitterest enemy in his latter years, and wrote critically of him in his memoirs, and in his famous "History of the Rebellion." Hyde's judgement is frequently accepted as the standard, yet it must be seen in the context of his animosity towards George arising from attempts to have him impeached for treason. Hyde wrote his major works late in life after having been exiled, so his opinion of George was coloured by the bitterness between them. He had, in earlier times, been full of admiration for George, and a staunch political ally. Hyde was a man of intense prejudices who became cantakerous and out of sorts with society and his contemporaries in later life; George was not the only prominent courtier to suffer severe criticism from him. Even Prince Rupert, the king's nephew, was represented as "little more than a swashbuckling troublemaker, invariably in the wrong in every dispute that arose."[2]

George reached his highest position at court during the first English Civil War, when he was Secretary of State to King Charles I. Both as a soldier and then as a close adviser to the king, he was in the thick of the action throughout the war. Many of the Royalists' failings during that Civil War have been laid at George's door. His conflict with the hero Prince Rupert, who commanded the Royalist army, has frequently been remarked upon as a chief cause of Royalist failings. George has been criticised as an incompetent general, a poor strategist and an unrealistic adviser, as opposed to the dashing prince, who impressed everyone with his bravery and panache on the battlefield. The charge of unrealistic optimism against George relates to the latter stages of the war, when he can be seen telling everyone that the Royalists are close to victory, and that everything will be all right. Yet correspondence shows that he was, in truth, fully aware of the king's plight, and pessimistic about the outcome of the war. It can be argued that at a time when many of those closest to King Charles accepted defeat, including Rupert, George's was a lone voice sustaining the Royalist war effort.

It must also be remembered that at the start of the war, George had no military experience whatsoever: he learnt as he went along. Yet time and again he was praised by seasoned soldiers for his courage and willingness to lead. In the years that followed he could point to several significant victories.

By the end of the war his opinion, which was influential, can be argued to have much merit. At critical points in the war, if some of his more visionary ideas had been followed, the outcome of the war may have been different and it will be one of the objectives of this book to examine these questions.

Less frequently has Rupert's performance been critically examined. Rupert's impulsiveness, his impatience and rudeness towards colleagues, led to rifts which could have been avoided. He was no diplomat, and made no attempt to win colleagues to his point of view. He was a professional soldier, and saw the war in terms of conflict to conclusion. Brought up in Continental Europe, his early military experience there led him to adopt harsh and mercenary tactics when laying siege to towns, creating resentment and antagonism in his opponents. He was therefore no help to the king in negotiating a peaceful settlement. Nor was he blameless on the battlefield. In the early stages he too often abandoned his colleagues in pursuit of the defeated, cutting them down and pillaging baggage trains before returning to the scene of the battle, too late to influence its ultimate outcome. Correspondence between Rupert and George throws an illuminating light on their relationship, and the mind sets of the two men. They were both at the heart of the Royalist campaign during the Civil War, and it will be argued that of the two George emerges with the greater credit.

George was not trusted by his contemporaries. His sudden changes of direction, his persuasiveness in debate, his rather daring (or madcap?) schemes, led to charges of inconstancy and, worse, treason. Many historians had very poor opinions of him. This is Derek Wilson, writing in The King and the Gentleman: "Digby was too much governed by his passions to have the intellectual stability necessary for a Royal councillor. He had entered the Long Parliament as a bitter opponent of the court but raised a troop of horse for the King in the outbreak of war. He had bayed for Strafford's impeachment, then opposed his Condemnation. He had championed Parliamentary privilege, then supported the arrest of the five members. He had been impeached for treason by the Commons and fled to Holland. He had served gallantly under Rupert, then fallen out with him. Anyone who had anything to do with George Digby learned not to trust him - except, it seems, the King and Queen."[3]

Yet he fascinated the leading men and women of his generation, and achieved high office in the service of two kings. The Venetian Ambassador described him as a young man combining "high birth with remarkable prudence and unequalled ability."[4] His optimism and positive approach in the face of misfortune often contrasted with the gloom of courtiers who wished they were somewhere else. This made him a congenial companion, a welcome presence to hard-pressed leaders. It can, and will be argued, that many of his changes of direction were driven by his convictions and moral courage, his desire to do the right thing, rather than caprice. This was not fickleness; it was a man at the heart of important decisions being honest with his colleagues and himself – even if it meant changing his mind. Would that some of our modern politicians possessed such integrity!

George was a valuable envoy, representing the king's interests to the rulers of Spain and France. Unusually among Englishmen of the age, he travelled widely and moved easily in Continental European society. Fluent in Spanish and French, and having lived for many years in both Spain and France, he was one of the first Europeans. Through his travel George had a wider vision of European affairs than most Englishmen, and therefore an appreciation of what was possible.

The aim of this biography is to present George in a fair light, and examine his influence upon seventeenth century Europe. Many of the charges raised against him, such as those of Derek Wilson, above, can be refuted and explained in rational terms. While much of the criticism levelled against him can be justified, he has not been given adequate credit for his achievements. In particular, apart from Ann Sumner's doctoral thesis, insufficient attention has been given to his Parliamentary career. There can be little doubt that he was a great orator, able to influence and persuade his fellow Parliamentarians with the power of his speeches and the force of his arguments. Many of his speeches resonate with modern politics, and stand as true today as they did then. He was a fearless defender of Parliamentary democracy and the rights of elected members, and what he stood for remains valid today. His words are still quoted from time to time in the Commons.

Perhaps most of all, however, the life of George Digby is an intriguing insight into the springs of power and influence in those momentous times, and his participation illuminates the developments which led to our modern democratic state. His story reflects that of seventeenth century England in general and the Royal court in particular.

Chapter 1.

Childhood.

In an age when patronage by the monarch was all-important to an aspiring young nobleman in England, George Digby's father had a lucky break. When the king's life was threatened by a group of desperate Catholics, who planned to blow up the Houses of Parliament while King James and his eldest son, Henry, were present, there was considerable alarm throughout the country. Guy Fawkes, the plotter whose task it was to lay the gunpowder trail and light the fuses, was captured and tortured into revealing the names of his conspirators, who were then pursued and killed or captured, to be tried and executed.

Nevertheless the Crown had been challenged. The plotters had planned to replace the king with his daughter, Elizabeth, a popular nine-year old with a strong personality. They proposed that she would be advised and guided by a prominent Catholic nobleman, the Earl of Northumberland. When the plot failed, Elizabeth was safe in the house of a wealthy merchant in Coventry. Her protector, Lord Harrington, was anxious to reassure the king that she was safe. He chose George's father, John Digby, to carry the good news to London.

The welcome confirmation of Elizabeth's safety brought John to the attention of the king. He took a liking to John, who was considered both handsome and socially accomplished with an education fitting a gentleman of the seventeenth century. John was made a Gentleman of the Privy Chamber and one of the king's carvers, which launched him on a career that was to take him to high honours. He was knighted on 16th March, 1607.

George Digby was thus born into a wealthy family which was highly considered by King James I, and enjoyed the privileges which such patronage derived. The Digby family had established itself in the fifteenth century in the Midlands as landowners. Arriving in England with William the Conqueror, successive generations had served the ruling monarchs as soldiers and administrators, steadily accumulating large estates in the process. Sir Everard Digby, Sheriff of Rutland, had fought in the War of the Roses on the side of Henry VI, and was killed at the battle of Towton. His seven sons all fought for Henry Tudor at Bosworth Field. George's grandfather was knighted at the siege of Zutphen in Flanders by Queen Elizabeth and died in 1586, leaving three sons of whom George's father, John, was the youngest, born in February 1580, the son of Sir George Digby of Coleshill, Warwickshire and Abigail, daughter of Sir Arthur Henningham. Unlike his warrior ancestors John proved to be a man of learning and attended Magdalen College, Oxford as a fellow commoner at the age of fifteen. He was therefore well suited to a life and career at court, and he seized the opportunity with both hands.

James I was by nature a peacemaker. The early years of his reign were marked by attempts to settle differences with England's neighbours. A festering war with Spain had been going on for twenty years, draining England's finances. The Spanish considered themselves as the champions of Catholicism and believed they had a mission to reconvert England to the "true faith." However, apart from religious differences there no longer existed any major contentious issues between the two nations. In addition Scotland had never been at war with Spain and James still considered himself to be a Scot. Upon accession to the throne he therefore wasted no time in negotiating peace with the Spanish, signing a peace accord on August 18, 1604. To cement the alliance, in 1611 he sought to arrange a marriage between Henry, Prince of Wales and the Infanta Anna, eldest daughter of the King of Spain. John

Digby was sent to Madrid as ambassador extraordinary to open negotiations.

This role provided John with the opportunity to display his abilities. He was by now married to Beatrix, daughter of Charles Walcot of Walcot, Salop and the widow of Sir John Dyve. Beatrix accompanied John to Madrid in June 1611, making the best of rather spartan living conditions. The Digbys, as Protestants, were not particularly welcome in so fervent a Catholic country and therefore were not afforded the hospitality and facilities which would normally be provided for so distinguished a representative of a major power. Madrid was to be the Digbys' home for fourteen long years as negotiations dragged on, first on behalf of Henry and the Infanta Anna, and when these came to nothing and Henry subsequently died, between Henry's younger brother Charles and Anna's sister the Infanta Maria. There were several breaks during this period when negotiations foundered, and John took on additional duties as a roving ambassador in Europe, but the family home remained in Madrid.

George was born in Madrid on October 15, 1612 and was baptised on November 5, the anniversary of the Gunpowder Plot. (Others have argued that he was born in England just prior to his parents' departure for Spain, but the relevant dates do not support this. When his mother left England for Spain she was accompanied by a young child, but this is more likely to have been Lewis Dyve, her son by a previous marriage. George's birth is recorded as occurring after Beatrix arrived in Spain). He spent much of the first thirteen years of his life in Spain and grew up speaking Spanish as fluently as English, and knowing Spanish society and domestic life rather better than that of England.

Madrid at that time was not a place where a foreigner could feel accepted. Although Spain was at last opening itself up to outside influence after a long period of introspection Madrid, which had been chosen as the new Spanish capital by Philip

II in 1560 as a showpiece to flaunt Spain's increasing wealth from its colonies, was a city of narrow, dirty streets which attracted the poor and unemployed from the countryside seeking their fortune from the nobility, who had accumulated vast riches from Spain's successful exploration of the Americas. The hot and dry climate affected foreigners' health, and led to constant crop failures and food shortages. Nevertheless, following the decision to move the capital from Seville, an ambitious building programme had created an environment of excitement and creativity which drew artists, craftsmen and adventurers to the city. A magnificent court was established where plays, masques and pantomimes were regularly staged.

George's schooling would have reflected the stimulation and intellectual development of Spain which was beginning to occur at that time. Unlike those growing up in England, his mental horizons would have been broadened, and his later life reflected the ease with which he moved in international circles. He was also to claim an intimacy with Spanish diplomacy. For part of his time in Spain he enjoyed the companionship of a remarkable cousin, Kenelm Digby. The elder son of the late Sir Everard Digby, one of the Gunpowder Plotters, Kenelm had been taken under the wing of George's father and had joined the ambassador to Spain in 1617 as part of his education. Nine years older than George, he was a larger-than-life character in every way. A huge man with a booming laugh, he displayed early academic brilliance and an unquenchable curiosity which was to make him one of the distinguished virtuosi of a very distinguished century. He was also socially accomplished and fitted easily into Spanish aristocratic society. As a Catholic he was later to play an important part in the negotiations with Spain over the marriage, representing John to the influential Spanish Catholic clerics. He became part of the Prince of Wales' entourage and was knighted in 1623 for his services in Spain. His influence was to be significant throughout George's life.

Those early days are likely to have been lonely ones for a foreign boy cooped up in the English embassy, mixing only with visitors from abroad, most of them statesmen. His nationality and religion would have precluded him from entering Madrid society in any significant way. Spanish social life was distinguished at that time by a stiffness and formality which would have made it difficult for the young George to make close friends among the local population. He was to grow up something of a "loner," content to follow his own instincts rather than consult others.

John Digby's skilled diplomacy and forthright views found favour with a monarch surrounded by sychophants. He also achieved some success in improving the lot of English merchants operating in Spain, who were experiencing discrimination, by exposing to the Spanish authorities some of the injustices suffered by them. Furthermore, perhaps John's most significant act was in 1613 to uncover the payment of secret pensions by the Spanish to a number of English politicians in return for their support at the English court. Notable among those being paid were the Howard family, the Earl of Somerset, the Earl of Northampton and Lady Suffolk. It was even rumoured that the king's favourite, George Villiers, later Duke of Buckingham, was on the list. When John revealed this on a visit to London in 1614, it created quite a stir, as these names represented a fair proportion of the most powerful families in the land. John thus made many powerful enemies, but the king was impressed by his integrity and fearlessness. As a reward, in 1615 he was made a privy councillor and vice-chamberlain. He was also granted the valuable possession of Sherborne Castle, a great estate in Dorset and in 1618 was made the first Earl of Bristol.

The well-known account of the injudicious and impulsive appearance in Madrid on March 7, 1623 of the Prince of Wales and Duke of Buckingham changed the nature of the negotiations, and John Digby's part in it. Frustrated by the way the proposed settlement was dragging, they took up the baton themselves. Buckingham, the dominant partner in this rash venture, attempted to take over negotiations, much to everyone's annoyance. His boorish behaviour offended the formal Spaniards, and led to clashes with John Digby, who was highly regarded by them. Buckingham became antagonistic towards John, and this was to lead to problems for the Digby family in later years. The negotiations finally foundered upon the Prince's refusal to embrace Catholicism, and Charles and Buckingham returned home disillusioned in October 1623. Greeted with relief by a nation becoming increasingly anxious that too much was being conceded to the Spanish, particularly in the matter of religion, Buckingham received popular acclaim. He had been feared and criticised for his influence over the king and his part in the search for a Catholic bride. Now the anti-papists and those merchants who stood for an aggressive foreign and colonial policy gave him their support. He used this approbation to lay the blame for the failed negotiations on John Digby's shoulders, accusing him of being sympathetic to the Spaniard's side.

John had commenced the negotiations in a spirit of reluctance: as a Protestant he did not approve of a rapprochement with the Catholics. He had become increasingly alarmed by the king's willingness to trade religious concessions for political advantage, most notably help in getting his nephew, the Elector Palatine, restored to his throne in Europe (Spanish Royalty, part of the Hapsburg dynasty, wielded great influence in northern Europe). But when the Earl of Bristol was recalled to England in January 1624 he was handsomely rewarded by the King of Spain, receiving a ring from him and an open offer that should he encounter difficulties on his return he would be welcome in any of Spain's dominions and accorded the highest honours.[5] Suspicions were thus sharpened, and Buckingham's hostility towards him made his homecoming less than cordial. Refused funds by the Crown, he was forced to sell his plate to finance the return journey. He was confined to his estate at Sherborne by the king, in whose eyes Buckingham could do no wrong. With him went his wife and George who, instead of being able to take his place as a gentleman in English society, found himself once again confined to a narrow, isolated existence.

Bristol mounted a spirited defence of his actions. Kenelm, who had been in Madrid throughout Prince Charles' sojourn there and had become one of the prince's entourage, was asked to intercede with the king on Bristol's behalf. The king merely responded that if he would admit his wrongdoing and humbly apologise, he would be restored to favour. But Bristol was a principled man, and was not prepared to yield. He implored Prince Charles to help him, and Charles went so far as to take Bristol's wife to see the king, but with no more success than Kenelm had enjoyed. Meanwhile Buckingham persuaded the ailing king to recall Parliament, where he presented his version of the negotiations. He was hailed as a national hero, and with James no longer able to rule with a firm hand it was Buckingham who virtually ruled England as its first minister.

When James died in 1625 and Charles acceded to the throne the influence of Buckingham became even more pronounced. Bristol's name was removed from the list of Privy Councillors and he was refused permission to attend the funeral. Worse still, Charles now claimed that Bristol had attempted to pervert him from his religion while in Spain. This accusation arose because John, recognising that the Spaniards would settle for nothing less than the prince's conversion, had questioned the prince about his religious convictions. It seemed to him at the time that the English were conceding everything asked for by the Spanish, and that perhapsCharles had made up his mind to convert. He received a very sharp reply: "I wonder what you have ever found in me that you should conceive I shall be so base and unworthy as for a wife to change my religion."[6] In reply to a plea from Bristol for reinstatement, Charles wrote back bitterly: "you know what your behaviour in Spain deserved of us, which you are to examine by the observations we made…. how much wrong, disadvantage, and disservice you did to the treaty, and to the right and interest of our dear brother, and sister, and their children; what disadvantage, inconvenience, and hazard you entangled us in by your artifices putting off and delaying our return home. The great estimation you made of that state, and the vile price you set this kingdom at, still maintaining that we, under colour of friendship to Spain, did what was in our power against them, which (you said) they knew very well." [6]

An action was initiated by the king against Bristol, requesting the Lords to summon him and make him answer for offences committed in Spain. Bristol requested that a counter-accusation by him against Buckingham should also be considered. The Lords decided to hear the king's charge against him first, followed by his charges against Buckingham, and he was detained pending the outcome of these hearings. On the same day Bristol despatched his son George, now a boy of thirteen, to the Commons with a petition pleading his cause and opposing Buckingham. By all accounts the impression he made was deep and long-lasting. He presented a strongly worded petition which laid the blame squarely at Buckingham's door:

"Humbly shewing, that being sonne and heire to the Earle of Bristol, and desireing rather to succeede to unblemished honor then any other inheritance; having understood that the honor and good name of the said Earle his father hath been much wronged by many sinister aspersions cast upon him by the Duke of Buckingham before both howses of Parliament, which dishonors will descend unto his posteritye (being upon Record) unless they shall be duely cleared:

Now forasmuch as the said Earle his father (as befiteth a Peere of this realm), hath for redress of his said wronges petitioned the howse of Peeres, where it is only proper for him to move: And hath there charged the Duke of Buckingham for the wrongdoing of him in the point of his honor and allsoe for haveinge abused theire Majesties and both the howses of Parliament, as will appeare unto this honorable howse by the annexed paper, which is a true coppie of the charge which his father hath given in against the said Duke of Buckingham:

He therefore humblie beseecheth this honorable howse in the behalfe of himselfe and of his whole family, who are part of the body of the Commons: That as the said aspertions have bene cast in both howses uppon the said Earle his father, the which he no way doubteth but he will fully cleare in the howse of peeres, soe you would be pleased in your high wisdomes to take some such course whereby satisfaction may be given unto this honorable howse for the clearing of the said aspertions, which is readie to be done by your supplyant in any sort this honorable howse shall think fitt; or els that nothing may remaine uppon record to the dishonor of the said Earle and his posteritye."[7]

This eloquent and persuasive speech from a teenager charmed the assembled House and presaged a future as one of Parliament's great orators. Nevertheless the Commons followed the Lords and brought formal charges of impeachment against his father. Bristol was sent to the Tower with instructions to prepare for a Star-Chamber trial. He continued to campaign actively, but fell ill in the Tower and this was used as an excuse to drop further proceedings. The Crown feared that a show trial would place Buckingham in a bad light. Consequently a rapprochement between the two protagonists led to Bristol being reinstated to the Lords in 1628. But he was still out of favour and Buckingham ensured that during his lifetime the Digby family was denied any further advancement. John retired to Sherborne, looking towards his accomplished son to make his mark upon society.

The original Sherborne Castle was built in the twelfth century and dominated the small Dorset town of Sherborne.

Originally it was given to Osmond, Earl of Dorset, by William the Conqueror. Norman by birth, Osmond became bishop and set a curse on anyone "that did goe about to pluck the same from that godly and pious use, it really being given to the Church."[8] This curse appeared to have some effect, for when King Stephen seized the castle by the pretext of persuading the bishop of Salisbury to annex it, he suffered misfortune until his early death. The rightful heir to the Crown, Maud the Empress and her son Henry, invaded England not long after the seizure. Sherborne was returned to the Duke of Somerset on a long lease. Within six months he lost his head and his sub-lessee, Sir John Hersey "declined in his estate untill he became so extraordinary poore that he was attained for ten pounds"[9] Thus the castle returned to the bishoprick until the thirty-third year of Queen Elizabeth I's reign, when she granted it to Sir Walter Raleigh. But even that popular hero, previously held in high esteem with the queen, was to be beheaded for treason under James' rule. Raleigh's widow is said to have beseeched the king on bended knees to permit her son to inherit his father's rights to the castle, but James had other intentions for it. Sherborne passed to the dashing young buck, Robert Carr, Earl of Somerset, the king's favourite. Even this favouritism was not to last, for in 1615 he was arrested for the murder of Thomas Overbury, and was committed to the Tower. Somerset was also suspected of having surreptitious dealings with the Spanish and John Digby was recalled to England to testify on this. The castle was granted to Bristol together with £800 per annum for upkeep.[10]

Sherborne was a substantial estate, although the building was inadequate and poorly sited. Bristol set about restoring and improving it. Raleigh had established a lodge in a shallow valley apart from the old, rather basic castle and had drawn up a detailed design for an ambitious country retreat. He had built a substantial mansion in the form of a letter H with four stories and four six-angled towers at the corners, but he did not hold the property long enough to see his dreams materialise. Bristol took up his design and added to it, with four wings, handsome balustrades and Italian window frames. Six new terraces were added together with a grove and a canal. The Digby symbolic ostrich and fleur-de-lys were added to ceilings and woodwork. He also added four new towers. This was the property which George was to inherit. The lodge remains today much as it must have been at that time, set in beautiful grounds.

Although Sherborne was somewhat isolated, depriving George of much social contact with people of his own age, his life there was to provide a valuable dimension to his education, for the great country houses of the seventeenth century were a focus for meeting and discussion. As travel was difficult and slow, itinerants would be accommodated overnight or sometimes for several days, the house-owner only too pleased to see new faces and learn the latest news. George would learn a great deal from visitors. His father's reputation drew to Sherborne some of the finest minds and leading statesmen not only of England but of France and Spain, where he had travelled extensively. Following the dispute with Buckingham, Sherborne became a focus for malcontents unhappy with James's reign and resentful of Buckingham's influence. It was in this atmosphere, with a sense of the injustice suffered by his father at the hands of the Crown, that George's political instincts were shaped.

George's part in the defence of his father against Buckingham had been noticed and resented by the new king. A warrant was issued on June 28, 1626, for George's detention along with his step-brother, Sir Lewis Dyve and Sir John Strangeways, for "stirring up of disaffection of divers of the members of both houses for the furtherance of their private ends."[11] It is not known whether he was actually arrested, but if he was he cannot have been detained for long as in August 1626, at the age of fourteen, he followed in his father's footsteps to Magdalen College, Oxford, where he spent several years. It was during this time that his brilliant mind was to expand and flourish. He was fluent in French and Italian before he went up, and soon mastered Latin and Greek. He enjoyed the study of classics and literature. At the time the regime at Oxford was centred on dialectic and logic, followed by rhetoric. The new sciences, including mathematics, were virtually ignored. Tutors coached their students in every aspect of life, not just intellectual studies. George formed a warm friendship with Peter Heylyn, the historian and divine, who was a very young but brilliant don from whom he derived a taste for theological discussion. Normally undergraduates were supposed to take a Bachelor of Arts degree after four years study, an MA following after a further three years. However in the seventeenth century the actual obtaining of a degree did not matter as much as it does today, being looked upon then in the same way as an apprenticeship, leading to a career as a teacher, priest or other professional. Less than half those who went up to Oxford emerged with degrees, and well-born gentlemen used the university as more of a finishing school. It would have been considered unnecessary, if not unusual, for the son of an Earl to obtain a degree. But George did indeed receive an MA, on August 31, 1636, exactly ten years after he had gone up to Oxford. King Charles and William Laud, then Chancellor of Oxford, visited the university at that time, and it was common practice for courtiers to receive degrees during such visits. George, undoubtedly, would have been among those attending the king. It is thus possible that he had in fact left Magdalen several years earlier, but as a returning scholar it would have been appropriate to have the degree conferred upon him.[12] As will be seen below, he was active in other fields well before 1636.

After he left Oxford he spent some time in Paris, rounding his education and honing his skills. He appears to have acquired a pedantry and stiffness from his earlier life in the excessively formal environment of Madrid. But the young Edward Hyde, later the Earl of Clarendon, was very impressed with the young man that emerged. "He returned again to his country and his father's house, the most accomplished person of that nation, or it may be that any other at that time, could present to the world, to which his beauty, comeliness and gracefulness of his person gave no small lustre."[13] At Sherborne, however, he was content to sink back into the bosom of family life and the entertainment which this gracious estate offered. But it was not long before his eyes turned towards those places where the future was being shaped: London, Parliament and the king's court, and his ambitions were about to be helped by a twist of fate.

Chapter 2.

Home In England.

On Saturday, August 23, 1628, the man who had prevented the Digby family from prospering in English public life was suddenly removed from the scene. The Duke of Buckingham was visiting Portsmouth as Admiral of the Fleet to review preparations for an attack on the French when he was stabbed to death by a discontented soldier, John Felton. By this time the popularity he had enjoyed on his return from Spain had waned, and his influence over the new young king was widely resented. His death therefore was celebrated in the streets, although the king took it very badly.

For George Digby and his father Buckingham's death meant that the main restraint to regaining favour at court had been removed, but recognition did not come overnight. Court patronage at this time was all-important: it led to the most prestigious posts, it brought influence and wealth. Without it even men as distinguished and experienced as John Digby had little power. But John was attracting around him many noblemen who were dissatisfied with the way the country was being ruled. He had been reinstated to his seat in the House of Lords at the beginning of the 1628 Parliament, and played a fairly prominent role there.

Upon his accession to the throne in June 1625 Charles had married the fifteen year-old daughter of Henry IV of France, Princess Henrietta Maria. Although she was a Catholic, this alliance was considered politically necessary in view of the antagonism which existed between England and Spain. The marriage had started badly; the princess had been brought up in a protected environment and was unprepared for public life in an alien country. Charles was impatient and cold towards her. Buckingham, who saw her as a rival at court, had adopted a hostile attitude and attempted to exclude her from court matters as much as possible. The assassination of Buckingham, on whom Charles depended so much as an adviser, confidant and friend, changed everything. The new young king transferred his emotional dependence to his wife. The couple discovered love. Henrietta Maria turned out to be a woman of strong opinions and forceful character, and she came to influence her husband increasingly. Most notably, she persuaded him to soften his policy of opposition towards Catholics.

This change of style in the monarch coincided with a desire among elected members of Parliament for their many grievances to be heard. Peace in Charles' domestic arrangements contrasted with all-out conflict between the king and Parliament. The king made an urgent plea for funds to be voted for the development of the navy in order to oppose Spain, who posed a threat at sea. The House of Commons saw his need for money as a lever they could use to have their grievances redressed. When they published the Three Resolutions in 1629, declaring enemies of the state anyone who encouraged popery, raised revenue through tonnage and poundage without Parliament's approval or paid such taxes, this amounted to little short of constitutional revolt. The gravity of the move was aggravated when members of the House of Commons locked the doors and forcibly held down the Speaker while the motion was read after he had refused to allow it. The king lost his patience and dissolved Parliament on March 10, embarking upon a period of personal rule which was to last until 1640. His conviction was that "kings make and unmake their subjects; they have power of raising, and casting down; of life, and of death."[14] Thus taxes, declarations of war and peace, the country's finances and the legal system were all in his absolute authority. This rigid belief in the divine right to rule led him finally to lose his head.

Unfortunately George's next appearance on the public stage - his first as an adult - was disastrous. In 1634, at the age of 22 he fell violently in love with a (unidentified) lady at court, and started to spend some time in London in pursuit of his love. On one of his visits a man called Crofts interposed himself between George and his lady, who may have been Crofts' sister. George reproved Crofts for his rudeness when they met later in the Privy Galleries during the Templars' masque, and in his subsequent account of the incident wrote that Crofts appeared to apologise and maintain that no discourtesy was intended. However, many months thereafter it came to George's ears that Crofts was letting it be known that not only had he been deliberately insulted but that George had actually kicked him. This was now the public rumour and George recounted how he sought Crofts out in the Spring Garden, close to the Palace of Westminster, where they could speak in private, and remonstrated with Crofts, pausing from time to time to allow him to answer. But Crofts was unrepentant and dismissive, "and by his scornful demeanour expressed rather a proneness to a new injury than to any satisfaction." George, in explaining the incident later to the king, wrote rather disingenuously: "... whereupon that the writer must confess that he was so warmed that he could not choose but to strike him with what casually he had in his hand, which was a walking staff that but a little before he had taken up in the green where he was looking on the bowlers."[15] Crofts defended himself with his sword, the fracas finally being broken up by the authorities, who arrested both men for fighting within the precincts of Whitehall where it was treason to draw a sword. Crofts' part in the affair was hushed up, for his sister was a maid of honour and Crofts himself was popular at Court. George and his step-brother Lewis Dyve, who was with him at the time, were committed to prison in the Fleet on May 31. The charge was a major one -

verging on treason - although George argued that the gardens were a common bowling place which charged an entry fee. His plight looked serious, but he set about energetically petitioning the king for his release with a rather one-sided account of what had transpired. The Digby family did not enjoy the support of the establishment in this plea. George's incarceration did not last long though, for he was released on July 2, having spent a mere 34 days in the Fleet. He attempted to mend some fences by writing to the Privy Council apologising for his "weakness in offending them" and that it "nowise proceeded from undutifulness." He beseeched them to "intercede with the King to restore him to a state of his grace, which he hopes he shall never forfeit again."[16] The experience was not a pleasant one and secretly he vowed vengeance on the court for the way he had been treated.

The following year, 1635, George married Lady Anne Russell, daughter of the Duke of Bedford. Born in 1615, she was described as "Her countenance, symmetrical in all its features, transparent in its tints, and illuminated with eyes that gave to its expression somewhat of an imperial, but by no means an imperious character, exhibits a luxuriant beauty sublimed above her sister's by the superior intellect beaming on her forehead. Her auburn hair, disposed on each side of her face in a multitude of ringlets, is bound in a Grecian knot behind with strings of pearls."[17] George had met Lord William Russell, Anne's brother, at Oxford and it is possible his acquaintance with his future wife stemmed from that friendship. The Duke of Bedford's children were renowned for their self-sufficiency, with all the daughters "suitably affianced" by the time they reached the age of fourteen. The Duke of Bedford and George's father were close friends and worked effectively together in the House of Lords, having similar political sympathies. It was therefore logical that their relationship should be cemented by such a union, but there existed genuine affection between the couple. As Lady Joanna Barrington observed, Anne was "to marry the Earle of Bristow's son at his return from travaile, their being setled a private affection between the younge couple."[18] Moreover George was on excellent terms with his father-in-law, helping Bedford negotiate a suitable marriage for his son John.

The Bedford family had much in common with the Digbys, being opposed to many of the excesses of the Court and disapproving of Buckingham's role there. Many felt the Duke of Bedford was destined for great office and it was a tragedy for England that he died before the outbreak of the Civil War. Very little is known about Anne up to this point in time, although she was to provide staunch support to George throughout the rest of his life. The early years of their marriage were tranquil and settled. Anne bore six children in the 1630's, one of whom died in infancy in 1637.

George was soon in trouble again for breaking the law. He had spent Christmas 1636 in London instead of in the country, whence non-resident gentlemen had been banished by law for fear of unrest. He appeared briefly in court in May 1637 and wisely retired to Sherborne thereafter. For the moment he remained there writing, reading and studying in many disciplines. He was made a Justice of the Peace for Dorset. He took a close interest in astrology, and his horoscope is still lodged at Sherborne Castle. He spent a great deal of time studying theology. He remained in constant touch with his cousin Kenelm who, having been born a Catholic, offered him a different perspective on religion.

During the decade of his personal rule Charles permitted a more tolerant attitude towards the Catholics. By 1636 a number of notables had publicly embraced Catholicism. Kenelm Digby, who as son of a Gunpowder Plotter had not been able to further his career at court, had converted to Protestantism in 1630 and had been rewarded immediately with an influential post at the Admiralty. It is possible that Kenelm had already returned to the Catholic fold by 1633, but it was officially announced late in 1635. This sparked a new round of debate between Kenelm and George, who remained staunchly Protestant. In an attempt to rebut Kenelm's arguments (and perhaps reinforce his own faith) George wrote a discourse on religion in the form of a controversy with Kenelm, pointing up the differences between Catholicism and Protestantism. There is evidence that he was somewhat shy of this effort, for whenever the book was aired in the company of friends he would take care to ensure "that someone else in the company should be able to produce some facetious discourse or copy of verses in English or Latin that he should not be looked upon as too grave or serious for his age." Although written in 1638 it was not published until thirteen years later.

George displayed in his writings of this period an excellent awareness of the current religious debate of that time. He subscribed to the notion of free thought promulgated by Viscount Falkland and the intellectual circle of writers, philosophers and poets known as the Tew Circle. The name was derived from the home of Falkland, Great Tew, which he kept as a country retreat for men of learning. George stood squarely between the extremes of Calvinism and Catholicism, supporting religious authority based upon the written scriptures. Kenelm, although a committed Catholic, also believed in free thought and defended freedom of action, but argued that the oral tradition of the Church and its infallibility were central to faith. George pursued his own theme to draw the conclusion that not only was church authority likely to be corrupted by its authority but so was government, and that "best of all, Monarchy, festers oft-times and swells into the worst of all Tyrannie."[19] Many of the points raised in George's letters were to appear central to lay Anglican thought in the 1630's, and it can be reasonably claimed that through his debate with Kenelm he was playing a leading part in the development of these themes – themes which were to become important when Parliament was reconvened and came into conflict with the king.

George talked to those who shared his sense of injustice at the way the court was behaving. He became a close friend of Falkland, who was also concerned with the excesses of the court, and who campaigned for religious tolerance. Although the country had remained reasonably quiet during the period of personal rule by the king, discontent simmered. The king's attempts to raise funds without Parliament had not been wholly successful and taxes imposed in order to renew the fleet - the infamous ship-money - had rankled with the citizens.

Charles had not helped matters when he appointed William Laud Archbishop of Canterbury in 1633. Laud was a man of strong convictions, unbending in his beliefs, a staunch supporter of the Anglican Church and adamantly opposed to the Puritans. For the king and his new archbishop the Anglican church was the only true church, and the rituals of the church were the symbols of continuity with the past. The Puritans, as their name suggests, campaigned for a "pure" religion bereft of symbols and the trappings of ceremony. They suspected Charles and Laud of being crypto-papists, pointing to the growing toleration of Catholics at Charles' court and the way the queen openly practised her faith. Laud sought to repress any differences of religious interpretation which did not concur with his own creed, using a hierarchy of bishops to impose order on the congregation. He viewed the Scots as a dissolute rabble with "no religion" and was itching to impose his ideas on them. In 1637 Charles gave him this opportunity.

The king ruled over Scotland without much heed for the nobles and lairds, hitherto an independent ruling class. Laud was encouraged to reconstitute mediaeval society in Scotland, with more control in the hands of the Church, administered by bishops sitting on the council in Edinburgh.[20] This enraged the nobles, who saw their power being usurped and their wealth threatened. A National Covenant was drawn up pledging maintenance of the Calvinist faith and protesting against any attempts to change it. The final straw came when a new Prayer Book based on the Anglican church was introduced in Scotland. This caused outrage and a rare sense of unity, with a near-riot in St Giles's Cathedral Edinburgh during which a stool was thrown at a priest. The supporters of the Covenant, the Covenanters party, emerged as the main opposition to the imposition of the Anglican prayer book, with Archibald Campbell, Earl of Argyll as its leader. Throughout 1637 and 1638 Charles and Laud attempted to impose the new prayer book, but the Scots were unbending. Any attempt to read the new service was accompanied by riots. Conflict became inevitable and Charles resolved to conquer Scotland by force.

The normal ways of raising an army in England were either by pressed recruits or apprentice militia trained-bands.. Both methods provided poor material. In the spring of 1639 Charles raised an army in the northern counties out of the trained-bands: peasants who lacked experience and discipline and had no enthusiasm for the cause. The Covenanters were ready to face the king at the border. Charles was uncertain as to the size of the enemy, estimates ranging from 12,000 to 20,000 men, and attempts to gain intelligence were easily foiled by the Scottish commander, Alexander Leslie, a veteran of the German wars who by contrast seemed to know a good deal about the English army. On June 1 Lord Arundel, Earl Marshal of England, crossed the Tweed and read out a proclamation by the king recalling the Scots as subject to obedience. Few people heard it, and nobody heeded it. When on June 3 the Scots failed to obey an order to remain ten miles from the border and were reported to be at Kelso, Henry Rich, first Earl of Holland, was sent with 300 horse and 3,000 foot soldiers to repel them. He made no allowance for the difference in pace of cavalry and infantry, and by the time he reached Kelso his tardy infantry were lagging far behind. The two armies faced each other, the Scots infantry, in Holland's estimation numbering as many as eight thousand, looking highly professional. A trumpeter was sent to request they withdraw, but came back with a counter-request from Leslie that the English withdraw. Fearing that the Scots significantly outnumbered his force Holland ordered the retreat, the cavalry wheeling and galloping away to jeers from the Scots.

To all intents and purposes the war had ended before it began. The king called a council of peers to consider his next step. The Earl of Bristol had taken no part in government during Charles' personal rule and remained out of favour with the king. He was permitted to attend the council, however, and spoke up strongly for the recall of Parliament in order to raise the necessary funds for a further campaign. The king reluctantly gave him a private audience of two hours during which he was partly persuaded by Bristol's arguments and agreed that the present campaign could proceed no further. Peace negotiations opened on June 11. Charles agreed to another Scottish Assembly and Parliament to discuss the future of their church. On June 19 articles were signed for the disbanding of both armies.

By the autumn of 1639 it was becoming apparent that the treaty Charles had signed was proving ineffective. The Scots had not disbanded their army and continued to oppose any religious impositions. It was clear now that their aims were political as well as religious, for they were also pursuing constitutional reform.[21] When on November 8 the king prorogued the Scottish Parliament the Scots ignored his command and continued to sit as the Lords of the Articles, saying that henceforth they would resist all attempts to govern them from England. This was unacceptable to Charles and in the view of the Earl of Northumberland was "…so offensive to the King that I do not see how a war can possibly be avoided."[22] Within weeks of the peace settlement preparations were afoot for the raising of a fresh army of 35,000 men.

Next to Laud, the king's closest ally was Thomas Wentworth, later created Earl of Strafford. A tall, austere Yorkshireman, autocratic and arrogant, he made few friends. But he was fiercely loyal to the king. He shared with the king and Laud a belief in the unquestionable authority of the sovereign. As an administrator in the north of England he had proved his worth, and Charles had appointed him Lord Deputy of Ireland. There he applied himself to raising revenue and managing the challenges he met by controlling the Irish Parliament effectively. Most importantly, he commanded an army of over 8,000 men who could be placed at the king's disposal.

In his hour of need, on January 12 1640 Charles recalled Wentworth from Ireland to London, ennobling him as the Earl of Strafford. The king was desperately in need of money. It was estimated that over £935,000 a year would be needed to keep an army in the field.[23] On his return in September 1639 Strafford had immediately turned to the king's council, who had profited hugely in the past under Charles. But attempts at persuading subjects to contribute were a dismal failure. In June 1639 a request for a loan from the City of London met with a lukewarm offer of £5000.[24] The aldermen refused to supply men from the trained-bands for the army, claiming their duty was to the defence of London only, and not far-off conflict.

Encouraged by the queen, a committee of court Catholics whose assistance to the king would be in their own interests, composed a letter to English Catholics asking them to appoint county representatives to collect money. To George's intense embarrassment, this committee was headed by Kenelm Digby along with another prominent Catholic, Wat Montague. Although the letter which was sent out was signed by Henrietta Maria, Kenelm's part in the fund-raising was duly noted by his enemies. It led to opponents accusing the Catholics of a popish plot to provoke war with Scotland, reminding the country that some of the committee were kindred of Gunpowder Plotters. Some money was raised this way, but not nearly enough.

The king's attempts to fund his campaign having failed, only Parliament could vote the necessary funds. He had no alternative but to recall Parliament, and writs were issued on February 12, 1640. This caused a great stir, for the people had not been represented in Parliament for over ten years, and electioneering became intensive. Competition for seats was fierce, washing away the old, established customs and social deference. Fired by his strong convictions and belief that fundamental changes were necessary, George was ready to take his place in public.

Chapter 3.

The Parliamentarian.

In March 1640 George was elected to Parliament as the member for the county of Dorset, although not without some difficulty. He actually received less votes (800) than the other two candidates, Richard Rogers and Sir Walter Earle (942 and 902 respectively), but they stepped aside.[25] It is probable that in keeping with the practice of the times both Rogers and Earle had stood for more than one seat, for they are both recorded subsequently as members of Parliament. In theory members of Parliament were elected by landowners and citizens of a certain status locally, but in practice these elections degenerated into contests between rival families, involving bribery and intimidation. The interests represented were almost exclusively local, and no proper party organisation existed. Parliament before 1640 was accustomed to dealing with local grievances brought by members and to voting supplies to the king. Not having sat since 1629, the list of causes which came before the House this time was long and diverse.

Parliament convened on April 14. The king's speech was short and to the point, making it clear that the purpose of this session was to grant him the subsidies he needed to oppose the Scots, whom he claimed had reneged on their agreement. As confirmation of their treachery he produced a letter from the Covenanters to the King of France requesting aid and denying Charles' authority. There was evidence that French arms and ammunition had been sent to the Scots. He demanded that Parliament confirm in retrospect the levies he had applied during the previous ten years of personal rule. The House was split, with many still pressing for their grievances to be addressed before the king's supply could be voted, while others warned that finance was essential for an army already in preparation. John Pym, the member for Tavistock, already tacitly accepted as leader of the opposition to the "Court Party," summarised the complaints in a long, clear analysis of Royal errors. Strafford, leading the king's supporters, underestimated the political skills of Pym, who outmanoeuvred him in the initial jousting. Instead of voting the required funds for Charles, Parliament ignored the Scottish question and turned to their own grievances. Pym assembled special committees to collect and examine complaints, and they drew up a list of grievances showing themselves to be much more interested in reform in England than Charles's campaign in Scotland. George had joined the discontented faction, opposed to the court's methods of administration, but it was not until April 20, a week into the Parliamentary session, that George first spoke in the House. His voice was to be heard more than once during this period and his reputation as an orator was to be quickly noticed.

Orders for the recruitment of trained-bands had been sent down in March 1640. Frantic attempts at raising funds ensued with the Lord Mayor of London told that the king required £200,000 from the City or else a demand for £300,000 would be enforced. The city merchants expressed alarm at the idea of a forced loan, arguing that this would debase the currency. When four aldermen were arrested for failing to provide information about the richest citizens in London discontent erupted. Apprentices gathered on the south bank of the Thames and marched on Lambeth Palace in their hundreds, causing Archbishop Laud to flee. Although the disturbance was quelled and an example made of a couple of the demonstrators, another riot occurred in Colchester when a rumour circulated that a local prominent Catholic was plotting for Irishmen to fire the town.

As the situation became more urgent the king fell back on levying unpopular duties. The Earl of Bristol suffered financially when the Court of Wards and Liveries ruled that a sum of £22,000 owed to him in back pension was more needed by the king at this time.[26] George chose this moment on May 2, 1640 to make one of his most powerful speeches to the Commons. Whilst emphasizing that he wished to see Parliament's grievances addressed before voting supply to the king for the Scottish war, he went on to attack those "Incendiary persons and firebrands of State" responsible for the problems in Scotland.[27] He pointed out that a war against the Scots would be "a Civill War...being wee are of the same Religion, under the same King."[28] He also spoke out against those promoting the war, the removal of whom would be "a safe and honourable cure" to the nation's problems. He warned that failure to extinguish the influence of these agitators could lead to unrest spilling over from Scotland into England. On May 4 Charles offered to abolish ship-money for twelve subsidies if Parliament would respond by voting supply the same day, but Parliament in committee could not reach a decision. George took part in the debate and suggested that, along with any answer they might give, this was a good opportunity to list the House's grievances.[29] Frustrated at the lack of progress, on May 5 Charles again dissolved Parliament.

George's father-in-law, the Earl of Bedford, was seen as a leader in the House of Lords, and behind the scenes was working to broaden the base of government. He consulted with George and his father frequently, and provided wise advice to the younger man. On July 19, 1640, George wrote to him thanking him for his good counsels, but maintained his individuality by adding "in this I shew an obedience to you only in that wherein mine own reason hath a share in the commaund."[30]

Strafford was emerging as the chief protagonist on behalf of the king, carrying the title of Chief Councillor.

He was absolutely committed in his support of the Crown. This meant riding roughshod over the opinions of elected members of Parliament, which was to lead to his downfall. The dissolution of Parliament had led to disturbances in many parts of the country, and the Earl of Bristol urged Strafford to recommend the calling of another session. Strafford refused, arguing that the processes of government were too slow in the current emergency. Strafford's immediate task was to raise a force which would conquer Scotland. He proposed to do this by establishing two armies, one in England and one in Ireland. His first problem was finance, but all attempts to raise funds by ship-money, forced loans and taxation were met with resistance. A press-gang army was raised in the South, but the recruits were mainly Puritans and bitterly resented their involvement. Desertion was wide-spread. Sensing an opportunity to prove their worth to the Crown, George and his brother John volunteered their services. John took part in the ensuing conflict with Scotland, but George remained at Sherborne training men.

The Scots were gathering their forces together, conscious of the preparations for war being made in England. Their leaders were prepared to submerge their differences in the common interest. Lord Conway, resident at Newcastle, expressed the opinion that the Scots did not have the power to invade but on August 20, led by Alexander Leslie they crossed the Tweed into England at Coldstream and marched steadily southward. With them went James Graham, 5th Earl and 1st Marquis of Montrose, later to be considered the king's staunchest supporter in Scotland. He had been the first to sign the Covenant and remained loyal to the Scots' cause until the beginning of the Civil War. However the despotism of the Scottish clergy and their unyielding attitudes soon caused him to have doubts in their cause, and he was to emerge as the principal opponent to Argyll.

The English army was divided, with a force led by Lord Conway at Newcastle, ready to face the Scots as they approached from Alnwick while the king stayed at York waiting for the remainder to assemble. The combined English force of 25,000 men and 2,500 cavalry was of similar size to the Scots army. As the Scots advanced on Newcastle, Conway was instructed to hold them back until the king's force reached him. But by August 28 the Scots were preparing to cross the Tyne at Newburn ford, four miles west of Newcastle. Conway sent a third of his troops to confront them, keeping the rest to defend Newcastle. The raw conscripts were no match for the Scots, however, and soon abandoned their positions, leaving the road to Newcastle open. The lack of money and preparedness had proved fatal: not only was the English army short of munitions and ordnance, but many of the infantry at Newburn had no firearms.[31] Conway, whose generalship had proved disastrous on several counts, failed to build proper defences at Newcastle. Ill-prepared to resist the Scots, he withdrew and marched south with the remainder of his army, not even putting up token resistance. The Scots occupied Newcastle.

The king, still residing at York, had received a petition requesting another Parliament so that those Royal advisers whom the two houses of Parliament considered responsible for their grievances could be brought to trial. The signatories included the Earls of Warwick, Bedford and Hertford but not Bristol, who supported the proposal but was still clearly out of favour, and therefore felt that he should refrain. In September 1640 the king decided to summon a Great Council consisting of peers, ostensibly to address these proposals but more importantly in an attempt to create a source of authority and funding outside Parliament. The leading peers of the Privy Council were critical of the king's policy towards the Scots, and seized this opportunity to force changes. Bedford was all for using the Council to push through major changes and redress grievances, but Bristol was more cautious. He took care not to be seen as in the Scottish "camp." Led by Bristol, the Council proposed that the king accept his defeat, make peace and use a new Parliament to attempt reconciliation between the Royalists and Parliamentarians. The king agreed and a delegation from the Council met the Scots at Ripon. The Council was able to come to terms with the Scots, yielding to all their political and religious demands and agreeing to pay their army £860 a day until a permanent treaty could be arranged. To find new money Parliament would have to be recalled yet again. Until new funds could be voted, the promise of a new Parliament encouraged George's father to secure a loan of £200,000 from City of London financiers. This enhanced the Earl of Bristol's standing with the king.

George remained at Sherborne, which must have been frustrating for such an active man. His standing with the king remained low, partly because he was a Digby but mainly because he had opposed the court so openly in Parliament. He was granted leave to train troops and horses for the Scottish war with the assistance of Lord Cottington, Lord Lieutenant of Dorset. The Council of Peers wrote to him assuring him that they would be "ready on all occasions to tell his Majesty of your forwardness to serve him in so advantageous a way."[32] The hands of his father and father-in-law, the Earls of Bristol and Bedford, can be seen behind this commendation.

With the country deprived of true Parliamentary representation for so long, the new elections in November 1640 generated unusual interest. Normally nominees were returned unopposed, with lords and gentry deciding who should sit, but for the Long Parliament, as this came to be known, at least 70 of the 259 constituencies were contested.[33] Many of the candidates were drawn for the first time from outside the gentry and rich merchants – yeomen, shopkeepers and craftsmen. As a consequence political and religious differences arose during these contests, and it was clear that the new Parliament would not be without a questioning, dissatisfied group of members. George was once again elected for Dorset, having stood for two seats, Milbourne Port and the County of Dorset, and been elected to both. He chose to serve Dorset, and his younger brother John took his place in the Milbourne Port seat.

The king had hoped that he would be able to exercise control over the new Parliament by having a number of men who supported him elected. The electorate thought otherwise. In the City of London the king's candidate for Mayor, the unpopular Sir William Acton, was rejected, and a compromise candidate, Edmund Wright, next in seniority to Acton, chosen by the Aldermen. Immediately a decision was made to postpone the promised loan from the City until Parliament met. The king's nominee for Speaker, Thomas Gardiner, was also defeated at the Parliamentary elections. There did not appear to be anyone who could fill the chair who would not be hostile to the Crown, and finally Charles decided on William Lenthall, a timid man whose inclination was to side with the majority and who was to prove no help to the king in the years to come. Ironically, the king's decision to reconvene Parliament was to lead ultimately to civil war, for expectations were very high among the elected members, and when their wishes were frustrated the atmosphere was to turn sour.

The popular party, as the new, lower class members of Parliament were known, "resolved to find fault with every thing that was amiss,"[34] but often could not express their discontent in a coherent manner. Whilst many members had visited the Continent, they were in the main country men preoccupied with their own homes and their environs. They were not adept at expressing their views cogently or coherently, and depended upon a relative few colleagues to voice their sentiments. In George Digby they found an educated, urbane champion who could be fierce in criticism of the bishops without losing his reverence; witty and expressive in his arguments without forfeiting their point and weight. He was helped by friends: Edward Hyde (later the Earl of Clarendon), Lucius Cary (Lord Falkland) and John Culpeper, all destined to become great statesmen, who advised the young George when to be prudent and when it was safe to attack. Falkland was famous for encouraging open debate on current topics and on encouraging the intelligentsia to tackle larger issues than mere parochial interests. The open house he held at his country residence, Great Tew, became a focal point for such intellectuals. Hyde was a member of the Circle, as was Kenelm Digby. There is no evidence that George ever visited Great Tew, and Hyde wrote that ".. he (George) was not a man of that exactness as to be in the entire confidence of the lord Falkland, who looked upon his infirmities with more severity than [Culpeper and Hyde]."[35]

George immediately made his presence felt in the Commons with a series of powerful speeches. Starved of the ability to express the opinions of the electorate for so long, the new Parliament assembled in a mood to air its grievances and protest against the curtailment of liberties which the country had suffered during Charles' period of personal rule. George caught the mood well in his first speech to the Long Parliament soon after its opening. It has lost nothing down the centuries, and in the sentiments expressed is as appropriate today as it was then. He started: "this meeting is to bemoane and redress the unhappy estate of the Commons…Our Lawes, our Liberties…our Religion all have bin by the endeavours of so many..so well secured and so much made our owne, now can scares be called ours…Our Lawes…which should run in an even streame, live now more to inflame their own Banks, and to overflow, and drowne those faites which they should gently refresh….Our Liberties…which should difference us from the slaves, and speak us Englishmen are held away…is not his offence and malice as great, who shall undermine my tenure, and surreptitiously deprive me of my Evidence, by which I shall hold my inheritance; as his, who by violence shall wrest it from me." This appeared to be a direct attack on the king; he was on dangerous ground. Skilfully he steered away by focussing his criticism on the bishops and ministers, ending with a ringing demand: "And lastly, if not penalty be found (though surely there is some) for such as have disguised religion in fantasticke dresses, if Heaven and Earth cannot but be angry to see it: and in their politics pride hath bin so long moulding a new state...for these innovations it will be lawful for you to innovate an exemplary punishment...let us endeavour to remove these imposters."[36]

George followed this with another powerful speech on November 10, when he presented the grievances for the county of Dorset. The County Court of Dorset had summarised the grievances under a short "memorial of heads which had been unanimously approved by the freeholders. These included the denunciation of ship-money – which they considered illegal – the press-gang system of recruiting to the army, the abuse of monopolies, the new Laudian canons and the oath required to be taken by church officers. He proposed a Select Committee to "draw out all that hath bin here represented, such a Remonstrance as may be a faithfull and lively representation unto his Majestie of the deplorable estate of this his Kingdome."[37]

George's prominence in Parliament led to his appointment on a number of influential committees. These included a select committee considering the status of Parliament in the governing of the country, which would ultimately emerge as the Grand Remonstrance;[38] a committee examining breaches of privilege in the Lords,[39] another examining the misdemeanours of Lord Lieutenants over the collection of taxes, and a study group making a case for annual parliaments.[40]

Relationships between the Houses of Commons and Lords had become strained. At the end of November a committee was formed in the Commons to examine questions of Parliamentary privilege and procedure. George was appointed to sit on this committee along with his brother-in-law, Lord William Russell, Sir Walter Earle, Hyde, Francis Windebank and Pym. A similar committee was formed in the Lords which included George's father, and throughout this period George can be seen working in close collaboration with his father. Their aims appear similar and their speeches reflect the same themes. Bristol, conscious of the disfavour in which he continued to be held by the king, was more circumspect than his outspoken son. He also chose to abstain on votes critical of the Crown, rather than to join the protest vote.

The question of Parliamentary privilege and procedure, and the resolution of tensions which had grown up between Lords and Commons was considered something of a sideshow compared to the petitions against grievances which were flooding in from the country, the towns and individuals. In the first week of Parliament over twenty were received, complaining of everything from ship-money, religious innovation and the work of the Star Chamber to personal grievances. Pym seized the opportunity to bring them together in a hard-hitting speech at the end of the first week, and was followed by George who sustained his attack by proposing that the House draw up a Remonstrance against the ministers responsible for Crown policy. The elegance of his speech is worth repeating in part: "You have received now a solemn accompt from most of the Shires of England, of the severall grievances and oppressions they sustaine, and nothing as yet from Dorsetshire; Sir, I would not have you think that I serve for a Land of Gotham, that we live there in Sun-shine, whilest darknes & plagues overspread the rest of the Land: As little would I have you thinke, that being under the same sharpe measure that the rest, we are either insensible or benummed, or that Shire wanteth a Servant to represent its sufferings boldly." He went on to list the grievances: Ship-money, pressing of soldiers, the multitude of Monopolies, the new Canon and the oath to be taken by lawyers and divines, the oath to be taken by Church Officers (thought to be illegal.)....."this Consideration, Mr Speaker, leades me to that which is more necessary farre, at this season, than any farther laying open of our miseries, that is, the way to the remedy by seeking to remove from our Soveraigne, such unfit judges, such pernicious Counsellors, and such disconscient Divines, as have of late yeares, by their wicked practices, provoked aspersions upon the government of the graciousest and best of Kings....and this leadeth me to my motion, which is, that a select Committee may be apointed to draw out of all that hath ben here represented, such a Remonstrance as may be a faithful and lively representation unto his Majesty of the deplorable estate of this his Kingdome, and such as may happily point out unto his cleere and excellent judgement, the pernicious Authors of it."[41]

This proposal was approved and George was chosen by Parliament along with Pym, Selden, Harley and Rudyard to catalogue their grievances, of which ship-money, monopolies and press-ganging were among the most serious. Parliament was also concerned to ensure that it was never again placed in the position of not meeting, as had been the case in the previous decade, and a bill was introduced calling for triennial Parliaments. George supported this with a most persuasive speech: "I rise not now with an intent to speake to the frame and structure of this Bill, nor much by way of answer to objections that may be made; I hope there will bee no occasion of that, but that we shall concurre all inanimously in what concerneth all so universally.....The essentialnesse Sir of frequent Parliaments to the happinesse of this Kingdome might be inferr'd unto you by the reason of contraries, from the woefull experience which former times have had of the mischievous effects of any long intermission of them...The Intestine distempers Sir, of former ages upon the want of Parliaments, may appeare to have had some other cooperative causes, as sometimes, unsuccessfull Warres abroad; sometimes, the absence of the Prince, sometimes, Competitions of Titles to the Crown; sometimes, perhaps the vices of the King himselfe…." Then, realising he had perhaps gone too far and risked the wrath of his sovereign: "I…..thanke God, wee have so good a King, under whom we may speake boldly of the abuse of his power by ill Ministers, without reflexion upon his person. What Friendship, what Union can there be so comfortable, so happy, as between a Gracious Soveraigne and his people? And what greater misfortune can there be to both, than for them to be kept from intercourse, from the meanes of clearing misunderstandings, from interchange of mutual benefits? The People of England, Sir, cannot open their Eares, their Hearts, their Mouthes, nor their purses to his Majesty, but in Parliament. We can neither hear him, nor complain, nor acknowledge, nor give but there. This Bill, Sir, is the sole key that can open the way to a frequencie of those reciprocal endearments, which must make and perpetuate the happiness of the King and Kingdom. Let no man object any derogation from the King's Prerogative by it. Wee doe but present the Bill, 'tis to be made a Law by him, his honour, his power, will be as conspicuous, in commanding at once that a Parliament shall assemble every third yeare, as in commanding a Parliament to be called this or that year….there is more of Majesty in ordaining primary and universall Causes then in the actuating particularly of subordinate effects…The truth is Sir, the Kings of England are never in their glory, in their splendor, in their Majestique Soveraigncy, but in Parliament. Where is the power of imposing Taxes? Where is the power of restoring from incapacities? Where is the legislative Authority? Marry in the King, Mr Speaker, but how? In the King circled in, fortified and evirtuated by his Parliament. The King out of Parliament hath limited and circumscribed jurisdiction, but wayted on by his Parliament, no Monarch of the East is so absolute in dispelling Grievances. Mr Speaker, in chasing ill Ministers we do but dissipate Clouds that may gather again, but in voting this Bill, we shall contribute, as much as in us lyes, to the perpetuating our Sun, our Soverraigne, in his Vertical, in his Noon-day lustre."[42]

He went on to press home the case: "...the frequencie of Parliament is most essentially necessary to the power, the security, the glory of the King. There are two wayes, Mr Speaker, of powerfull Rule, either by Feare, or Love...Let a Prince consider what it is that moves a people principally to affection, and dearnesse, towards their Soveraigne. He shall see that there needs no other Artifice in it, than to let them injoy unmolestedly, what belongs unto them of right." He also addressed the perceived cause of the king's impatience with Parliament: "...wicked Ministers have bin the proximate causes of our miseries, but the want of Parliaments the primary, the efficient cause. Ministers have made ill times, but that Sir, hath made ill Ministers...Let his Majesty heare our Complaint never so Compassionately" (this referred to ship-money) "Let him purge away our Grievances never so efficaciously. Let him punish and dispell ill Ministers never so exemplarily. Let him make choyce of good ones never so exactly."[43]

The king responded on January 25, 1641 with a speech to both Houses in which he rejected the Triennial Bill as a direct encroachment on his prerogative.[44] Amendments to the Bill by the Lords, endorsed by the Commons, seem to have satisfied him however, and he passed the Bill on February 16. This success enhanced the reputation of both George and his father with Parliamentarians, and did not seem to have done them any harm with the king, for Bristol was appointed to the Privy Council on February 19. It also encouraged both Bristol and George that the king would listen to their advice and could be reasonably persuaded, although George was of the opinion that the queen had brought her influence to bear on the king's decision.

George's main target, the bishops, led a hierarchial system of church government inherited from Roman Catholicism and Archbishop Laud's efforts to strengthen their authority aroused suspicion and opposition. The popular party wanted the episcopacy abolished altogether, fearing that anything less would be a stopgap measure. George had reservations about this, arguing that it could result in "a Pope in every parish."[45] The argument split the popular party, and both Hyde and Falkland distanced themselves from the proposals. The Scots were also in favour of removing power from the bishops and introducing a democratic ecclesiastical organisation, based upon Presbyterianism.

The first serious challenge to the king came with a petition for the abolition of the episcopacy, "root and branch," signed by 15,000 citizens.[46] It was presented to the House on February 8 by Isaac Pennington, a cloth merchant from the City of London and a zealous Puritan. Many members were critical of the bishops, but most favoured reform of church government and limitation of the bishops' powers and exclusion from the House of Lords. The Earl of Bedford and John Pym entered negotiations with the king for reform rather than abolition, and George was among those who supported this approach. He also drew attention to the popular pressure which had accompanied the petition, with 300-400 people crowding into Westminster Hall in support. He considered this "a thing of the highest consequence." He urged the House "not to be led on by passion to popular and vulgar errors."[47] He argued that the manner of the petition's presentation was sufficient grounds for rejecting it. The next day several thousand citizens went to Westminster and demonstrated peacefully in favour of the petition. They also adopted a threatening attitude towards those they perceived were opposed to their views. George was aghast at the methods employed, which showed every sign of having been orchestrated by Pym. He protested in the House, deploring "irregular and tumultuous assemblies of people, be it for never so good an end."[48] He could see the dangers that mob rule presented to the court and was troubled by Pym's hostility towards the king.

In this debate George questioned whether the problems experienced under episcopal government were institutional, or the result of failings by the bishops appointed. He expressed concern over the alternatives to episcopacy and believed that a method of controlling the bishops through Parliament could be devised. "Sir, if I thought there were no further design in the desires of some, that this London Petition should be committed, than meerly to make use of it as an Index of Grievance, I should wink at the faults of it, and not much oppose it. There is no man within these Walls, more sensible of the heavy Grievance of Church Government, than my self; nor whose affections are more keen to the clipping of those wings of the Prelates, whereby they have mounted to such insolencies, nor whose zeal is more ardent to the fearing them, so as that they may never spring again. But having reason to believe, that some aim at a total extirpation of Bishops, which is against my heart....I cannot restrain myself from labouring to divert it, or at least, to set such notes upon it, as may make it ineffectual to that end."[49] The main question he posed the House was: if the bishops were removed, by what would they be replaced? Nobody had proposed an alternative. He warned against allowing petitions opposing an established law, and said he could not vote for abolition until he was shown a form of government not subject to similar problems – and he believed this was an impracticable utopia. George had a suggestion: with the bishops' powers curbed, a standing committee made up of members of both houses could be set up to consider grievances against the bishops and to advise on the best way to govern the Church. The House resolved to send the petition to the committee on church affairs, which was barred from considering whether the episcopacy should be abolished or reformed. This committee recommended the removal of bishops from the House of Lords and the exclusion of clergy from secular offices[50] and these measures were approved by the Commons on March 10/11. Had the problem of the bishops been straightforward, this proposal would have been eminently sensible, but the question was a political one, of the influence of the church and the authority of the king, and George's ideas received short shrift. But now the attention of Parliament was to be drawn away to a much more serious issue, which would have far-reaching consequences.

Chapter 4.

Strafford.

Pym had turned his attention to the king's chief ally, the Earl of Strafford. Strafford had not been prepared to lay down his arms against the Scots and had been bitterly opposed to the conciliation offered them by Bristol. He was detested by Parliament for the support he had given the king and for his attempts to control the Commons. He also found himself under investigation for his government in Ireland. There remained considerable nervousness in England surrounding Catholic intentions, and Strafford's strong army in Ireland had led to rumours of a new Catholic plot. Under Strafford the Catholics had enjoyed unusual freedom and advancement in Ireland, and this was anathema to Pym, who above all feared and detested popery. The king's wife Henrietta Maria, who showed increasing influence over her husband, was known to be actively campaigning for further tolerance for Catholics. She sought to protect Catholics in her court. The friendship between the king and the Papal Nuncio to London, the Scotsman George Con, who had arrived in 1636, was apparent to all.

Aware of the threat posed to him, and Pym's challenge to the king, Strafford persuaded Charles to arrest the Parliamentary leaders. At the last moment the plan was abandoned, but not before news of it had reached Parliament. On November 11, 1640, Pym moved that the House be cleared and the doors locked. He wished to propose that a case be drawn up against the Earl of Strafford. The impeachment listed a number of charges, many of them without substance. By far the most serious was the accusation that Strafford had plotted to bring the army back from Ireland to subdue protest by dissidents (which would include Parliament) in England. That, under Article twenty-three, amounted to high treason. George supported this proposal, referring to Strafford as "that grand Apostate to the Commonwealth."[51] Whilst George and his father were supporters of the king, they had no love for Strafford, and wished to see his power and influence diminished. It is clear that when George railed against "ill Ministers" and "evil advisers" of the king, he was referring to Strafford.

Only the voice of Lord Falkland was heard in disagreement, warning gently against proceeding too fast on inadequate evidence. But for Pym speed was of the essence if he was to trap Strafford before he could assemble his formidable legal skills, and the impeachment was carried to the House of Lords the same day. Strafford, hearing what was happening, hurried to the Lords, but the peers, smarting after years of his arrogance, shouted "Withdraw, withdraw."[52] That afternoon he was taken to the house of Maxwell, Gentleman Usher of the Black Rod, where he was kept in custody, and later transferred to the Tower of London while the case for his impeachment was drawn up.

George was one of a committee of seven members nominated to draw up the charge. He proposed that some lawyers be appointed to the committee, and Selden, Palmer, Whitelocke and Maynard were selected. It is thought by commentators that George made this proposal not because more legal expertise was needed, but rather to provide a modifying influence on the committee. He was clearly concerned at this stage by the implications of impeachment, for on February 26, 1641 he proposed that the charge be changed from impeachment to the lesser charge of attainder: "the best and only way of attaining our ends in doing Justice… was to doe it by Bill rather than by Judgment; because much scruple might remaine with the Lords and others of the quality of the offences, to bee Treason."[53] He also reminded the House that a charge of treason would require evidence from more than one witness. Although committed to removing Strafford, George would not at this stage have considered impeachment as threatening Strafford's life. Impeachments carried out during the Parliaments in the 1620's preceding the king's period of personal rule had merely led to loss of privileges, and George probably thought that a successful action against Strafford would lead to his disqualification from Royal service, which would meet his aims. The introduction of Triennial Parliaments, heralding in a more effective Commons would, in George's view, solve the problem of evil counsellors.

George's standing had not been improved by a Committee formed on January 28 1641 to question his cousin Kenelm with others in the queen's circle about their role in raising money for the northern expedition. Kenelm had written to George on October 1, 1640 acquainting him with their actions.[54] In a debate on March 15, 1641 it was agreed that the papists assisting the queen, namely Kenelm, Walter Montague, Toby Matthew and her secretary, John Wintour, should be removed from her service. Concern was expressed that if Wintour was removed he may be replaced by a Frenchman. George seized upon this concern to point out that the queen had supported the Triennial Bill and had helped Parliament's cause through her growing influence on the king and the sensible policies she helped to advocate.

The queen had been under pressure from Parliament for some time, and had even suggested she may return to France. The Commons were concerned at the influence she wielded over the king, and were particularly worried about her Catholic activities. On February 16 the Commons resolved that no priest or papist should be admitted to the queen, and no mass said in her court.[55] She responded by sending a message to Cardinal Richelieu in France reqesting support, but he advised her to be patient. When she then suggested she may go to Ireland, this merely heightened the tension over the role of the Irish army.[56] A crucial issue was whether the queen would be permitted to retain her French Catholic servants, and the king supported her. On March 15 the Commons discussed the matter, and George put the queen's case. Although his intervention was to no avail, his standing with the Royal family was significantly enhanced by this interlude, and thereafter he was regarded as a close ally of the queen. Unfortunately, given the prevailing mood of Parliament, it was simply another cause for resentment against him.

Parliament paid no heed to George's proposals to alter the charge against Strafford. The committee wasted no time in confirming the charge of treason, and on March 22 Strafford was brought to trial in Westminster Hall, the grand chamber adjacent to the House of Commons. Strafford's trial formally began with the reading of his impeachment for high treason. Pym saw the successful indictment of Strafford at the heart of his political strategy. If he could destroy the king's most influential lieutenant in the teeth of opposition from the Crown, he would establish Parliament's rights once and for all. The king had sought to secure the Lords by promoting a number of his critics, including the Earl of Bristol, to the rank of Privy Councillor without admitting them to his inner cabinet. The Lords initially took exception to the case brought against one of their number, but Strafford's many enemies persuaded their fellows not to oppose the proceedings. Strafford was impeached on the grounds of "endeavouring to subvert the fundamental laws…and to introduce an arbitrary and tyrranical government against law."[57]

Pym opened the case against him, arguing that whilst individual charges might not appear to be treason, the overall intent was unmistakable. Strafford responded by demonstrating flaws in the factual evidence and casting doubt upon the witnesses. In the early exchanges George was seen to be frequently participating on the side of the prosecution, defending witnesses against Strafford's skilful challenges and pointing out that Strafford had offended so many people that it would be difficult to find witnesses who were not prejudiced against him. One of the charges brought against Strafford concerned an accusation that he had incited the king against Parliament, and the Earl of Bristol was called as a witness.[58]

The charges against Strafford relied upon a discussion with the king during a meeting of the small Council of War eleven months earlier. Secretary of State Henry Vane had made notes of the meeting, which included the alleged offer by Strafford to bring the Irish Army to England. These notes had been left at his home and had been found by his son when searching for some cabinet papers his father had requested. Recognising its significance in the Strafford trial, he had made a copy of them and passed them to John Pym. Pym lodged the copy as evidence with the Clerk of the House of Lords together with the proposed impeachment. The key sentence read: "His Majesty might, by the Irish army reduce the Kingdom here." The evidence against Strafford was flimsy, with only one witness in support of the charge. The note of the Council meeting was therefore a crucial issue, and George was later to claim that he had agreed to support the accusation on the grounds that Pym had promised him conclusive evidence in the form of some notes from the Council meeting. George did not expect the charge to be supported merely by one witness, the person who had taken the notes. This witness was Vane, who provided verbal evidence of the fateful Council meeting. It emerged that of all the people present only he could remember the actual words. His records were chaotic and he proved to be unreliable, contradicting himself several times and showing reluctance to produce written evidence. In Parliament George made much of the issue of reliable evidence: "…This I was assured would be proved before I gave my consent to his accusation, I was still confirmed in the same belief, during the prosecution, and fortified in it most of all since Sir Henry Vains preparatory examinations by the assurances which that worthy member M. Pimme gave me, That his testimony would be made convincing by some notes of what passed at the juncto concurrent with it, which I ever understanding to be of some other Counsellour, you see now proved but a copy of the same Secretaries notes discovered and produced in the manner you have heard, and those such disjoynted fragments of the venemous part of discourses, no results, no conclusions of Counsels, which are the onely things that Secretares of State should register; there being no use at all of the other, but to accuse and to bring men into danger."[59]

Vane reacted in a horrified manner when his son, Sir Harry Vane, surfaced to testify that there was a record of the meeting, although this turned out to be roughly scribbled notes. At around this time Pym's copy of the fateful Council proceedings, which had been entrusted to the Chairman of the Committee, Bulstrode Whitelocke, went missing from his desk in his private chamber, when only three people were present. George being one of them, he was accused of having stolen it. It reappeared a little later, but with a critical change: "His Majesty might, by the Irish army reduce the Kingdom *there*." The change from "here" to "there" implied either Ireland or Scotland but certainly not England, and altered the entire sense of what Strafford was reported to have said. Moreover another important paper deposited in evidence went missing and from Strafford's answers it appeared that he had been given sight of it. Whitelocke protested that only the Select Committee had access to the paper, but they all denied that they had shown it to Strafford, with George protesting as vehemently as anyone. Years later, when the King's papers were captured at Naseby, it is asserted that a copy of this paper in George's handwriting was found. Whitelocke's diary records "long afterwards att the battle of Naseby, the Kings Cabinet being taken, among the papers in it was a Copy of these notes under the L Digbyes hand, wherby Wh was cleered, & the conveyer of the paper to the King, & from him to the E of Strafford, was discovered."[60]

Strafford's ability to challenge the prosecution and expose the flaws in their case meant that the case against him was crumbling fast, and Pym realised that he could no longer pursue the accusation of impeachment with expectations of success. He thus suddenly dropped the prosecution and switched tactics. On April 10 Sir Arthur Haselrig introduced a Bill of Attainder in the Lords. This was nothing more than a restatement of the charges, but the procedure was basically different. Instead of requiring a majority to convict Strafford of certain crimes the Bill of Attainder would, if successful, lead to an Act of Parliament declaring that Strafford's death was necessary to state security, and could be passed if a majority felt the presumption of guilt was strong enough. It did not require legal proof. The change was crucial. Much to George's horror, his original suggestion had returned to haunt him.

By now George was having doubts. The more he examined the case the less he liked it. He still felt that Strafford was dangerous and out of control but he could not justify to himself the basis for the charge of high treason. (Clarendon, in his Four Portraits suggested that George had perceived he could improve his standing with a court increasingly distressed by the accusations against Strafford, and saw his opportunity to speak out. This is somewhat at odds with the odium he now attracted, and the courage with which he persisted in arguing his case). Strafford argued that there should be settled rules of law, and Pym was shifting the goalposts. George agreed with this.[61] Pym asserted that Strafford had abrogated power to himself illegally, and that this was subversion. George acknowledged that he had exercised martial law, that he had monopolies and that he had given the king dangerous advice, but he questioned whether this constituted treason. Moreover, under an Elizabethan statute conviction for treason required two witnesses, and Pym had only one.[62] He remained unconvinced that the most serious charges were proven, or that Strafford was actually guilty of subversion.[63]

As we have seen, throughout the early part of his Parliamentary career George could be seen working closely with his father and father-in-law, the Earl of Bedford. His ideas, while distinctly his own, were clearly influenced by the views of the two politically experienced lords. The Earls of Bristol and Bedford were becoming increasingly disturbed by the situation. As members of the Council of War, they were now attempting to form a middle party which would re-establish the influence of the House of Lords and hold the balance between king and Commons. Bristol, now a Privy Counsellor and at last back in favour with the king, opposed the Attainder and came to Strafford's defence, winning approval from the king for his stand. It is possible that he brought his considerable political weight to bear on his son, but nevertheless what George did now required considerable courage.

From April 15 in the Commons the Bill of Attainder was debated for several days, with George prominent. His keynote speech in opposition to the death sentence for Strafford was a model of logic, eloquence and persuasive argument, displaying great moral courage and integrity at a time when emotions were running high and the majority of the House was baying for Strafford's blood on any pretext. It is worth reproducing at some length:

"I know, Master Speaker, that by some things I have said of late, whilst this Bill was in agitation, I have raised some prejudices upon me in the course....Truly sir, I am still the same in my opinions and affections upon the Earl of Strafford, as that I confidently beleve him the most dangerous Minister, the most insupportable to free subjects that can be charactered....in a word, I beleve him still that grand Apostate to the Commonwealth who must not expect to be pardoned it in this world, till hee be dispatched to the other. And yet let me tell you Master Speaker, my hand must not be to that dispatch, I protest, as my conscience stands informed, I had rather it were off. In prosecution, upon probable grounds, we are accountable onely for our industrie or remissnesse; but in judgement we are deeply responsible to God Almighty, for its rectitude, or obliquity...the same ground whereupon I with the rest of the five...brought down our opinion, that it was fit he should be accused of Treason, upon the same ground, I was ingaged with earnestnesse in his prosecution...to deale plainly with you, that ground of our accusation, that I put to our prosecution, and that which should be the basis of my judgement of the Earle of Strafford, as unto Treason, is to my understanding quite vanished away. This it was Master Speaker: his advising the King to employ the Army of Ireland to reduce England."

He then referred to interrogation of Sir Henry Vane by Pym (three times under oath). The first time asked about the Army of Ireland "he said positively in these words, I cannot charge him with that...Some dayes after, he was examined a second time, and then deposes these words concerning the King's being absolved from rules of Government and so forth, very clearly; But being pressed to that part concerning the Irish Army, againe can say nothing to that. Heere we thought we had done with him, till divers weeks after, my Lord of Northumberland and all others of the Junto, denying to have heard any thing concerning those words of reducing England by the Irish Army, it was thought fit to examine the Secretary once more, and then he deposes these words, to have been said by the Earl of Strafford to his Majesty: 'You have an army in Ireland, which you may deploy heere to reduce...this Kingdome'....Onely let thus much be infer'd from it, that he who twice upon oath, with time of recollection, could not remember any thing of such a businesse, might well a third time misremember somewhat; and in this businesse the difference of one Letter, here for there, or that for this, quite alters the case, the latter also being the more probable, since it is confest of all hands, that the debate then was concerning a war with Scotland...Whereupon I accused him with a free heart, prosecuted him with earnestnesse, and had it to my understanding bin proved, should have Condemned him with innocence; Whereas now I cannot satisfie my conscience to do it. I professe I can have no notion of any bodies intent to subvert the Laws treasonably, but by force, and this designe of force not appearing, all his other wicked practices cannot so high with me.... I do not say but the rest may represent him as a man worthy to die, and worthier perhaps than many a traitor, I do not say but they may justly direct us to Enact that the like shall be Treason for the future. But God keepe me from giving judgemente of death on any Man... upon a law made *a posteriori*. Let the marke be set on the dore where the Plague is and then let him that will enter dye. I know Master Speaker, there is in Parliament a double power of life and death by Bill, a Judicial power and a Legislative; the measure of the one is what's Legally just, of the other what's prudentially and politically fit for the good and preservation of the whole. But these two...are not to be confounded in Judgment. Wee must not peece up want of Legality with matter of convenience, nor the defiance of prudential fitnesse, with a pretence of legall Justice. To Condemne my Lord of Strafford judicially as for Treason, my conscience is not assured that the matter will bear it. And to do it by the Legislative power, my reason consultatively cannot agree to that, since I am persuaded neither the Lords nor the King will passe the Bill, and consequently that our passing it will be a cause of great divisions and combustions in the state.

And therefore my humble advice is, that laying aside this Bill of Attainder, wee may think of another, saving only life, such as may secure the State from my Lord of Strafford, without endangering it, as much by division concerning his punishment, as he hath engaged it by his practices. If this may not be hearkened to, let me conclude in saying that unto you all, which I have thoroughly inculcated to mine owne conscience upon this occasion: Let every man lay his hand upon his heart and sadly consider what wee are going to doe with a breath, either justice or murther....doubtlesse he that commits murther with the sword of Justice heightens that crime to the utmost. The danger being so great, and the case so doubtfull, that I see the best Lawyers in diametrical opposition concerning it. Let every man wipe his heart, as he does his eyes when he would judge of a nice and subtile object: The eye if it be pretainted with a colour, is vitiated in its discerning. Let us take heed of a blood-shotten eye of Judgment. Let every man purge his heart clear of all passions; (I know this great and wise body politic can have none; but I speak to individuals from the weaknesse which I find in myself). Away with all personal animosities, away with all flatteries to the people in being the sharper against him, because he is so odious to them; away with all feares lesst by the spring of blood they may be incenst; away with all such considerations, as that it is not fit for a Parliament that one accused by it of Treason should escape with life....I doe before God discharge myself to the uttermost of my power: And do with a clearer Conscience wash my hands of this man's blood, by this solemn protestation, that my Vote goes not to the taking of the Earl of Strafford's life."[64] His point about lawyers being opposed to the prosecution was true: prominent lawyers such as Orlando Bridgeman, John Selden and Robert Holborne defended Strafford.

Few were swayed. Falkland made a reasoned speech in favour of attainment. His standing in the House, and the conviction he obviously felt had a great impact. George once again drew attention to the influence of the crowds agitating outside Parliament. He was alarmed that many members seemed unwilling to resist this pressure. There was evidence that George's criticism of Vane, his unreliable evidence and the rather chaotic state of his papers, was borne out, for in answer to George's speech a member referred to the fact that "it was a great providence of God, that a copy of the paper hee [Vane] had burned should have been taken, produced, and attested in the manner it was."[65]

It all had no effect. After three readings of the Bill, on April 10, 12 and 15, the vote was conclusively 204 to 59 in favour of Strafford being attainted. Interestingly one of Pym's closest supporters, Hampden, left at the beginning of the division and did not return, having refrained from voting. There is speculation that at the time he was pursuing negotiations with the king.[66] The Earl of Essex, an important figure in this process, was convinced he should die. The Earl of Bedford made a last attempt to persuade Essex to change his mind, suggesting that it would be sufficient if Strafford was stripped of all offices. Essex was adamant: "Stone dead hath no fellow."[67] Strafford's fate was sealed.

From being one of the leaders in Parliament, George became one of its most reviled members. His colleagues felt betrayed; they had become totally committed to destroying Strafford, and George's change of heart was less than helpful. He was called to explain himself to the House, but when he did he was further condemned.

In a desperate last attempt to save Strafford, Charles summoned the Commons to the House of Lords. There they found him seated on a throne in his full regalia. He begged that Stafford be exiled, banished, anything but death, and hinted darkly at reprisals if they chose to disobey him. He had been advised by the Earl of Bedford that the Lords were still by no means convinced of Strafford's guilt, and that a direct appeal to them could sway their decision. Instead they received a peremptory statement that he could not in conscience sign the Bill, as the Royal prerogative overrode Parliament. This was not well received, and at the crucial moment when the king badly needed advice the Earl of Bedford took ill.

On May 3 about 5000 people gathered at Westminster, accusing those who had voted against the Attainder as "Enemies of Justice," and demanding that they perish with Strafford.[68]

When Bristol's coach emerged some protesters surrounded it shouting "We know you are an apostate from the cause of Christ, and our mortal enemy; we do not therefore crave justice from you, but shall, God willing, crave justice upon you and your false son, the Lord Digby."[69] George's name headed a list of "Straffordians" posted in Old Palace Yard. Talk of plots and assistance from foreign powers swept London. The ports were closed. It was rumoured that the French had agreed to supply ten regiments to the king's army at York or Portsmouth and had taken the Channel Islands, that a Spanish army was preparing to invade, that the Catholics had set fire to the House of Commons. When the Lords arrived at Parliament to debate the Bill of Attainder, they could hardly find their way through the crowds shouting out furiously for "justice."[70] Thoroughly alarmed, they supported the Commons, voting 26 to 19 in favour, Bristol abstaining. This was achieved by a political faction in the Lords which supported Pym pushing through a crucial motion setting aside the normal rules of evidence which called for two witnesses.[71] On May 8, the Earl of Bedford died, removing a staunch supporter of the king and Strafford.

Strafford was duly found guilty of treason and beheaded on May 12, 1641 on Tower Hill, the king signing the fatal warrant. The battle lines were drawn and individuals were taking sides. Parliament and the king were irreconcilable, and the execution of Strafford created a dangerous animus. George, by supporting the Crown, had clearly chosen his allegiance and Parliament, perceiving George and his father to be influential in gathering together around the king those opposed to Pym and his tactics, turned on him angrily. He found himself in grave peril

Chapter 5.

Driven Into Exile.

The king had hoped that Strafford's blood would appease the Commons, and that they would be in a more cooperative mood thereafter, but the opposite was the case. Parliament's victory had emphatically reasserted it's influence, even if many citizens were having second thoughts about Strafford's fate. Pym and his followers pressed for more reform, passing a number of Acts without debate, including the Triennial Bill. The more hot-headed members of the Popular Party chose this moment to debate the Root and Branch Bill in the Commons, aiming to remove bishops altogether. George, under heavy criticism from antagonistic members, was unable to make any impact on Parliament. Pym sought to strengthen ties with the Scots by allowing the Presbyterians in the Commons to propose the abolition of episcopacy and the secularisation of cathedrals and university colleges. Ship-money was made illegal along with other means of raising revenue such as knighthoods, tonnage and poundage, and forestry.

George chose this moment to aggravate the animosity felt towards him. He arranged for his speech against the attainder of Strafford to be published and distributed in London. Five hundred copies were printed, and the pamphlet was soon the talk of the nation.[72] The speech was publicly burned, and the Parliamentary leaders passed a resolution "That the Lord Digby's Speech contains within it matters untrue and scandalous...and that the publishing of that Speech, after a Vote passed in the House upon the said Bill, and Offence taken to it....is scandalous to the Proceedings of this House, and a Crime....That the Speech shall be burnt in the New Palace at Westminster, Cheapside, and Smithfield,....That both Houses do move his Majesty to forbear to confer any Honour or Imployment upon the Person of George Lord Digby, who hath declared so ill of the Parliament."[73] In January 1642 George published "Lord Digbie's Apologie for Himselfe" in which he blamed his step-brother, Lewis Dyve, for publishing the speech without asking his consent.

By publishing his speech on Strafford without the permission of Parliament, a clear breach of privilege, George had placed himself in danger of being sent to the Tower, but the king and queen now saved him. Henrietta Maria had been as energetic as anyone in attempting to help Strafford. She had invited the leading Parliamentarians to meet her in an attempt to persuade them to drop the charge, often offering inducements of one sort or another. One of the few who had agreed to come to the queen by the back stairs was George, by now despairing of his position in the House. The Commons had ordered that his name be included in a list of fifty-nine members who had voted against the charge. This list was posted publicly, and proceedings commenced to have him excluded from the House. But on June 9 1641 the king announced his elevation to the House of Lords as Baron Digby. He was now one of Charles's closest advisers, on all the standing committees in the Lords. This was to provide a respite from his foes, for Pym was reluctant to attack a member of the House of Lords and thus further widen the differences between the two Houses.

George's views were more in sympathy with the Lords, and they in turn were fascinated by this energetic newcomer. He retained the friendship of Edward Hyde, later to become Earl Clarendon and one of the most powerful man in the country after the king. Three years older than George, the son of a lawyer, Edward Hyde had made a career in law. His family were moderately wealthy but not of the aristocracy, and this flamboyant young nobleman must have dazzled him. But

Hyde commented of George: "He was called up by writ to the House of Peers, as fit to move in that sphere, where he no sooner came than he gave fresh life and vigour to it, the real temper of that House retaining a vigorous affection to the King, Church, and Government, and consequently very inclined to follow his example, and to be swayed by his reason, who always delivered himself with noble advantage, and was now known to be trusted by the Court, and so like to carry on their designs in the method prescribed there...and truly, if the too great activity and restlessness of his nature would have given him leave to have sat still, and expected, and made use of those advantages...it is very probable, the wisdom and temper of the one House, with the concurrence it would have found from the major part of the other, which was far from being corrupted, would have prevented those calamities, which, under the specious authority of the Parliament, were afterwards brought upon the Kingdom."[74] For Hyde was later to blame George for starting the Civil War.

The tide was running strongly against the Crown. The Venetian ambassador reported that the Commons were seeking measures against its opposers, and of these "the Earl of Bristol and his son are the most threatened and we expect to hear of some severe measures very soon."[75] The king, alarmed at the direction the Commons was taking, cultivated the army officers among the court circle. He still controlled the army that had been raised for the invasion of Scotland, and although the commander, the Earl of Essex, was loyal to Parliament, a number of the Protestant officers were devoted to the king. Some of these officers also sat in the Commons and often attended the queen. This group formed the beginning of a rather sinister, extreme group and were encouraged by the queen. The rumour was of a conspiracy between the army in the north, the force guarding the Tower and France to threaten the nation.[76] Pym was aware of this so-called movement and in May, after the king had tried to send troops to secure the

Tower, moved the Commons to dismiss several of the group from office on the grounds they were part of an "Army Plot" to dissolve Parliament and arrest its leading members.

Suspicion was focused on the queen. Some officers saw the crowds as threatening the safety of the members of both Houses, and proposed that the army offer to restore order in London, but there was little support within the army for such a move. There was a suspicion that some members of Parliament were encouraging civil unrest for their own ends, and those who disapproved of the presence of the crowds at Westminster, such as Falkland and George, "from that time forward joined with the king."[77]

Pym obtained agreement that in future all appointments to the household of the queen or her children should be made only with consent of Parliament.[78] In July a bill abolishing the Star Chamber and its kindred courts in Wales and the north was passed, fundamentally changing the relationship between Parliament and the Crown and bringing to an end the direct judicial powers of the Crown. Charles, without his closest friend and adviser Strafford, signed the new laws without much thought.[79] Pym was cleverly pursuing a well thought-out plan to reduce the influence of the Crown and increase that of Parliament. The legislation which followed the death of Strafford was to be far-reaching. The Crown had been decisively stripped of sovereignty in most important matters; as yet Parliament had not yet assumed the mantle. The king was dependent upon a House which in turn could only act with the consent of the king. In response he turned to the House of Lords for support, appointing a number of lords sympathetic to him. The Earl of Bath, Lord Dunsmore and Lord Seymour were made Privy Counsellors, and Edward Nicholas, Clerk of the Council, was designated Secretary of State. Son of a country squire, Nicholas had followed his father into the law profession and thence secured his position with Buckingham through a family friend, John Dacombe. By the time Buckingham died his reputation was established at court, and he was appointed Secretary to the Commissioners at the Admiralty. He was seen increasingly at court, and came to be relied upon by the king for secretarial duties of various kinds. Thus at the age of 47 he was in the right place at the right time when a new Secretary of State was being sought. Many of the new appointments appear to have been recommended by the Earl of Bristol, George's father. The most interesting perhaps was the elevation of the Duke of Lennox to Duke of Richmond, for he was married to the only daughter of Bristol's old, now dead, enemy the Duke of Buckingham. Nicholas had, of course, once been secretary to Buckingham. Thus Bristol can be seen working to bring together those loyal to Charles in opposition to Parliament.

The latter half of 1641 was a period in which the Digbys' fortunes flourished. Bristol was appointed Gentleman of the Bedchamber on August 8, while George was made Ambassador to France. The retiring ambassador, the Earl of Leicester, had returned to England on July 26, and the Venetian ambassador described his replacement, George, as a young man combining "high birth with remarkable prudence and unequalled ability."[80] He never took up the position. Although the Lords passed a resolution appointing him, this was rejected by the Commons. Despite this setback, he retained the goodwill of the king. His father clearly felt that his own appointment signified his reinstatement in the eyes of the king. Bristol wrote: "It has pleased the King, after many years, totally to remove from me the markes of his former displeasure by commanding me to wait on him as Gentleman in Ordinary of his Bedchamber."[81] Both father and son can be seen in 1641 to be working very hard in the Lords to represent the king's views. Ironically, one of the tasks carried out by George was to oppose the demand to remove the king's "evil counsellors," which included the bishops.

While the Digbys remained in London to manage the king's affairs, on August 10 Charles left London for Edinburgh, hoping to negotiate an alliance with the Covenanters and perhaps assemble a northern army which he could hold in reserve against his enemies in London. Pym made a last-minute attempt to stop him. The king merely replied that he was glad to find himself so desired in both kingdoms. The king's journey was seen by many as a flight from England, and he was mobbed by members of the public imploring him to turn back.

On Monday, November 9, Parliament met to review the news of Charles' negotiations with the Scots.. They were alarmed that the king no longer referred to the Scots as rebels, but this topic was rapidly overtaken by the desire of members to vent their frustrations at the many perceived wrongs they suffered. Culpeper made an impassioned speech attacking ship-money, monopolies and the damage done to trade. The next day George took up the themes in what Peyton describes as "a most excellent speech."[82] In addition to the themes that Culpeper had raised, he returned to the constitutional issue of the clerical claim to legislate. Although aimed at the bishops, he was obliquely criticising the king's assumption of legislative supremacy over Parliament.[83]

On October 21 a debate took place over a bill to take away the votes of bishops in the Lords. It was passed in the Commons against the opposition of Falkland and Hyde but failed to carry the Lords. A demand for removal of the king's evil counsellors, aimed at the episcopacy, was opposed in the Lords and agreed to be deferred, with the Earl of Bristol and George prominent. Nicholas drew the king's attention to the Digbys' work: "…the singular good service that was in that business done by those two noblemen, and especially the sonne, who…did beyond admirac'on."[84]

On October 23 1641 bad news came from Ireland. The Catholics fearing that Parliament would pursue a more aggressive anti-Catholic policy, rebelled. They pledged their loyalty to the king, and Pym claimed that some of the leaders, notably Philem O'Neill, had been encouraged by the king. But in truth they were rebelling against a Dublin government appointed by the king, and the Irish Catholics were in fact resisting English rule. They feared that thousands more English Protestants would be introduced to Ireland as settlers. They marauded across the island, driving English settlers from their homes. Soon horrific stories, not all of them invented, began to circulate in England of the outrages and cruelties inflicted on Protestant settlers by the insurgents. This rebellion presented Parliament with a dilemma. An army was required to repress the Irish, but members feared to vote the necessary resources in case the king turned these forces against Parliament.

On November 22 the Grand Remonstrance was introduced in the House of Commons. It's purpose was to demonstrate that the king was unfit to choose his own counsellors or control the army.[85] But it was also a criticism of the House of Lords, and Charles described it as "an attempt to incense the people against us and the House of Lords."[86] It made a plea for him to change his counsellors, and it set out the terms on which the Commons would vote the king funds. These terms addressed a long list of grievances, including popery and the role of bishops. Hyde led the opposition by declaring that he was not against the Remonstrance in principle; on the contrary he supported the proposal that a short statement concerning the business of the present Parliament should be presented to the king. But, he argued, a long and detailed catalogue of complaints covering Charles' entire reign would merely anger the king and alienate the House of Lords. Falkland followed this up by asking what the populace would think of the Commons should they rake over events so far in the past as to be part of history. Culpeper added that the Remonstrance was probably unconstitutional, as it was really addressed to the electorate and not the king. These powerful speeches drew the moderate elements of the Commons together in opposition to the motion. George appears not to have spoken in this debate, presumably embarrassed by his initial support for the Bill. Pym showed flexibility by offering to drop the odd clause, or amend another while remaining insistent that the Remonstrance as a whole stand. Finally at one o'clock in the morning with three hundred and seven members still present a vote was taken. By eleven votes the Remonstrance was passed, although many of the leaders voted against it, including Culpeper, Falkland, Sir Ralph Hopton and "all the best lawyers."[87] On leaving the House, Oliver Cromwell was heard to say that had the Remonstrance been rejected he would have sold all his possessions and emigrated to America. In fact the Remonstrance was seen by many as being inflammatory and provocative. Men such as Hyde and Culpeper, who wished to cajole the king rather than confront him, were horrified at what reaction it might bring. Hyde was also concerned that the Lords, who had not been consulted, might bring a counter-remonstrance.[88]

The king could make no real progress with the intransigent Scots. By encouraging first one side and then the other, Charles merely aggravated the differences which already existed between the factions in Scotland. He returned to London on November 25, believing he had cemented an alliance with the Covenanters, but this was far from the case. He was cheered as he rode through London, the people relieved at his return.

The Remonstrance was presented to the king on December 1, and later published. The king's answer, published on December 20, was based upon a draft reply by Hyde. This was intended to be a private note, but George caught sight of it and was so impressed with Hyde's reasoning that he recommended that it should be shown to the king. Hyde was horrified. Still in the House of Commons as the member for Saltash, Hyde was one of the leading critics of the path Parliament was treading and increasingly concerned by the Remonstrance and

Pym's tactics. He recognised that should his authorship leak out he would be ruined in the House of Commons. George, backed by the king, assured him that the authorship would not be revealed. With this assurance Hyde had little option, and the note was sent to the king. He later wrote that when the reply was published, over the name of the king and with the full backing of the Privy Council, it was well received, "…and it was very apparent to all Men, that the King's Service was very much advanced by it."[89] Although Parliament sought every means at its disposal to discover who had written the response, they never identified Hyde. This episode did Hyde's cause much good in the eyes of the king, who shortly thereafter offered him the post of Solicitor-General for his "many good Services." [90] Hyde refused the post on the grounds that he was not yet ready for such an honour, particularly as it would mean replacing the encumbent, St John who, he remarked, "..though the Solicitor will never do much Service, He will be able to do much more Mischief if He be removed."[91] Offered an alternative post, he turned that down as well, saying he could do more service to the king where he presently was.

Meanwhile the king was very pleased with the Digbys, and Bristol and his son were frequently talked about as having increasing influence over the king. In early December George was being talked of as a candidate for Secretary of State to replace Vane, and his father as Groom of the Stole.[92] The Digbys seem to have been on friendly terms with the powerful Villiers faction, who still held considerable sway at court. The bitter animosity between Bristol and the Duke of Buckingham was now history. Although George was not appointed he managed to persuade Culpeper to become Chancellor, with Falkland as Secretary of State. Falkland, an intelligent but modest and retiring man, would only accept the position if Hyde agreed to assist and advise him, which Hyde was delighted to do. Thus George was able to assemble around the king a powerful quartet of advisers who respected each other's views and were all men of integrity and moderation. His skill at having appointed such moderate men in positions of such influence gave the lie to the opinion of some observers that George pressed for ultra-Royalist views. He can also at this time be seen to be advancing Hyde's career significantly.

George also advised the king that it was important to re-establish the Crown's influence in the Commons. Opposition to the Remonstrance had been strong. Charles should seek to drive a wedge between Pym and the more moderate of his supporters. Pym was aware of the precariousness of his position, and reopened the attack on the bishops, who were supporters of the Crown. He indulged in some rabble-rousing, inciting the apprentices to demonstrate against the bishops.

Mobs continued to besiege Parliament, and even sought to influence individual members. Sir John Strangeways was surrounded by some 200 people demanding that he vote for the "putting down of bishops." He told them that "they must desire in a legal way what they would have legally done."[93] Some of the crowd then attempted to break into the House of Lords, but were repulsed by the Earl of Dorset, whose guard fired above their heads to disperse them. Strangeways, a close friend of the Digbys, told the Commons that he had received information "of a plot or conspiracy for the destruction of some of the members of this House....and said that he was informed that some of the members of the House were either contrivers or consenters to it."[94] There was evidence that a member, Captain Venn, had sent a message to his wife telling her to send the citizens to Westminster with their weapons, but this was the only concrete evidence Strangeways had and the claim was ignored by Parliament.

George and his father came under strong attack from the Commons. The Earl of Bristol was accused of attempting to broker a truce between Holland and Spain, mediated by Charles. His role in the Spanish match was resurrected, and he was accused of trying to convert the king to Catholicism.

On December 23 George provoked the Commons further by accusing them of invading the privileges of the Lords and the liberties of the subject. On December 29 Pym, among others, pressed the Lords for Bristol 's "removal and for justice against George."[95]

George sought to have Lewis Dyves appointed to replace Sir William Balfour as Lieutenant of the Tower of London. Balfour was a Puritan, unpopular with the king and not well-liked in the country either. Charles offered him £3,000 to resign and when he refused, dismissed him.[96] Parliament immediately declared Balfour to be a most excellent and trustworthy officer, and opposed the dismissal. No doubt the unpopularity of George in the Commons contributed to the opposition to his brother-in-law. Dyve was not in London at that time and the king needed to replace Balfour immediately, so George was forced to cast about quickly for a substitute, and "Col. Lunsford hearing of it, and obtaining the letters of many popish Lords, hee presented himselfe unto the King, as a very true and loyall subject ...and thus by great conivance he was elected to be Lieutenant of the tower, although indeed hee was a great signior of the Papists." These rumours caused the apprentices to take to the streets in protest again.[97]

Thomas Lunsford was a soldier with an unsavoury past. Several years previously Lunsford had narrowly escaped trial for murder, and was said, improbably, to roast the flesh of babies.[98] Two captains in the City's trained bands, Randall Mainwaring and Maximilian Bond, brought a petition to the Commons against Lunsford, arguing that he was "a man given to drinking, swearing and quarrelling...(who)...may be tempted to undertake any ill design."[99] A petition was raised claiming that Lunsford's control of the Tower would be prejudicial to the City, and it was reported that merchants were withdrawing bullion from the mint within the Tower.[100] It is highly questionable whether George was involved in the appointment of Lunsford, as he hardly knew the man,[101] although some historians[102] believe that it is likely that George, rather than the very moderate constitutionalists, Falkland and Hyde, would have influenced the king in this instance.

George remained concerned about the unrest on the streets, and in particular argued that the rioting in the vicinity of Westminster meant that Parliament could not function freely. On December 27 he was appointed to a Committee along with his brother-in-law, the Earl of Bedford to enquire into the disturbances and to prepare a conference to discuss the matter in the Commons.[103] On December 28, George moved that Parliament should reconvene at a safer place.[104] The House of Commons took exception at his comments, accusing him of complaining that the Commons was encouraging unrest and thus infringing upon the rights of the Lords. There may have been some substance in this, for George and his father were becoming increasingly concerned at Pym's animosity towards them. There was even talk of impeaching the two, with Cromwell moving the proposal and being supported by John Hotham, of whom more later.[105] Proposed charges against the Digbys were eventually dropped quietly, but it was clear that they were regarded as enemies of the Commons.

The breach between Crown and Parliament was by now serious. The king was suspicious of Parliament, seeing it as a threat to his sovereignty. The blunders made by the Crown had encouraged the Parliamentary leaders to believe they could make progress with their grievances by bringing pressure to bear on the king. The role of the bishops was central to the dispute. Parliament felt they wielded too much influence in the House of Lords. They were also unpopular with the London demonstrators who stopped coaches as they emerged from Parliament shouting "No bishops" and "No popish Lords." Asked to disperse, they replied that they were afraid to return home as Colonel Lunsford and his soldiers lay in wait for them. Three days of demonstrations against Lunsford ensued aimed at having him replaced, a demand supported by the Commons but opposed by the Lords. On December 27 Lunsford was at the Commons lobbying for arrears of pay when he was confronted by the apprentices. He drew his sword and attacked them, wounding several. In the ensuing slanging match the epithet Roundhead arose for the first time, as a description of the unkempt, bullet-headed apprentices. The term Cavalier was already common, used to describe armed officers such as Lunsford who were hard-drinking, foul-mouthed and quick to use their swords. There were signs of the emergence of disgruntled professional soldiers waiting for their pay arrears and looking for new commands in Ireland.[106] In fact the king had finally yielded to the Commons' demands and had dismissed Lunsford the day before this confrontation, although this was not known by the apprentices. He was replaced by Sir John Byron.

Chased out of Westminster Hall by officers with drawn swords, the crowd massed in Palace Yard and barracked members of Parliament as they entered or left the House. George again argued that the threat posed invalidated much of the work of the present Parliament as it infringed the rights of members but this was opposed by the Lords as it was recognised that this could create a precedent.[107] On December 28 the demonstrators succeeded in preventing twelve bishops from entering the Lords. Any that attempted to approach the House were surrounded and jostled, and several feared for their lives. Thomas Smith wrote at this time that the bishops had attempted to make this "Parliament no Parliament, and so to overthrow all Acts passed and so to cause a dissolution of it for the present." Pym saw his opportunity and moved the Commons to vote for the impeachment of all the bishops. The Lords endorsed this, and the dozen bishops were bundled off to prison. The next day Archbishop John Williams, encouraged by George, protested that if bishops were forcibly expelled by mob rule their absence would render the House of Lords incomplete and its legislation invalid. The Commons reacted to this pressure by voicing the suspicion that this was a ploy by the king to have Parliament dissolved.

There was some substance to this claim. In addition to Lunsford's swashbuckling assault on the apprentices, the king had asked the Mayor of London to restore order to the streets using the trained-bands. However these bands were unreliable, and had much sympathy with the demonstrators, so Charles called on his forces from the Tower under Byron to help. He also accepted an offer of protection from Lunsford, who moved to guard the palace with 120 men.[108] The consequent build-up of Cavaliers in the vicinity of Westminster led many members of Parliament to fear that the king was about to expel them by force. They requested that the Earl of Essex be appointed to guard the House, and incidentally to control the unruly demonstrators, who concerned them almost as much as the king.

There was now a serious danger of the authorities losing control. The Commons found themselves caught in the middle. Afraid that the king intended to challenge them, they looked to their electorate for support, but at the same time they were alarmed that the popular riots could not be contained and controlled. On December 30 between three and five hundred young men of the Inns of Court marched to the palace pledging their allegiance to Royalty, whom they believed to be in danger, and offered their services for the "suppression of these tumultuous assemblies."[109] As a consequence the unrest subsided somewhat, and the Commons assured the king that it would co-operate in seeking to control the mobs.

Chapter 6.

Parting Of The Ways.

There now occurred one of those defining incidents which was to accelerate the plunge towards civil war. Clarendon later called it "...the worst judged, and worst executed gamble of his (Charles') career." The king was resentful of criticism levelled at the queen, his wife, a Catholic who was suspected by Parliament of encouraging rebellion in Ireland. On January 2, 1642 a rumour reached the king that the Commons intended to impeach his wife.[110] George is thought to have been responsible for bringing this to the queen's notice[111] although Clarendon believed it was Lady Carlisle who warned the queen.[112] There is no evidence that Parliament intended to seize the queen, but it is possible that the rumour, which spoke of a meeting at the house of Viscount Mandeville (previously Lord Kimbolton) in Kensington involving Essex, Saye, Wharton, Pym and Fiennes was started in order to provoke the king.[113] Alarmed by the appointment of the Earl of Essex to guard Parliament, the queen and George advised the king to resist the deployment of Essex's men and to offer instead two hundred of the trained-band under Lord Lindsey, the king's commander.[114] The king was urged to assert his authority over Parliament, and to resist any attempts to usurp his position. It was argued that the riotous assemblies outside Parliament had been orchestrated by a small group in the Commons which owed its power and influence to mob violence.

Pym informed a bemused Commons that a villainous plot was about to be hatched. Some shops were shut and citizens started to arm for self-protection. Inspired by George, with the hysterical support of the queen who was afraid that she was about to be impeached of high treason,[115] the king impeached Mandeville, the son of the Earl of Manchester and leading Puritan agitator in the Lords, and five members of Parliament, Pym, Hampden, Holles, Heselrigge and Strode. They were accused of high treason for "they have endeavoured…by force and terror to compel the Parliament to join with them in their traitorous designs, and to that end have actually raised and countenanced tumults against the king and Parliament."[116] Although there was no direct evidence of the five actively plotting, it was claimed that they had directed others to incite violence. Among those cited were two radicals, neither of whom was an MP. John Fowke, a Levant Company trader, soon to be a common councillor, and Randall Mainwaring, captain of the London trained-bands, were accused of going from house to house in London encouraging inhabitants to go to Westminster and demonstrate. The Puritan Venn was also implicated, and there was evidence to show that he had organised some of the protests, although he was also seen calming the crowds.[117] In fact it is unlikely that Pym and his followers instigated the unrest, though they did use it for their own purposes.

It could be argued that the case against the five would stand up just as well as the impeachment of Strafford. As early as September 1640 the king had stated that he would not forget his subjects' treasonable correspondence with the Scots, and their behaviour in the Commons clearly amounted to an attempt to alienate the people's affections from the king. They had also encouraged a foreign power (the Scots) to invade England, and had passed legislation which subverted fundamental laws and placed great power in the hands of citizens. It was also claimed that Pym was working closely with the London radicals to stir up sedition.

The Attorney-General, Edward Herbert, announced the impeachment in the Lords on January 3, 1642. It was plain that the Lords were much troubled by the proposal and they refused to order any arrests until they had determined whether the Attorney-General was acting within the law. Ironically the Earl of Bristol's impeachment in 1626 had been declared unconstitutional, and it was clear that Mandeville's was as well.[118] It was planned that at this point George should demand the imprisonment of the five. Sitting next to Mandeville, he missed his cue to rise and accuse him of treason, and "never spake the least word." He is said to have been most surprised at the impeachment and to have whispered in Mandeville's ear "That the king was very michievously advised and that it should go very hard but he would know whence that council proceeded; in order to which, and to prevent further mischieve, he would go immediately to his majesty."[119] Shortly thereafter he left the chamber. As he was the only person on the order to have named Mandeville, having not spoken in the House no action could be taken against the peer. George's surprise may have been genuine, for there is evidence that Mandeville was added to the list at a late stage, possibly on the strength of the rumour about the meeting at his house. The order was in the king's hand and erasures on the document clearly indicate that Mandeville's inclusion was an afterthought.[120] It is probable that the original intention was to call him as a witness and it is possible that George was not informed of the change or primed to respond, although Mandeville was a rival to George and was talked about as a Secretary of State in preference to George, who may have sought to have him removed.

The House of Commons, alerted to the move in the Lords, sent in a request for a conference with the Lords, claiming that the accusation was a breach of privilege. A committee was formed to consider the precedents for such a move, and the Earl of Bristol was among those appointed to the committee. The king made public the articles of treason against the five men, arguing that no Parliamentary privilege could protect them against treason. The king's supporters in the Inns of Court were alerted to be ready to defend the king at Westminster.

That evening George met the queen to discuss what should be done. Throughout the affair the queen had adopted a stronger and more aggressive stance than the king, probably because she recognised how unpopular she was and was afraid of impeachment. George was equally unpopular in Parliament, and together they decided to urge the king to move against the accused members.[121] The king met in Council with Culpeper, Falkland and Nicholas to consider their next move. The queen is said to have told him: "Go, you poltroon! Go pull these rogues out by the ears or never see my face again!"[122]

The same night two Members of Parliament, John Venn and Isaac Pennington urgently requested the Mayor to provide a trained-band to protect Parliament against an attack by the king. Hearing of this, the king issued an instruction to the Mayor forbidding him to help the Commons, and threatening to use force against any crowd trouble.

An order was issued for the arrest of the five accused, but when the serjeant-at-arms was sent to the Commons to arrest the members on the morning of January 4 the House replied that this involved their privileges and they were questioning its legality. It was seen as a direct threat against Parliamentary rights. So in the afternoon Charles, accompanied by four hundred swordsmen, came to the House. As he approached, Pym requested leave of the Speaker and left with the other accused. The doors of the Commons were flung open and Charles, accompanied by his nephew, the Elector Palatine, entered and approached the Speaker between rows of silent, standing members. The king requested that the speaker give him his chair. From there he addressed the House, accusing the impeached members of treason. He was met with a stony silence, and when he called for the five to come forward he found they were not present. The king was forced to acknowledge that the coup had failed. "Well!" he said, "since I see all my birds have flown, I do expect that you will send them unto me as soon as they return hither." He left with the cries of "Privilege! Privilege!" ringing in his ears.[123]

The fate of the five accused lay in the hands of the people of London. George urged the king to allow him to take Colonel Lunsford and half a dozen gentlemen to fetch the fugitive members from their refuge in the City.[124] But this was too rash a venture even for the king. He did however issue a proclamation ordering the City to surrender the five, and confronted the meeting of Common Council at the Guildhall to explain his reasons for going to Parliament and demanding they be handed over. He argued that they were dangerous men and that neither he nor Parliament would be safe if they were allowed to remain free.[125] The Council replied that the five were protected by privilege of Parliament, to which he replied: "No privileges can protect a traitor from a legal trial."[126] The London trained-bands turned out to protect Parliament, but with the king's ally Sir John Byron in charge at the Tower and Lunsford's men on hand Charles felt he could still take the members by force if he could find out where they were. George was sent to Surrey to collect more volunteers. Battle lines were drawn.

Mobs took to the streets again shouting "Privilege! Privilege!" The king, in his preoccupation with the charge against the five, had misjudged the strength of feelings among the population. He realised that London was lost. Four thousand armed squires and freeholders poured out of Buckinghamshire to protect their Member of Parliament, John Hampden. Sailors and lightermen marched through cheering crowds in the City, offering to live and die for Parliament.[127] The next day the Commons met in committee at the Guildhall (close to where the five members were hiding, in a house in Coleman Street) to issue a proclamation declaring as public enemies anyone who assisted the king in his attempt to arrest the five. The breach between king and Commons was final. Clarendon had no doubt about the significance of this episode:

"In one stroke of unimaginable idiocy the King had destroyed everything they (Hyde, Culpeper and Falkland) had been working for. He had made a present of the middle ground to his most implacable adversaries."[128] War loomed.

It was not long before George's part in this scheme was fully known. By now he "..had almost the whole nation his enemy, being the most universally odious of any man in it."[129] He was soon to be in worse trouble. London was in uproar, with shops shut and bands of unruly citizens roaming the streets. The king, fearing for his life and even more for that of his unpopular wife, had retired to Hampton Court on January 10 to remove himself from the ferment in London, possibly on the advice of George, who was accused by Parliament of advising the king to flee. On January 11 the five accused returned to Parliament. They were accompanied along the river by a flotilla of gaily-decked craft packed with cheering throngs of townsfolk and many of their fellow Parliamentarians. As they passed the empty Palace of Westminster they called out: "Where is the King and his Cavaliers?"[130]

At Hampton Court a group of between forty and fifty soldiers were clamouring for pay due them from the northern expedition. They were persuaded to return to their quarters in Kingston-upon-Thames and George was sent to pay them. He took a coach- and-six, and with him went the unpopular Colonel Lunsford in another coach with one servant. George's part in the proposal to wrest the Parliamentary five from their refuge in the City had become general knowledge, and in the hothouse atmosphere which prevailed in London a rumour immediately circulated that he was armed and that Kingston was packed with horses and ammunition. This part of it was true: Kingston did have a large store of ammunition, and it is possible that in the feverish atmosphere that prevailed George and Lunsford planned to use it. It was reported that Lunsford had ridden into the town with some three hundred troops and had been drinking, swaggering and swearing, to the terror of the townsfolk. They were quoted as saying that "they should see bloody times ere long." When news of this reached London it was reported that "Colonell Lunsford was risen up in Rebellion at Kingston-upon-Thames, and had thousands of men there, and that he would come against England and cut all the Protestants throats."[131]

General Philip Skippon was summoned by Parliament to defend London. Orders to secure the peace were given to the Sheriffs of Surrey, Berkshire, Buckinghamshire, Oxfordshire and Middlesex. Lunsford was arrested and imprisoned in the Tower. George was ordered to appear before the Lords and explain himself. On January 15, 1642 Sir Philip Stapleton made a speech in the House accusing George and Lunsford of high treason. The list of misdemeanours George is supposed to have committed included deserting Parliament, betraying a position of trust, opposing the entire House on Strafford's attainder, mixing with public enemies (Lunsford), and taking up arms without the permission of the king or Parliament.

George recognised that life had become very uncomfortable in England. He resolved to leave the country. He decided to go to Ireland, but having journeyed to Wales found it difficult to secure a boat to take him as Parliament had decreed that a special licence was required by anyone wishing to go to Ireland. He stayed in Carmarthen until he found a French barque, Le Olive Shampanell, willing to take him to France. No sooner had he set sail than the weather deteriorated and for eight days the ship hugged the Welsh coast riding out the storm. The Vice-Admiral of the Fleet, Sir John Pennington, was also sheltering from the bad weather and he imprisoned George on his ship and requested instructions from Parliament. George produced a warrant, dated January 13, signed by the king giving orders to Pennington for him to be transported "beyond the seas" to France or Holland. Finally George was released and made his way to Deal. There he again met Pennington, and dined with him on his flagship before boarding The Lion's Whelp, a despatch boat bound for Holland on January 16, 1642. Before the ship sailed he received a letter, the contents of which are unknown but which caused him to disembark and turn back towards London.[132] At Canterbury he was stopped by the mayor, who knew of his flight because letters from Lewis Dyve in London had been intercepted there. Arguing that he was on his way back to London to obey the summons of the Lords, he was released and recommenced his journey towards London. Once out of Canterbury however, he changed course and returned under cover of darkness to Deal, where he finally sailed for Holland on The Lion's Whelp. Later George was to refer to this incident in a letter to Dyve, in which he claimed that he would have actually returned to London had he not been stopped at Canterbury.[133]

It was as well for George that he did leave England at this time, for another plot was discovered shortly thereafter. John Pellam, a boy employed at the castle in Sherborne, gave some of his friends from the town gunpowder to make fireworks, and the source of this supply was revealed to their parents when they asked their children from whence it had come. The militia were called and a search of Sherborne Castle uncovered a vast store of arms in the cellar: two hundred barrels of gunpowder, three hundred muskets, fifteen hundred small arms - pistols, carbines and harquebusse - pikes and lances. The steward was interrogated but said that they belonged to his master and that only he could answer. Then a wagon full of arms and ammunition was stopped at Bagshot, then again at Hartford Bridge. It contained 38 cases of pistols, saddles, four small locked trunks, bullets, two swords and three barrels of gunpowder. It was also in the charge of one of George's servants.

Parliament used the incident involving Lunsford to bring a charge against George. They claimed this amounted to levying war against the king. Further evidence was presented concerning the discovery of arms and ammunition at Sherborne. George referred to this accusation as "a great treason of mine plotted and discovered at Sherborne."[134] On 26th February, 1642, the House of Commons impeached George on a charge of high treason, which read:

"1. That in or about the month of January he had maliciously and traitorously endeavoured to persuade the King to levy war against his liege subjects within this Kingdom, and that he did actually levy forces within the realm to the terror of His Majesty's subjects.

2. That he had falsely, maliciously and traitorously endeavoured to raise a dissension between the King and his people and to possess His Majesty that he could not live in safety of his own person among them, and did thereupon persuade His Majesty to betake himself to some place of strength for his own defence;

3. That he endeavoured to stir up jealousies and dissensions between the King and his Parliament, and to that end did wickedly advise the framing certain false articles against Lord Kimbolton, Denzil Hooles, etc., and did persuade His Majesty, accompanied by divers soldiers and others in warlike manner to come in person to the House of Commons and demand the said House then sitting, to the apparent danger of His Majesty's person and in high violation of the principles of Parliament."[135]

Chapter 7.

Exile.

George took refuge in Middleburg, capital of Zeeland, at the Sign of the Golden Fleece, an inn, under the name of Baron Digby of Sherborne. He was soon assailing friends and colleagues with ideas, schemes and advice. To his half-brother Lewis Dyve he wrote: "If the King declare himself and retire to a safe place I shall be able to wait upon him from hence as well as out of any part of England. Besides this I found all the ports so strict that if I had not taken the opportunity of Sir John Pennington's forwardness in the King's service it would have been impossible for me to have gotten away at any other time."[136]

When the coup against the five in Parliament failed Charles's position was seriously weakened. His first priority was to secure the safety of his family, and after a brief stay at Windsor the entourage moved on to Dover, where the queen and her younger children embarked for Holland on February 23, 1642 taking with her the crown jewels and urgent requests for military help addressed to the Prince of Orange and King of Denmark. The king rode along the cliffs waving his hat in farewell before turning back to Hampton Court.

With the queen went the king's nephew, Prince Rupert. A significant volunteer to the king's lists, he was the third son of the king's sister Elizabeth, who had married the Elector Palatine, Frederick V. He was born in Prague in 1619 and was educated at the University of Leyden. He had seen active service in the Netherlands and the Thirty Years' War. He had impressed everyone with his bravery, and brought to the Royalists skills and tactics which were unknown in England. Unfortunately he was also arrogant, quick-tempered and lacking in courtly manners, and had made many enemies in his young life. He joined the queen's entourage in Holland and immediately quarrelled with her other supporters including George. In addition to both men vying for the queen's favour, they were temperamentally poles apart: George, the quick-witted strategist with a silver tongue; Rupert, the seasoned military campaigner used to having his own way in a direct, rather crude manner. Their enmity was to have a profound effect on the Royalist forces during the civil war which followed.

Henrietta Maria was received with great courtesy by the Prince of Orange. Her daughter Mary was pledged to be married to William, the Prince of Orange's son, a match acceptable to both sides. However there was strong anti-Catholic feeling among the Dutch Calvinists which made her presence something of an embarrassment. The Dutch and English were trading and colonial rivals, and there was a suspicion that Charles had turned to the Spanish for assistance in his war against the Scots. The United Provinces still suffered from the military presence of the Spanish.

George did not welcome the queen publicly to Holland, recognising that his presence would be an embarrassment for all concerned, but he wrote privately in the warmest terms. He referred to preliminary discussions he had conducted with the Prince of Orange concerning aid, but it is clear that these had gone nowhere for the prince showed no sign of helping the queen materially. The stadtholder of The Hague, Frederick Henry, obtained for her a loan of 300,000 guilders on his own credit, but was not willing to provide the arms she requested. She soon left the Hague for Breda to supervise the sale of her jewels. Although most of the dealers were very reluctant to handle the valuables, nearly £130,000 was raised from the sale. With this money she purchased ordnance, gunpowder, firearms and saddles, and thereafter a steady stream of ships supplied arms through Royalist ports in north-east England.[137]

It has often been asked: why George went to the United Provinces, and not France, the country most likely to receive him warmly. It can be seen that he initially tried to get to Ireland, and when that failed he tried to make for France only to be arrested before he could leave England. So his ultimate decision to head for the United Provinces may have been out of necessity. But it does seem that he carried instructions from the king to seek aid from the Prince of Orange. The Venetian ambassador reported that "he is taking instructions and letters from his Majesty to the Prince of Orange to support his failing authority."[138] The Prince does not seem to have taken to George, describing him as "impetuous." Nevertheless George remained the chief negotiator on behalf of the queen, reporting regularly back to her on progress. And despite the Prince's remarks, progress there was. He promised support, and gave the Royal party four cannons together with thirty thousand guilders, which were used to pay off the queen's debts in Holland. Some ammunition was also sent to England.

Around this time George received a letter from Thomas Elliot in York who was worried that the king might be tempted to come to an accommodation with Parliament "…but I hope what he shall receive from the Queen will make him so resolved that nothing but a satisfactory equal to the injuries he hath received will make him quit the advantage he hath."[139] George responded by recommending to the queen that "Charles should take himself to a safe place, where he may avow and protect his servants from rage and violence."[140] Another of George's letters to the queen referred to the wisdom of her "having withdrawn from a country unworthy of her." He also wrote to Secretary Nicholas in justification of his position: "My sudden coming out of England, I believe, will have caused various discourses little to my advantage; but my comfort is that my enemies were before so rancorous that I can neither gain nor lose with them by anything I do. And my friends, among whom truly I rely upon you in a prime place, I hope are so settled in their good opinion of me, that they will not easily entertain vulgar prejudices of me....no fear for myself, severed from the King's service, has contributed the least thought towards this absence of mine."[141] Unfortunately Elliot's letter and those written by George from Holland were intercepted by Parliamentary agents and read out in Parliament. The most damaging extract was advice to the queen to persuade the king "to put himself in some secure place, excusing his departure as not having fled from justice, but from the hands of traitors."[142] Parliament was sufficiently alarmed by these missives to send a message to the king beseeching him: "Yet we are farre from reflecting any thing upon the Queen, or expecting any falsification from her Majestie; But impute all to the bold and envenomed spirit of the man; Only we most earnestly beseech Your Majesty to perswade the Queen, that she will not vouchsafe any countenance to, or correspondence with the Lord Digby."[143]

Whether he knew of the interception or not, George continued to advise the king to withdraw to a safe place where he could muster support. This advice, together with a letter to Dyve, in which he wished the king was in Holland and added: "God knows, I have not a thought to make me blush towards my country, much less criminal, but where traitors have so great a sway, the honestest thoughts must prove most treasonable,"[144] were again intercepted. Unlike his peers, George had become aware early in the process of Pym's ultimate aims. The intercepted letters were clearly inflammatory, but it was difficult for Parliament to find anything in them which could be considered treasonable.

A year later George published an "Apology"[145] which in fact sought to demolish the charges put forward by Parliament. He starts: "It may be wondered that after well nigh a year's groaning under the most unsupportable burden of public displeasure and censure I should now consider myself so much as in a general calamity to make an apology to the world." He went on to explain his actions and refute the claim that he was raising armed forces. He argued that the publishing of his speech to Parliament on his rejection of the charges against Strafford was necessary in order to correct the misreporting which was rife at the time. As for the intercepted letters, was it not conventional to tell any lady that a country was unworthy of her??

In November 1641 an ordinance orchestrated by Pym had been issued proposing that Parliament assume the defence of the kingdom, reinforcing the impending conflict – the so-called Militia Bill. It provided for protection of the country against "Papists and other ill-affected persons who have already raised a rebellion in the Kingdom of Ireland."[146] Although not expecting the king to agree to this bill, he was repeatedly asked to pass it. When he refused, Parliament finally resolved in March 1642 to issue it themselves and to take over the defence of the kingdom. This was effectually proclaiming the power of Parliament and its right to act for the good of the country independently of the king.

A key element in the looming war was likely to be the fleet, the only potent and organised armed force in the land. Parliament had moved swiftly to take control through the well-respected Lord High Admiral, the Earl of Warwick, a Puritan. Officers and seamen, who had not been paid, were happy to back the anti-Royalist factions. By controlling the fleet, Parliament also deterred foreign assistance to the king. The king resisted this strongly, recognising its importance in any armed conflict to come. Messages were sent from Parliament to the Governor of Hull and to Colonel Goring at Portsmouth to secure their arsenals and reject any overtures from the king.

In March 1642, recognising the weakness of his position in London, the king travelled north, to the bitter resentment of the people of London and the concern of Parliament, who saw him as deliberately distancing himself in order to wage war against them. Through Royston, Cambridge, Huntingdon,

Stamford and Lincoln he attracted great crowds, for the general populace were not yet in a mood to acknowledge that the person of their sovereign was not to be paid allegiance. The Earl of Pembroke and Holland were despatched to Royston by Parliament to beg the king to return. They urged him to dispense with "his wicked counsellors" of whom George was cited as the most evil, and that if he would do so Parliament would support him. The king angrily retorted that he had many grievances of his own, that the House was wild and irrational, and that he had no evil counsellors.[147] Charles spoke of peace and reconciliation, careful not to provoke the war which he was now certain was coming, declaring that he had been forced to leave his home for fear of his and his family's safety. Finally on March 19, 1642 he reached York where he set up court, and prepared for conflict. Most of the House of Lords travelled north to be with him, but he had no army to speak of. The Earl of Essex and Holland formally declined to join him and were dismissed from their positions at court.[148] Overtures by the king to Lord Fairfax and his son Thomas, who commanded a strong following in Yorkshire, were rejected. The king embarked upon a series of meetings in key towns in the midlands and north to drum up support, and the locals responded in great numbers, enthusiastically assuring him of their allegiance. In the main these were the nobility and gentry, men of substance.

George's campaign for funds in the king's cause provoked a sharp difference of opinion with his father. The Earl of Bristol had been incarcerated in the Tower under suspicion of being involved in yet another plot against Parliament. In poor health he was eventually found not guilty and released. He disagreed with his son's tactics, and believed more could be achieved through quiet diplomacy. On May 20, 1642 he made a speech in the House of Lords, warning that the country stood on the brink of disaster. He reminded the House of the grievances which had been presented to the king, and maintained that the king had met their demands through the actions of Parliament.[149]

The exiles continued to strive for any foreign aid they could muster in aid of the king. George was among the most active in this effort. There were rumours that a force from Denmark was preparing to invade after Charles's uncle, King Christian IV had been approached by Henrietta Maria. Moreover, George was reported to have been seen in Elsinore, negotiating supplies.

Close to York, the port of Hull was also a stronghold of Puritan sentiment. Much of the town's trade was with Holland, and many of its inhabitants were Dutch immigrants with a Calvinistic background. Moreover, exposure to trade with European countries had led to greater availability of imported books and new ideas which influenced the inhabitants. These tendencies led the townsfolk to be more in sympathy with Parliament than the king. More importantly from a strategic point of view, a large quantity of arms and ammunition was stored in Hull in readiness for the Scottish war. With additional weapons bought from Holland and collected from other parts of the country, Hull had become the largest arsenal in England, capable of equipping 16,000 men. Control of these arms could prove critical in the forthcoming conflict. Parliament despatched Sir John Hotham to Hull on January 11, 1642 as Governor in order to secure the arsenal. Hotham was a member of one of the oldest and most influential Yorkshire families. Although aligned with Pym politically, he was by no means an anti-Royalist. This paradox was to cause him considerable problems. His brief was not to deliver up the town or supplies "without the King's authority signified by the Lords and Commons in Parliament."[150]

The Elector Palatine, Frederick, husband of the king's sister, Elizabeth, had died in 1632 and had been succeeded by his oldest son, Charles Louis, who had joined the king, his godfather, in York. He and the brother of the king, James, the young Duke of York, travelled to Hull to persuade the Governor to pledge his allegiance to the king. They were received with great civility and every sign of cooperation. Next morning Sir Lewis Dyve appeared to announce that the king was on his way to Hull. The Mayor of Hull, a Royalist, prepared for a ceremonious reception. When Hotham heard of this, and that the king was accompanied by a troop of cavalry, he panicked. He could see that if he allowed the king into Hull he would almost certainly lose control of the castle and magazine. So on April 23, 1642 he closed the gates and lifted the drawbridge. The king had no alternative but to withdraw to York. The Elector and Duke of York quickly followed rather shamefacedly, having been at dinner when the king approached and therefore having missed the opportunity to appeal to the people of Hull to welcome him. The Elector Palatine, feeling he had been humiliated, returned to the Continent. The king complained to Parliament that the Duke of York and his party had been detained, and demanded immediate action against Hotham. Instead Parliament sent orders to Hotham to load the arms and ammunition onto ships of the Parliamentary fleet under the Earl of Warwick which had been despatched to defend Hull. This was achieved, and the main arsenal removed from the town. Hull remained a key port however, not least for its strategic importance as an entry point from the Continent.

With the king safely established at York, George could not resist the urge to return. A number of the king's supporters assembled in Holland, including the princes Rupert and his brother Maurice, Lord Denby, Colonel Cockram, the Irish leader O'Neill and Sir Lewis Dyve, George's step-brother. They did not conceal their preparations, as a Parliamentary spy reported back: "...They have fitted themselves with armour of proofe, and all other accoutrements of warre, they have been very merry, and have drunk many healths to their good voyage, and in their cups have made dividents of the Parliament mens lands."[151] On July 6, 1642 with between eighty and ninety Cavaliers George, Rupert and Maurice embarked upon the Lyon with a supply of arms and ammunition, with a second ship, the Providence, to follow with more ammunition and baggage on board. A violent storm which raged for three days tossed the small ship about unmercifully, preventing them from continuing, and finally it returned to Holland, where most of the passengers disembarked. George tried again, and carrying several letters from the queen, he sailed back across the Channel disguised as a French merchant. He went first to see Edward Hyde, still in London, who wrote later that he was completely deceived by the disguise, and was thoroughly alarmed at the risk George was running. Two days later Hyde was dismayed to see George in the street talking animatedly with his father, but it seems that even the Earl failed to recognise him, and merely enquired of Hyde when George had gone: "That Frenchman tells me he is working for you. Well, he's a real wit, and I should say you have gotten yourself a proper man. What use do you put him to?" George made his way to York, lying up in a hideaway by day and meeting the king at night.

George was not impressed by the situation he found in York, despite the relative comfort of the court (made possible by the generosity of Edward Somerset, Earl of Glamorgan, who gave the king over £120,000 of his personal fortune). He decided that he could better serve the king abroad, where he could help in the assembly of much-needed arms and ammunition from Holland. Others of the king's entourage decided to join him, among them Ashburnham, Berkeley, Pollard and Wilmot, and they set sail in the Lyon. On the way to Holland they met the Providence in the Humber estuary with a shipment of arms for the king. Berkeley, Pollard and Wilmot changed their minds and decided to join this ship, leaving George and Colonel Ashburnham to continue on towards The Hague. Hotham had received intelligence that a ship carrying ammunition was near the port of Hull, and despatched one of his captains, Paget, in the Mayflower to intercept it. The delay caused by the transfer of George's colleagues and discussions between the two groups gave time for the Parliamentary squadron to catch up with the Providence. Fortunately its captain knew the coast well and ran the ship aground in a creek near Burlington, saving the cargo, which was unloaded with the help of local villagers sympathetic to the Royalist cause. The other ship, the Lyon, was stopped however, and Ashburnham, Sir Edward Stradling and George captured. William Ashburnham, a prominent member of the Royalist party, was well known to the Parliamentarians, and a valuable catch. George, with great presence of mind, managed to disguise himself again as a Frenchman, shaving his moustache and beard and switching clothes, so that even his own friends could not recognise him.[152] He was also very seasick, and spent the return journey to England in the hold, out of sight, where he was able to destroy any incriminating papers undetected.

Still professing illness when they landed at Hull, George was able to persuade his captors to find a quiet spot in which he could recover. Hotham knew him, and if he was discovered his life would be in mortal danger, yet it hardly seems possible that a member of the crew of the ship on which he had sailed would not have betrayed him. In broken English he now requested a private audience with Hotham, saying he had important secrets to confide. To his alarm, he was received in a room full of guests, including several gentlemen recently returned from France. Undeterred, George spoke of his military service and his purpose in coming to England, which was to offer his sword to the king. Fluently in French he answered the questions that came from the assembly, until the probing began to become uncomfortable and the suspicions of his questioners grew. He requested a private audience with Hotham, saying he had information which could not be imparted in public. The governor was not inclined to grant it, afraid for his own safety, but drew George aside into the deep recess of a window, out of earshot of others.

George immediately asked him whether he knew who he was. Startled, Hotham said no. At this point George revealed his identity, adding that he trusted Hotham was sufficiently honourable to resist turning him over to his enemies. The governor, aghast at this news, was not concerned about honour at this time, but much more concerned about the construction others would put on the fact that the notorious and much sought-after traitor, Digby, had been accommodated in Hull and given an audience in safety by him. Hastily he called the guard to take him away and watch him carefully, explaining to the curious assembly that the Frenchman had given him very valuable intelligence about the queen's plans. Hotham said he would see George again the following day.[153]

By now George had fully recovered his poise, and saw Hotham as a weak and vacillating man, unsure of the confidence of Parliament and terrified of making a mistake. In fact Hotham was ambitious, devious and prone to temptation. George was playing a very dangerous game, but he planned to play on the governor's weakness, and by flattering the man and talking up his sense of honour persuade him to consider how he could serve the king. He reinforced this message by adding that he was sure the king would prevail in any conflict, as the crowned heads of Europe were coming to his aid, and that the man who dared to start this process by assisting him now would achieve great glory and recognition. Specifically, he proposed that Hotham deliver Hull up to the king, thus securing peace.[154]

Hotham was extremely agitated, seeing clearly the risks inherent in choosing either side incorrectly. He could not undertake to deliver Hull to the king, as the citizens and armed forces there were not well disposed towards the Crown, and his own son was a Parliamentary agent who was virtually spying upon his father. But he promised that "…if the King would come before the town, though with but one regiment, and plant his cannon against it, and make but one shot, he should think he had discharged his trust to the Parliament, as far as he ought to do, and that he would immediately then deliver up the town; which he made no doubt he would then be able to do."

So Geoge hurried off to York, revealing himself and his plan to an astonished king. Further attempts had been made to take Hull, the Earl of Northumberland carrying out a raid without success. It was decided that Charles should move closer to Hull by mustering a force of four regiments at Beverley, a few miles from Hull, while George returned to Hotham. The Earl of Lindsey built three forts commanding the Humber River, and set about besieging Hull. Unfortunately Hotham had been correct to feel apprehensive about his position. He continued to play both sides, keeping up a correspondence with the Royalists. These letters finally came to the notice of Parliament, who kept him under constant surveillance. Although aware of the surveillance, Hotham and his son continued to intrigue. Finally on June 28, acting on the word of Captain Moyer of the merchant-man Hercules, lying outside Hull, that Hotham was plotting to hand over Hull to the Royalists, 100 seamen were sent to secure the town and Hotham was taken prisoner. Hotham was to pay for his vacillation with his life; he and his son were condemned to death for betrayal. Parliament sent 500 fresh troops to Hull under the command of a seasoned commander, Sir John Meldrum, a Scot who had seen service on the Continent. 1500 men followed later, supported by two men-of-war, The Unicorn and The Rainbow. These warships, on arriving in the Humber, opened fire on the three forts, destroying them all. The banks of the rivers Humber and Hull were cut, flooding the surrounding fields for four miles.

There was little prospect now of Hull yielding to the king, although Charles had given the appearance of laying siege to the town, erecting batteries and digging trenches.

While the king was standing outside the gates on July 11 he was approached by the Earl of Holland with a final plea that he abandon his preparations for war and return to London. The king replied that first he should open the gates of Hull as a sign of good faith, and when Holland refused to agree, Charles departed with the parting shot: "let all the world now judge who began this war."[155] George and Ashburnham were sent back from Hull to the king with expressions of regret and loyalty. A small expeditionary force under the command of the Earl of Lindsey was sent out to assess the situation, but they found the fortifications being strengthened, and were fired upon from the walls.

Through the summer of 1642 the king roamed the north, drumming up support for his cause. Many of the volunteers were Catholics who had suffered from Parliament's attitude towards them. This fostered the story that the king was at the head of a papist army.[156] The Parliamentary representative for Yorkshire, Lord Fairfax, held considerable influence and his son, Thomas, made it known he was ready to defend Parliamentary interests in the north. On June 3 the king visited Heyworth Moor to enlist support from local Royalists, but the Fairfaxes appeared with several hundred supporters and a petition requesting Charles to return to Westminster. This was presented by being thrust onto the king's saddle, but the king ignored Fairfax, provoking strong resentment among the Yorkshire gentry.

The king and his small entourage turned south towards London, hoping to enlist local support as they journeyed. His advisers urged him to make one last effort to secure peace, but this was instantly rejected by Parliament. Charles' betrayal of Strafford counted heavily against him in these early months, as potential supporters paused at the thought that they, too, may be deserted. The landed gentry were reluctant to commit themselves to his cause when they may have to answer to Parliament later for their actions. George's brother, John, set about obtaining horses in the country around Sherborne, and was called to account by Parliament.[157] On August 22 the dejected Royal party, numbering no more than one thousand, reached Nottingham where, in driving rain, they set up the Royal standard and a proclamation denouncing the Commons and their troops as traitors was read out. Thus war was formally declared.

Chapter 8.

Civil War.

The raising of the king's standard at Nottingham did not provoke major conflict immediately. Skirmishes erupted in isolated bursts throughout the country, although outright war was not yet apparent. But almost immediately the king received bad news. Portsmouth, governed by George Goring, was besieged by sea. Although Goring had received sufficient warning when the fleet declared for Parliament, he had neglected to stockpile supplies. He sent word that unless relief was forthcoming immediately he would be forced to yield within days. Unfortunately the nearest Royalist force, commanded by the Marquis of Hertford in the south-west, was itself coming under pressure. Lord Hertford, a staunch Royalist, had returned to his home county, Somerset, to raise troops. He was accompanied by Lunsford, Sir Ralph Hopton, a professional soldier who was to command the Royalist army in the south-west, and Kenelm Digby's brother, John, who had gained an outstanding reputation for bravery in the north as part of the king's army which faced the Scots at Newcastle, and was able to provide a valuable supply of men and horses. Parliament was also busy recruiting men to their standard and at Wells had assembled a force of some six hundred foot. John Digby with a hundred volunteers charged and dispersed this force, killing seven, wounding many more and capturing their chief officers without a single loss on his own side. But it was plain that the local population sided with Parliament, and when news came that the enemy was approaching Wells the Royalists withdrew to Sherborne in nearby Dorset, Hertford setting up his headquarters in Sherborne Castle. George's wife,

Anne, was living in the New Lodge and offered the Royalist officers use and accommodation of her home as well as the old castle.

A Parliamentary force of five hundred foot, eight troop of horse and twelve cannon advanced from Bristol to challenge Hertford. It was led by Denzil Holles, one of the five Parliamentarians who had held the Speaker in his chair while the Commons passed the Remonstrance Bill, and who had survived the king's attempt to arrest him in 1642. He was accompanied by Charles Essex, an experienced army officer, and William Russell, the Earl of Bedford. Although the young Bedford was Anne Digby's brother, he did not agree with his father's allegiance to the king, and had chosen the Parliamentary cause on the outbreak of war. Preparing to defend the Royalist position Hopton took his cavalry to the edge of the town while Hertford manned the castle with infantry. In fact these two generals were so successful in defending the town that Bedford was forced to camp a mile outside in open fields, where he mounted a barrage of artillery against the castle and town, to little effect. Hopton's cavalry were able to take advantage of the open terrain to mount rapid skirmishes on the Parliamentary army, and this was followed by an attack from the castle which surprised the besiegers and caused some casualties. This spread alarm among the locally recruited Parliamentary force. For four nights they had camped in the cold, getting very little sleep, and Bedford's troops had begun to desert in numbers. The harvest was due and the "country fellows that were wont to have their bellies full of good beef, and then to their beds, would not long endure hunger and cold on a bleak hill."[158] Consequently Bedford sent word to the castle that he would retire if the Royalists undertook not to molest his force. Hertford retorted: "They came upon their own council and might get off as they could." Bedford withdrew to Yeoville, harrassed by Hopton's cavalry and infantry sent out from the castle.

In Sherborne Museum there is another explanation for the retreat by the Parliamentarians, who possessed overwhelming advantage in numbers. It is said that when Bedford sent word that he had instructions to destroy the New Lodge, Lady Digby rode out alone to her brother's camp and told him that if he attacked the Lodge he would find his sister's bones buried in the ruins. He was subsequently called to Parliament to justify his actions, and is said to have been cleared.[159] However he does appear to have issued instructions that his sister and her children were not to be harmed. He later defended his actions with Denzil Holles: "We for our part will gladly lay down our lives…but truly we would die like men and with men and not like fools in the company of heartless beasts, with whom we have no more wit than to engage our honour and lives."[160]

Meanwhile George remained at Nottingham, where the prevailing atmosphere was one of depression. The king was having second thoughts about the war, particularly as it became apparent that the Royalist cause was not at all popular, and difficulties were being experienced in raising troops and arms. George had been joined there by Hyde and Falkland, and this triumvirate formed an inner council to the king, with George appointed as military governor of Nottingham. The king received a number of entreaties from his followers to reopen peace negotiations. A brief skirmish at Coventry, in which the Royalists suffered losses, persuaded the king that his position was weak, and Southampton and Culpeper were sent to Westminster to enquire what terms could be advanced for peace. The Lords were receptive, but the Commons at first would not see Culpeper. Pym advised caution. His opinion was heard in silence, and the decision was made that until the king took down his standard and recalled his denunciation of treason against members of Parliament they could not negotiate. An offer proposing that both sides withdraw accusations of treason was also rejected, even though the king offered to strike his standard if this was agreed, and would consent to a thorough reformation of religion. Parliament demanded instead that he cease protecting delinquents. The prospect of peace had the immediate effect of drawing to his side those property owners who were fearful of having their possessions confiscated. Before long, the Royalists had assembled a force of 10,000 men.

No Royalist commander-in-chief had been appointed. The most senior soldier was the Earl of Lindsey, sixty years old and without active service for over twenty years, holding the rank of General-in-Chief. This position was only recognised by the infantry, many of whom he had introduced to the Royalist forces himself. Prince Rupert had returned from abroad not without some difficulty: sent for by the king, he had attempted to land at Tynemouth but was challenged by a Parliamentary ship called the London, and finally got ashore in a boat at Scarborough. He was appointed to the position of Lieutenant-General of the Horse, and was seen as independent of the General-in-Chief. Before leaving Holland Rupert had quarrelled with both George and Henry Jermyn, Henrietta Maria's chancellor, and had antagonised most of the queen's retinue. Henrietta Maria herself warned her husband that while Rupert would obey orders, he was headstrong, young and inexperienced, and not to be trusted. The young prince quickly alienated both Hyde and Falkland as well with his impetuousness and bad manners, and their disquiet was heightened by his appointment as Lieutenant-General of Horse, a position more senior than many of the king's older, more experienced generals. To make matters worse, the king let it be known that in his commission was a clause exempting Rupert from all orders issued by anyone other than the king himself.

Rupert and George had taken an instant dislike to each other. George saw the prince as a soldier without the tactical sense to command an army let alone participate in the king's war council, and let his feelings be known. He made caustic remarks about the low-class company kept by the Prince. Rupert was infuriated, and forced an abject apology out of George, who explained that he had merely told someone that "where there was a friendship of honour with so gallant a Prince...les petit gens should be kept at a greater distance."[161] An amusing incident illustrates the gulf between Rupert and George. The king requested two petards from George as military governor. George had no idea what a petard was, and had to wake Rupert for assistance.[162]

The Earl of Essex, commander of the Parliamentary forces, left London on September 9, 1642 and by adding to his force as he travelled west, approached the king's headquarters with nearly fifteen thousand men. The king, outnumbered, decided to move to Shrewsbury, which supported the Royalist cause and where it was hoped more recruits could be attracted from the west. Rupert and his brother Maurice created animosity by demanding money from the owners of country houses along the way. This practice was common on the Continent but when they demanded two thousand pounds from the citizens of Leicester in return for immunity from plunder, and they reacted in fright by sending five hundred pounds, the king showed his disapproval of the action, though he kept the money.

At Shrewsbury the Royalist position began to improve. The king's command was strengthened by the arrival of Patrick Ruthven, another experienced soldier who had held high command in the Swedish army, and brought with him some professional Scots officers. Recruits flocked to the standard from Wales and the north. Money came, too, from the Earls of Newcastle and Glamorgan and the king's cousin, the Duke of Richmond. Silver plate, donated from such institutions as Oxford and Cambridge, was melted down and a mint set up at Shrewsbury to pay the army. By October the king's army consisted of six thousand foot and the basis of a cavalry force under Rupert's training.

The Parliamentary forces under the command of Essex were by now advancing towards Worcester, where Rupert protected the road to Shrewsbury. Worcester was difficult to defend, as its walls and gates had decayed during the peaceful reigns of Elizabeth I and James. On September 23 Rupert ordered an evacuation and retreat to the north. He took half the cavalry out into open fields south of Worcester to await the enemy and cover the evacuation. With him went Lewis Dyve and George Digby, who had been given command of an infantry brigade. Rupert chose his ground carefully which was just as well for soon, before they expected it and while they were dismounted and resting under some trees, having removed their armour, there was movement on the Pershore road near the village of Powicke and a group of 500 well-armed and mounted men appeared, outnumbering the Royalists three to one. The Parliamentary force had crossed the river Teme by Powicke Bridge, intending to cut Rupert off from the rear. Fortunately for Rupert they approached down a narrow tree-lined lane which opened out into the field. His force did not have time to put on their discarded breast-plates before mounting their horses and charging. By waiting until sufficient of the enemy were at the entrance to the field before he charged, Rupert was able to scatter the force and inflict severe casualties in the confined lane before they could escape. Roughly half the force were swept into the river, their commander killed, and the rest forced back nine miles to Pershore, crossing the Severn at Upton. Essex's cavalry were stationed there, a fighting force which was in later days to prove their courage. But at this stage in the war they were relatively raw recruits with no experience of battle, and when they saw their colleagues' retreat and the pursuing Royalists, they broke ranks and retreated in disorder.

Dyve was wounded in the skirmish, along with Prince Maurice and Wilmot, but George came through unharmed. None of the Royalists were killed. They claimed victory at

Powicke Bridge, but did not have the resources to defend Worcester and retreated, leaving it to Essex's force to march in the next day. The mayor was arrested, the magnificent cathedral sacked and the famous organ, loved for miles around, torn down. However the victory at Powicke Bridge was well known among the king's men and overnight Prince Rupert became the hero of the Royalist army. This success encouraged new recruits, who now poured in from the surrounding countryside. By the beginning of October the king had six thousand horsemen in addition to Rupert's cavalry.

On October 12, 1642 the decision was made to march on London. The first night was spent at Wolverhampton, where new Welsh levies joined the king, bringing his force to thirteen thousand men. There George, out reconnoitering with three regiments of foot and some cavalry met Hollis with a similar force, and was forced to retreat after a sharp encounter. The pace of the advance towards London was leisurely, for the king was next entertained by Sir Thomas Holt at Aston Hall near Birmingham, before moving on through Bridgnorth, Kenilworth and Warwick where crowds turned out to cheer him and to join up. By the time they reached Edgehill, west of Banbury, the force had swelled to fifteen thousand foot and eight thousand horsemen. Within two days of the king's departure from Shrewsbury the Earl of Essex had turned back from Worcester to intercept him, and such was the slow pace of the Royalists that he was able to catch up with him on October 22 at Wormleighton, a few miles north of Banbury, although much of his artillery, two of the strongest infantry regiments and one regiment of horse together with their ammunition was still a day's march in the rear. Essex had also been weakened by the need to post garrisons at Worcester and elsewhere.

The Parliamentarians stood between the king and the main road to Banbury, Oxford and London. Rupert had recognised the strategic significance of the escarpment at Edgehill, and by marching under cover of darkness, was able to establish his cavalry on the summit before the Royalist infantry arrived and took up positions on high terrain. The steep slope made it unsuitable for cavalry although they dominated the valley below and hence the approach of the Parliamentary force, so Rupert ordered his men down to the lower slopes. There was some debate about the wisdom of engaging the enemy so soon, but the Royalists were conscious of the fact that their opposition were weakened by the absence of the regiments which had not yet arrived.

Dissension within the Royalist ranks complicated the situation. The commanders had already disagreed about the route from Shrewsbury. Rupert was behaving in a high-handed and arrogant manner. He had already upset Lord Falkland by objecting to receiving the king's commands from him. The seasoned and loyal campaigner, the Earl of Lindsey, was General of the army as a whole, but Rupert also insisted to him that he would only take orders from the king. Lindsey, having protested at the perceived insult, was now confronted with a battle plan with which he disagreed, laid down by Rupert in his most peremptory manner. In front of his troops Lindsey threw his baton to the ground and declared that if he could not be a general he would die a colonel at the head of his regiment.[164] He was replaced by Sir Jacob Astley, a mature and competent general who had once been Rupert's tutor. It is somewhat surprising that this spat, resulting in a change of battle plan to one with which the army was not familiar, and a change in the high command, did not result in a disaster.

At three o'clock in the afternoon of Sunday, October 23 the first full-pitched battle of the Civil War commenced with a heavy artillery barrage by both sides. They roared at each other for an hour before Rupert's cavalry were given the order to charge. Rupert had ordered his men to hold their fire until close enough to be sure of their targets, and the result was devastating. Attacking the enemy's left flank, they quickly routed their opponents and caused enormous confusion as they rolled over the enemy lines. Such was the instant success that Rupert's men were reluctant to stop and return to the support of their fellows, instead pursuing the panicking Parliamentarians off the field.

On the opposite, left flank George was acting as second-in-command of Henry Wilmot's cavalry. There they faced three incomplete regiments, two under Sir Phillip Stapleton and one under Sir William Balfour. Wilmot encountered greater resistance than Rupert had experienced. The Royalists found themselves fired upon by musketeers concealed in hedges and ditches lining the terrain of their advance. Sir Arthur Aston and his dragoons appeared in support of Wilmot to force these men back, and Wilmot rushed forward, disappearing over the horizon in pursuit of the enemy. With him went George, now a colonel in charge of four troops, of which three were used in the action. They were, in the main, well-connected gentlemen and experienced soldiers.[165] Thinking the battle was won, the reserve cavalry followed triumphantly. By evening both armies were exhausted. Rupert had returned in time to turn back the Parliamentary infantry, but the outcome was indecisive.

The next day found both armies confronting each other, but so exhausted and depleted by casualties that they were reluctant to resume the conflict. The Royalists occupied the battlefield, and were able to identify wounded survivors and rescue some of their fellows. On the second morning Essex withdrew from the field back to Warwick as his position lower down the hill was the more vulnerable, and at once Rupert was after him, attacking his baggage train and capturing valuable correspondence. In the process many of the Parliamentary cannon were abandoned and four ammunition wagons blown up.

The way to London was now clear. The king, after resting at Aynhoe, advanced on Banbury. The garrison at Banbury Castle was eight hundred strong with a troop of horse under

Lord Saye and Sele, a Parliamentarian leader in the Lords and a great landowner in these parts. Left unprotected, the garrison immediately surrendered and many enlisted in the Royalist army. The king stocked up with food and clothes before moving on to Oxford which was reached on October 29. "They came in their full march into the town."[166] The king was anxious to establish a base at Oxford, close to London but strategically placed for the midlands and the west. At the start of the war the town had been evenly split in its sympathies for the two sides and when a Parliamentary force under Lord Sayle and Sele occupied it they did not encounter too much resistance. But the Roundheads bickered among themselves, sword fights in the streets becoming commonplace, and the townsfolk were badly used by the soldiers. Thus by the time the king first rode in, his colours flying triumphantly together with those he had taken at Edgehill, the town welcomed him. He set up his quarters at Christ Church, with surrounding colleges commandeered by his staff.

George and his father set up their quarters at George's old college, Magdalen, with a large retinue, at the east end of the new Royal headquarters. He had maintained close ties with the college, and used his contacts to recruit undergraduates to his regiment. He was given command of the dragoons with instructions to guard the eastern approaches to the Royal headquarters, the most likely route for an attack from London.

The king set up a war council which was to accompany him on his travels, which when in Oxford met at Christ Church College, and George was appointed to this council. Rupert was of the opinion that with a victory under their belt they should press on quickly to the capital, seize the city and dissolve Parliament before the opposition could regather themselves. Essex was still believed to be at Warwick. The Earl of Bristol advised caution and resisted such a move, and George also opposed Rupert.[167] Rupert's opinion held sway, however, and the Royalist army was soon on the move again, down through Reading, leaving George and the Earl of Bristol with a troop of horse and dragoons to defend Oxford. Essex wrote to Westminster pressing them to call out all available troops to defend the capital. Volunteers erected posts and chains across the streets, money was raised and trained- bands took up arms again. Armed men flocked into town from the surrounding counties, and earthworks were thrown up on the approaches. The two youngest children of the king, Henry and Elizabeth, who had been taken by Parliament when Charles left Westminster, were moved from St James's outside the walls into the City for their own protection, but also as a bargaining counter.

Many citizens were critical of Parliament, and called for peace. A Peace Party had emerged among the remaining members of Parliament, with the Earl of Pembroke (who had entered into correspondence with Hyde offering his services to the king) arguing in favour of immediate peace negotiations. On October 29 the Lords proposed the reopening of negotiations, and two days later Edmund Waller proposed the same in the Commons. The City of London, appalled at the prospect of a prolonged war on finances, supported the proposal. Accordingly a letter was sent to the king requesting an opening to peace talks.

The king received this missive at Reading. Some of his advisers counselled against talks, but the Earl of Bristol was among the leading voices pressing for a negotiated peace. He was apprehensive that Rupert's brutal style of waging war would alienate Londoners already antagonistic to the king. He was also said to be horrified by the sight of Englishmen shedding their fellow countrymen's blood.[168] Charles, shaken by the loss of his young cousin Lord d'Aubigny and the two generals, Lindsey and Verney, was inclined to accept Bristol's advice and proceed cautiously, avoiding pitched battle. He asked the Londoners to appoint commissioners for the peace talks.

Rupert, scenting the weakness of the opposition and believing he could achieve a quick victory led an attack on Windsor with his cavalry, hoping to sever the water traffic route from the Thames Valley to London, but could make no impact on the well-defended castle. Meanwhile Essex, taking a more northerly route to avoid Rupert, crossed the Chilterns at their eastern end. By dint of forced march he had caught up and was close to London. The citizens of London were extremely relieved when he marched in, and he was immediately directed to impose martial law on the city. Gathering together the London trained-bands he turned and marched towards the king, with drums beating and flags flying.[169] The king responded by moving forward to Colnbrooke, where he met the Earls of Northampton and Pembroke together with three members of Parliament, who presented a petition requesting him to nominate some place outside London where committees from both Houses could meet to negotiate. The terms hinted at appeared favourable, but the question for the Royalists was whether Parliament could be trusted or whether they were merely playing for time. Finally the king responded by promising to refrain from further action while negotiations continued.

If there was ever the possibility of peace at this time it was quickly demolished. In direct contravention to the king's orders, early on the morning of November 12 the Royalist cavalry led by Rupert appeared out of the mist in the streets of Brentford, brandishing their swords and uttering threats. Although there were professional soldiers garrisoned there, the main Parliamentary force consisted of untrained volunteers, "butchers and dyers" as the Royalists called them, who scattered at the first charge. Many were cut down by the cavalry, the rest driven into animal pens and forced to surrender. Denzil Holles, the Parliamentary commander, who had distinguished himself at Edgehill, fought back furiously, and many a tidy garden was wrecked in the battle. But his men were no match for Rupert, and they were ruthlessly slaughtered. Rupert's troops then ran amok, entering houses and plundering valuables, clothes, food and drink, and destroying property. Essex sent barge-loads of ammunition upstream in an attempt to augment the supplies of what was left of the defenders, but Rupert's men attacked them from the gardens of Syon House with withering fire, and the supplies did not reach Brentford. Over five hundred prisoners were taken along with fifteen cannon and a large amount of ammunition.

As the Earl of Bristol had feared, Rupert's ruthless treatment of the citizens of Brentford and the breach in the cease-fire had a galvanising effect upon the citizens of London. Indignant at the outrages of Brentford and fearful for their own safety, the trained-bands united with the army returning from Edgehill. They were augmented by thousands of apprentices, tradesmen and even some Members of Parliament. In all twenty-four thousand armed men massed at Turnham Green, determined to resist any further advance by the Royalists. They manned every doorway, window, ditch and garden. Barriers were set up along the main roads into the capital, and cannon wheeled up to support the infantry. The two armies confronted each other in an uneasy lull of activity. Crowds of sightseers rode out of London to observe the expected battle. Skittish, they reacted to any movement in the Royalist ranks by scattering, taking with them many new recruits who then quit the field permanently. The Royalists were tired, hungry and outnumbered, and the position did not favour the use of their greatest asset, their cavalry. Essex, on the other hand, was reluctant to test his motley and inexperienced army in an all-out pitched battle which, if lost, would leave the entry to London unprotected. Finally the king turned away, directing his army back to Kingston while he visited his house at Hampton Court. From there, after a day, he went to Oatlands before withdrawing to Reading, a heavily fortified Royalist stronghold, taking his army with him.

In Reading the king called a Council of War on November 22, and George joined him from Oxford. The time George had spent with his father in Oxford had moderated his views, the experienced diplomat's alarm at the escalating war leading him to advise caution. At Westminster both Houses debated whether to continue the war. The House of Lords was in favour of a peace treaty, but it soon became clear that Pym and his supporters intended to press forward with the war. A demand was sent to the king that he abandon his supporters and return to Westminster. This was bound to be rejected, and hostilities were resumed.

Leaving a garrison under the command of Sir Arthur Aston, the king retired to Oxford where he had set up his court. The town was heavily fortified with trenches and earthworks, and a mill for gunpowder and a sword factory had been established. Supporters of the king poured into the town, offering whatever they could to the war effort, and cattle were plundered to provide a good stock of food. With garrisons at Abingdon, Wallingford and Reading a strong front towards London was presented, while further garrisons at Banbury and Brill protected the rear and flank.

George having parted from the king when he left Reading, moved to Wantage, learning on the way that five hundred dragoons of the Parliamentary force were on their way to Marlborough under the command of Sir Edward Hungerford and Sir Nevill Poole, with a further thousand to follow.[170] Marlborough had a reputation for being strongly anti-Royalist and, located as it was squarely on the road to the west and not that distant from Oxford, could be an irritant to the Royalists. On George's suggestion a detachment of cavalry set out on a forced march to the town, arriving there at five on the morning of December 2, 1642 with a regiment of four hundred horse in order to surprise them and give the enemy "a warm breakfast."[171] It was evident that there was a fairly light garrison defending the town, contrary to the strong force he had expected. The townsfolk reported that there were no commanders, and they were dependent upon two Scotsmen sent by Essex to fortify the town. George proposed to Wilmot, who was in command, that they attack the town immediately, as its capture would open a line of communication from Oxford to the south-west. When he demanded the town's submission the townsfolk played for time, sending urgently for reinforcements. His demands were made on a Saturday, and men arriving in town for the market were ordered to stay and defend the town.

The Royalists delayed the attack until Monday, December 5, when they opened up with a fusillade from their heavy artillery. The town was particularly vulnerable, built as it was along a broad high street with several inns which were difficult to defend. Soon the defences were breached. George entered from the south while Lords Grandison and Wentworth attacked from the north and west. Barricades had been erected in many of the streets and the attackers suffered intense cross-fire from the neighbouring houses. The defending governor and officers retired to the church and resisted strongly from there. Eventually the houses were set on fire and the defenders smoked out. Soldiers ran amok in the streets, cutting down any citizens whom they encountered irrespective of their sympathies and whether they were soldiers or not, burning and plundering.[172] Cartloads of plate and clothes were taken. Bales of cloth and "two hundred pounds worth of cheese"[173] were carried off to Oxford, and the townsfolk sued for peace with money. George was personally named as a commander who stripped and searched prisoners for valuables before tying them up without food. A citizen who pleaded poverty because he had eighteen children was reputedly told by George to go and drown them.[174] George was called a "prime beast" and acquired a fearsome reputation as a consequence. Marlborough was the first garrison taken on either side in the war.[175]

The capture of Marlborough was regarded as a triumph by the Royalists as it gave them control of the road to London from the west and therefore the power to divert the wool trade coming from Wiltshire to London. It also reopened communications with Wales, from whence the Royalists were drawing so much of their strength. George's reputation as a Cavalier commander was established, although prior to the onset of the Civil War he had had no experience of military action. As it had been his idea to take Marlborough, he gained considerable credit from the Royalist side. On the way back to Oxford, George with three cavalry regiments was surprised by a Parliamentary force at Wantage, not far away, and barely escaped. Fifty men and some ladies, including Lady Jermyn, were captured.

Pym pointed out to his Parliamentary colleagues the futility of attempting to negotiate peace with the king, whom he represented as devious. Evidence of appeals by the Royalists for help from abroad fuelled suspicions in London. To counteract this propaganda George suggested a broadsheet be published weekly to redress the balance. The paper, Mecurius Aulicus, first published in January 1643, "communicating the Intelligence and Affairs of the Court to the rest of the Kingdom" was smuggled into London, and became very popular. Published weekly at a penny, it served to counteract many of the pamphlets issued by the London presses. George supplied it with a stream of relevant information. Edited by a lively young man, John Birkenhead, a Fellow of All Souls, it swiftly developed into more than just a chronicle of events and took on a satirical tone.

By now it was difficult to determine how the two armies were deployed and it was possible to come across the enemy anywhere. George had become head of Charles' secret service by offering to pay for it. He also took charge of the postal services, which increased his power and influence. Here he was in his element, for he liked nothing better than intrigue, and the posts put him at the centre of Royalist intelligence gathering. It was decreed that all Royal orders had to be countersigned by him. He also used the respite from the battlefield to raise money for the war effort and prepare his dragoons for the next campaign by replenishing ammunition stores.[176]

After a quiet spell during the winter months, the Cavaliers ventured out at the beginning of February 1643 to attack Cirencester, an important communications link with the south-west. A heavy snowfall in late January had prevented the Parliamentarians from reinforcing the garrison there, and although well fortified with heavy walls they had been built for a bygone age and would not resist the siege cannon applied by Rupert. On the morning of February 2, 1643 Prince Rupert, seconded by Wilmot and George overpowered the town in two hours, taking twelve hundred prisoners, six pieces of ordnance and a large store of arms and ammunition. Rupert established a garrison there, providing a valuable strategic stronghold on the road to the west, and providing added protection to Oxford. Half-naked and starved, the prisoners were paraded through the streets of Oxford and herded into St Michael's Church. On the way back to Oxford Rupert took Malmesbury to secure most of Gloucestershire for the Royalists.

Whilst they were absent, Parliament had presented new peace terms to Charles. Moderate in tone, they drew a distinction between the king and his advisers, who they accused of plotting against the state and not serving his interests well. Prepared to come to amicable terms with the king they excluded the Royalist generals from this armistice, citing by name, amongst others, the Earl of Bristol and George. They demanded that Bristol be "removed from your Majesty's Counsels and…be restrained from coming within the verge of the Court and…not bear any employments concerning the state or Commonwealth."[177] It seems that despite his moderate stance the old earl was being categorised with the king's other, more hawkish advisers. Parliament also made clear that George and Newcastle would be exempted from pardon.[178] Predictably this had the effect of causing these generals to counsel the king strongly against peace and for the prosecution of the war. Even Bristol now came out in favour of war. Peace talks received a further setback when a letter between the king and queen was intercepted in which Charles admitted to caring nothing for the treaty, but was "full of designs" for continuing the war[179] Pym used this information to persuade Parliament to vote the necessary ordinances to wage the war.

In March Rupert moved on the port of Bristol. Strategically it was very important, being the second largest in England, but it was strongly defended. An army reported to be in the region of ten thousand advanced to the walls, encouraged by two residents, Richard Yeamans and George Boucher, who had arranged to open Froome Gate on the signal of bells rung at St John's and St Michael's churches. The plot was discovered in time, and nearly a hundred plotters were arrested and imprisoned in the castle. Rupert had no alternative but to fall back.

Whenever possible George had remained in touch with his patron, the queen. He had heard that the queen was determined to rejoin her husband who, now he was settled in his headquarters in Oxford, felt confident enough of the control the Royalists held over strategic parts of England to attempt the reunion. In February 1643 she set off by ship with a consignment of arms escorted by the famous Dutch admiral, Maerten Tromp and managed to survive a hazardous sea trip from Scheveningen to Bridlington. The stadtholder of The Hague willingly supplied the arms as he was pleased to be rid of her: "…because otherwise it appears the queen will not leave, but will continue to stay here to the noticeable disservice of the country."[180] She made her way to York to provide a rallying point for Royalists. She was anxious to rejoin her family, and a passage had been cleared south through Newark, Tamworth, Ashby-de-la-Zouch, Lichfield and Stratford-on-Avon. Unfortunately the Parliamentary army had responded immediately by driving the Royalists out of Stratford and laying siege to Lichfield, which had surrendered on March 4. This setback caused her to delay her journey south.

Rupert and George travelled north with a force of 12,000 horse and dragoons and between 600 and 700 infantry to meet the queen, leaving Oxford on April 1. They set about clearing a way between Oxford and the north. First on April 3 they attacked Birmingham, a centre for tradesmen which had since the beginning of the war produced fifteen thousand sword blades for Parliament. Its inhabitants were strongly Parliamentarian and obdurately independent, and opposed the advance of Rupert. He soon subdued the town, and in retribution stripped it bare of money and any other valuables he could find before setting fire to eighty houses and maltreating the inhabitants, causing outrage.

The Royalists' progress was blocked at Lichfield by a Parliamentary garrison which abandoned the lower town and secured the Cathedral Close there. This Close had been developed into a formidable stronghold with deep ditches and reinforced walls surrounding it. When negotiations over surrender failed to make any progress, the Royalists were forced to lay siege, and Rupert with great thoroughness set about draining the moat and mining walls so thick that no battery could make an impression on them. He reinforced his relatively small force with local inhabitants, and finally succeeded in blowing a twenty foot hole in the wall with a mine on April 21. He recruited the subchanter, a Mr Turnpenny, to guide the infantrymen once they were in the Close. But as soon as the wall was blown, George impulsively jumped the moat on his horse and led his men into the castle where he found himself dangerously exposed. He was rescued, covered in mud and shot in the thigh, and not very popular with Rupert, although his daring drew expressions of admiration from others. The Royalists suffered heavy casualties, but so did the defenders, and the next morning they surrendered. George, handicapped by his wound and at odds with Rupert, returned to Oxford. The siege had taken eleven days, and seriously delayed Rupert's plans to capture territory in the north.

As soon as he had recovered from his injuries, George set out for the north again. Word reached him that the queen was embroiled in the northern campaign. She was in favour of an all-out attack on Leeds, controlled by the Fairfaxes, but the experienced soldiers and wiser heads considered this too dangerous. She therefore remained some time in York, still a Royalist stronghold, frustrated at the lack of action and unable to travel south in the absence of the Earl of Newcastle, whose wife had died. In any event, while Leeds was in enemy hands the Royalists were reluctant to spare troops to escort her south. She finally started out on her southward journey on June 4. Before that she had sent on ahead a consignment of much-needed arms and ammunition which arrived at Woodstock outside Oxford on May 13. Now, at the head of three thousand foot, thirty companies of horse and dragoons and one hundred and fifty baggage waggons, she marched with the Earl of Newcastle, calling herself "She-Majesty Generalissima." She reached Newark on June 18 and stayed there for two weeks, recruiting supporters and hoping for signs of dissension in the Parliamentary ranks. Finally, at the head of two troop of horse George met her at Ashby-de-la Zouche. Essex sent out cavalry to intercept her, but somehow she evaded contact and reached Stratford-on-Avon on July 11, staying with William Shakespeare's granddaughter at New Place. By then she lead a formidable army, as Secretary Nicholas reported to Rupert: "…the Lord Digby writes, that the forces of Leicester and Coventry consist of twenty-eight troops of horse and ten companies of foot."[181] On July 13, after fifteen months of separation, she was reunited with her husband and two eldest sons at Edgehill, and the party, including George, returned to Oxford on the 14th amid wild celebrations.

Success in the west country for the Royalists had forced the Parliamentary commander, Waller, to fall back on Bristol, but by now Rupert had returned from the north. He besieged Bristol, where the garrison had been reduced to one thousand men in order to strengthen Waller's force. Although Bristol was strongly fortified, its townsfolk did not wish to see their city destroyed, and the Parliamentary commander was forced to surrender. Waller and his troops, recognising that the city was lost, had moved on to the Parliamentary stronghold of Gloucester. The king, accompanied by Rupert and George, took command of the siege on Gloucester which followed. But attempts by the Royalists to capture this important city faltered in the face of resolute defence, and the siege was finally lifted on September 5 by Essex, marching in from London. The king's forces withdrew.

Around August 28, during a brief visit by the king to Oxford from the siege of Gloucester, George's brother-in-law, the Earl of Bedford, appeared. Never very enthusiastic about the Parliamentary cause, he had been made increasingly uncomfortable by the extremist attitudes prevailing in Parliament and had no wish to be in conflict with the rest of his family, who were all Royalists. With him came the Earls of Holland and Clare. The king was unsure whether to receive them and accept their allegiance. Rupert took it upon himself to introduce them, incurring the fury of the queen. The king was feeling more confident about the outcome of the war, and could not see how these newcomers could benefit him.[182] They were sent away, and returned to London, resentful of the treatment they had received.

Essex recognised that although he had been successful in saving Gloucester, London was dangerously exposed in his absence, and he was soon on the road again, feinting, twisting and turning to avoid the Royalists. The opportunity to block

Essex from a return to London was missed through the king's lack of a sense of urgency, and a chase ensued, the two armies matching each other across the Cotswolds. Rupert went ahead with his cavalry to harry and delay Essex's retreat. Despite lashing rain and high winds, by an amazing forced march through Lechlade Rupert caught up with Essex at Farringdon. Well to the rear at Alvescote near Burford, the king sent George to Rupert asking for advice on their next move. It was decided that Wantage would make an appropriate rendezvous, but the same day at Auburn Chase Rupert's force ran into the rear of the enemy, riding through them at close quarters. A Roundhead officer turned and advanced on the pursuers, peering into the leaders' faces before discharging his pistol at George at point-blank range. For some reason the pistol misfired and George merely suffered temporary blindness from the powder flash.[183] Hyde wrote that "…this may be reckoned one of those escapes of which that gallant person hath passed a greater number in the course of his life than any man I know."[184] Although the Cavaliers were forced to retreat they had succeeded in diverting the Roundhead march.

Rupert did not wait for the king at Wantage but pressed on to Newbury, 16 miles away, intent on stopping Essex from reaching Reading. George, despite his narrow escape, accompanied him and was involved in the action which followed, although there is some evidence that he was not present during certain stages of the battle.[185] This may be explained by his temporary blindness. The Royalists reached Newbury before Essex, and there proposed to stand. Essex realised he would have to fight, as he could see no safe way round the town. Neither army was in a fit state for a prolonged battle, as they were short of sleep and food and the weather, windy and wet, was against them. The fighting was fierce and fragmented as much of the terrain was in small fields surrounded by ditches and hedges. The Royalist musketeers began to run short of ammunition, so despite the unfavourable terrain Rupert's cavalry rode to the rescue, outflanking the Parliamentary infantry and storming their rear. Both sides suffered heavy casualties, and withdrew from each other at nightfall, with the Royalists suffering the worse due to the fusillade they faced from either side of the lanes. Percy, General of Artillery, reported to the king, who by this time had joined Rupert, that only ten barrels of gunpowder remained, and in view of the heavy losses it was decided to withdraw to Oxford. Essex braced himself for the resumption of battle in the morning, but with dawn came the realisation that his enemy had left the field, and the road to London was open. The king returned to Oxford and Essex continued towards Reading. The tenacious Rupert would not relent however and pursued him, forcing him to relinquish Reading on October 3 and press on to London, exhausted and with a much diminished force.

Chapter 9.

The King's Chief Adviser.

Dissent among the Royalist leaders had been growing since the capture of Bristol, and there was now open hostility between them. The queen's presence at Oxford exacerbated the situation. Rupert and Maurice, staunch in their support of the king, wanted maximum freedom to pursue their war aims. The queen gathered around her a small band of influential courtiers, including Henry Jermyn and George. She took to advising her husband on the course the war should now take. She was in favour of marching on London, a view not held by Rupert. The king, unfortunately, did not like large gatherings of advisers, and preferred to deal with his courtiers individually. His devious nature caused him to strike inconsistent agreements with these individuals, and this divisiveness fostered uncertainty and hostility among them.

Falkland found this falling out very sad, and was becoming steadily more disillusioned with the war. A negotiated peace now appeared very unlikely and conflict in Scotland was increasing. Added to this the king was planning to involve the Irish army in his campaign. Even a Royalist victory could only be accomplished with more pain and suffering, followed possibly by the collapse of democracy. This most sensitive and civilised of men saw little hope in the future. Hyde wrote that he had observed "...a kind of sadness and dejection of spirit had descended (upon him) since the beginning of this unnatural war which had clouded his usual cheerfulness and vivacity."[186] The death of Mrs Moray, "a handsome lady at Court who was his mistress and whom he loved above all creatures"[187] depressed him even more, and he was observed at the siege of Gloucester sitting alone and morose, exclaiming almost dementedly and frequently in a high voice: "Peace! Peace!"[188] He could not come to terms with the times and the way his countrymen were tearing each other apart. Having courted death at the siege of Gloucester by walking his horse daily beneath the walls, the end came at Newbury when he deliberately and slowly walked his horse past a gap in the hedge where enemy fire was heaviest, and was killed. Thus the king lost one of his steadiest and wisest advisers, and George lost a friend who had more than once protected him from his wildest impulses.

The queen's arrival marked an improvement in George's fortunes. Her interests included the selection of counsellors. There was a vacancy as a result of the death of Falkland, and she had worked closely with George in the Netherlands and knew his capabilities. The king wanted to give the post of Secretary of State vacated by Falkland to Hyde, but he and the queen did not get along well, and Henrietta Maria preferred George. George's first inclination was to refuse, not wishing to stand in the way of his friend, but Hyde persuaded him to take the post, saying it required knowledge of foreign languages and foreign politics, in which he himself was lacking.[189] Later, when Hyde and George had fallen out, Hyde was to describe George as "having an ambition and vanity superior to all his other parts and a confidence peculiar to himself, which sometimes intoxicated and transported and exposed him."[190] It is interesting that this view, expressed much later, was in such contrast to Hyde's enthusiasm for George's appointment. George had the advantage of speaking fluent French at a time when negotiations with the French to secure aid were ongoing. A new French ambassador, the Comte de Harcourt, had arrived and the queen was optimistic that she could persuade him to back the Royalist cause. Her hand was strengthened by the fact that both Richelieu and King Louis XIII, her brother, had recently died, leading to a much more fluid situation at the French court.

On September 28, 1643 George was appointed Secretary of State and admitted to the Privy Council. This Council now consisted of Hyde, Richmond, Cottington, Culpeper, Nicholas and George, though Nicholas was soon complaining that he had less standing than previously, due to the queen's influence. It was by now widely recognised that George carried the most influence within the Privy Council. Command of his regiment passed to Thomas Weston, and his military career in England was effectively at an end. It is possible that the injuries he sustained near Newbury were more serious than first made out, and hastened his retirement.

George threw himself into his new post with great zeal, demonstrating both the best and worst of his character. He was constantly in attendance, missing hardly any council meetings. Gardiner wrote of him that "Charles had a man to whom he could confide secrets of which it was well to keep the honorable Nicholas in profound ignorance."[191] With such an inside track George began to dominate Council meetings. Sir Philip Warwick described him as "eminent with his tongue or pen."[192] With his appointment the king laid down that in order to tighten up procedures (for the first time) all Royal warrants were to be countersigned by one of the two secretaries (George or Nicholas).[193] George's analysis and speed of thought dazzled his peers, but then just when everyone was settled on what to do – usually what he proposed – he would think up some brilliant new scheme, which was often wild and unpractical. Unfortunately, whilst this tendency was widely reported by his contemporaries, his correspondence was in general so formal that little evidence of these schemes exists, and the council minutes do not report them either. Orders were peremptorily changed, driving the army leaders to distraction and creating more squabbling. Gardiner wrote that "Statesmanship became in Digby's hands a mere policy of intrigue."[194] Hyde wrote: "…

he did often involve himself in very unprosperous attempts. The king himself was the unfittest person alive to be served by such a counsellor, being too easily inclined to sudden enterprises, and as easily amazed when they were entered upon."[195] He added that George had "that excess of fancy that he too often, upon his own recollections and revolving the grounds of the resolutions which had been taken, upon the suggestions of other men, changed his own mind; and thereupon caused orders to be altered, which produced, or were thought to produce, many inconveniences."

At the same time his influence can be seen to have tempered some of the wilder and more aggressive army commanders. Whenever there was the opportunity to seek negotiation and peace talks, he preferred that route to warfare, and during his time in office he attempted several secret rapprochements. His vision and knowledge of other countries caused him to seek solutions to the Royalist problems from overseas. The Archbishop of York commented that George was "a man of good fortunes, parts, industry and honour."[196]

In contrast to his mercurial political manoeuvres and rather rash schemes, there is evidence that George applied himself diligently to the mundane tasks associated with his post. He conscienciously dealt with numerous warrants, and was influential in several important appointments, most notably that of Ormond to Ireland. But his practical experience of war was also valuable. He considered efficient supply of arms and ammunition vital, and his correspondence is full of detailed application to this task.[197] The picture emerges of a hard-working Secretary devoted to the aim of winning the war for the Royalists, but one more inclined to seek peaceful means of achieving this aim than all out war.

George has often been portrayed as an "ultra-Royalist" who believed there was no alternative to war if the king was to prevail; the "evil counsellor" who stood between the king and a peaceful settlement. Yet there are a number of contemporary commentators who bore testimony to his flexibility and readiness to negotiate. Daly, in his book believes that George was prepared to negotiate and saw the stance taken at any time by the Royalists as tactical.[198] He did from time to time initiate secret negotiations for peace[199] and his close collaboration with his father, who was known to be alarmed by the war and seeking a peaceful settlement, points to his desire to find the best possible means of resolving the dispute.

Most importantly George's dominance of the Royal councils meant that his voice and opinions received precedence over those of Rupert's, who was in any event no diplomat and no match for George in political debate. His military responsibilities were such that he missed many of the council meetings, and paid only fleeting visits to the court. This left the way open for George's opinions to prevail. It was remarked that "Rupert stormed enemy strongholds, Digby attempted to reduce them by treachery."[200] "The army is much divided," wrote Rupert's agent in Oxford, Arthur Trevor, "and the Prince at true distance with many of the officers of horse."[201]

Rupert's single-minded concentration on the detailed administration of the war effort and the tactics to be applied, regardless of the feelings and opinions of others, had made important enemies, most notably Wilmot and Harry Percy, youngest son of the Earl of Nothumberland, who had been appointed General of the Ordnance on the queen's revommendation. Rupert blamed Wilmot for allowing Essex to relieve Gloucester, and Percy for not supporting the force at Newport Pagnall, which had been forced to surrender. Critics remarked that the town could have easily been defended by the Royalists. The loss of this strategic position once again opened the flow of supply from the midlands to London.

After a long illness, Pym died on December 8, 1643 of bowel cancer, depriving Parliament of its leader and arch-schemer. He had been one of the few Members of Parliament to have served before and after the decade of King Charles' personal rule, and as such had enjoyed a natural authority in the House. When the king accused him of high treason his attitude hardened to the point where he would brook no compromise, and resisted all efforts at peace settlements. His death opened up the prospect of greater flexibility.

For the first time in many months there appeared to be a real possibility of peace. George was delegated by the king to open negotiations with Sir Basil Brooke, a prominent Catholic. At the same time Charles wrote to the newly-elected mayor of London, Sir John Wollaston, attempting to enlist his support for a rapprochement. At around the same time an approach was made to the Earl of Bristol by a Parliamentarian, Thomas Ogle, being kept prisoner in Winchester House. In a letter dated October 17, sent through Lieutenant-Colonel Mosely, one of the officers at the Aylesbury garrison, he suggested that the Independents, for fear of the growing influence of the Presbyterians, would switch their allegiance to the king. It was believed that London was tired of war, and that many of its most influential figures would welcome peace. As proof of the seriousness of his claims Ogle wrote that if he was allowed to escape Aylesbury would be delivered up to the Royalists. Ogle asked the king to write to the keeper of Winchester House, Devenish, instructing him to allow his prisoner to escape. Bristol, asked to enter secret negotiations, received Mosely's assurance that he would yield Aylesbury, and further assurances were received from Thomas Riley, Parliament's scout-master general, offering some hope of desertions.

George and his father embraced this idea with enthusiasm, and a safe conduct warrant was sent to Devenish via Mosely. Ogle was duly allowed to escape and arrived in Oxford on January 3. Unfortunately both Moseley and Devenish were relaying back to Parliament all that was discussed. Worse still, when on George's advice Rupert took a small force to Aylesbury, trudging through the snow, he discovered it was a trap. Colonel Moseley refused to open the gates and he was forced to retreat. Fortunately for him the winter weather prevented Essex from acting in concert with Mosely to defeat Rupert's force, but during the retreat 400 troops were lost in flooded rivers as the snows thawed. Furious, Rupert prepared to hang Ogle, but George intervened to save him.[202] Rupert, already annoyed with George for having led him into the trap, felt even further aggrieved.

The queen and Rupert frequently disagreed, and her influence on the king was such that he usually took her side. She believed strongly that Charles should not open peace negotiations but fight to the finish, and her many letters to him reflect this sentiment. She extracted a promise from him that he would take no major decisions without consulting her first, and he gave every appearance of complying with this wish. Thus her influence in the Royalist camp was great. Protestants and Catholics revived old grievances, and many of the leaders looked to their own interests rather than the common good. The king had been lavish in the rewards which he bestowed on supporters in return for money and military service, but the proliferation of new appointments and honours merely exacerbated the jostling for position. George was invited by the City of Oxford to become its High Steward in place of Lord Saye and Sele, who had been made Lord Lieutenant of Oxfordshire and Gloucestershire by Parliament but had been forced by Royalist dominance in these counties to retire to London. Rupert blamed George for anything which went wrong, and the queen's support for him and antagonism towards Rupert widened the rift. Rupert believed by now that everyone was against him, though his biographer avers that Wilmot and George fought bravely for him. In March 1644 Jermyn wrote to Rupert that he had kept a particular watch on George and was confident that he had not failed in anything.[203]

The Parliamentarians were no more united. It was rumoured that many of the leading Parliamentarians were moving their possessions out of the country, to Holland and New England. Without the unifying leadership of Pym, the Parliamentary cause threatened to fall apart. Militarily, the campaign was not going as well as hoped. Essex was showing increasing signs of independence, ignoring the wishes of Parliament and waging his own campaign in the manner he thought fit. Thus in August 1643 Parliament decided to formally unify the Eastern Association and East Midlands armies. Commanded by the Earl of Manchester, who would be subject only to Parliament and independent from Essex, they drew men from the East Anglian counties of Essex, Cambridgeshire, Suffolk, Norfolk, Bedford and Huntingdonshire, a region hitherto relatively unaffected by the war.

After the debacle of the Aylesbury raid, the animosity between George and Rupert reached fever pitch. Rupert was already at odds with Wilmot, whom he blamed for allowing Essex to relieve Gloucester, and with Harry Percy, towards whom Rupert showed unconcealed scorn. Rupert's enemies now sided with George. Rupert told the king to choose between him and George. Fortunately the king ignored his request. The queen and Rupert had never liked each other, and his absence on the battlefield in these stressful times put him at a great disadvantage. In November 1643 the Duke of Richmond took it upon himself to defend Rupert to the king. He wrote in response to Rupert's concern that George was criticising him: "Upon receipt of yours…perceiving your Highness, from a hint taken of a letter from Lord Digby, was in doubt that at Oxford there might be wrong judgements made of you and of business made in your quarters, I made it my diligence to cleare it with the King (who answers for the Queen)."[204] However the king could see that Rupert was the most effective commander he had, although George, Wilmot and Culpeper would have happily seen him go.

George had formed a friendship with James Butler, Earl of Ormond, the leading Protestant nobleman in Ireland, whom the king made a Marquis in 1642. When George became Secretary of State he wrote to Ormond introducing himself, and the two struck up an immediate rapport, although Ormond would gently chide George for his exuberance. George supported Ormond strongly in the Council at Oxford, and with the queen urging her husband to bring an army from Ireland to his aid in England, the leadership in Ireland was becoming a key issue.

Ormond had been able to negotiate a truce with the Catholics in Ireland on September 15, 1643. A modest measure of religious freedom was granted them in return for a year of peace. The king hoped that he would be able to draw on English regiments freed from duty by a peaceful Ireland to support his campaign on the mainland. In November 1643 Ormond was appointed Lord Lieutenant of Ireland, and one of his first actions was to send a force to Wales, where it was initially successful in gaining control and in making inroads into Parliamentary territory in Cheshire. One of the officers to be noticed was a surly young captain called Monck. His reputation was such that the king wrote him a letter of thanks when he came over from Ireland, little knowing how grateful his son would be to Monck later, for he was destined to play a crucial part in the restoration of Charles II to the throne. In December 1643 Monck was presented to the king in Oxford by George, who had a high opinion of him and recommended that he be given a significant command.[205] Monck was critical of the way the king's army was organised, and refused command in it. He was allowed to return to his regiment near Nantwich. On January 25, 1644, his regiment and the other troops brought over from Ireland were defeated by Fairfax and most of the officers joined the Parliamentarians. Monck refused to do this, and was detained in the Tower of London for two years.

George Digby: Hero and Villain

In January 1644 a munitions ship bringing arms to the Royalists from Dunkirk was forced to take refuge from a Dutch ship in the port of Arundel and there fell into Waller's hands. Among papers aboard were several letters from George to various secret confidantes of the court containing promises and offers in the Queen's name. The papers were proclaimed seditious by Parliament, and several arrests followed.[206]

George remained actively engaged in securing arms. He sent a servant, Richard Shirley, to Ireland to buy arms. The letter that he took as authority assured sellers there that if they supplied Chester, Beaumaris or Bristol with arms or gunpowder they would obtain reasonable rates.[207] Merchants were prepared to sell arms to both sides, but at a price. In February 1644 George wrote from Oxford to Ormond informing him that he was negotiating with merchants to ship arms and ammunition to Chester, Bristol or Minehead, and that he would pay for them promptly with cash.[208] It has been suggested that George indulged in a bit of private enterprise, buying arms privately and selling them at a profit. Although some bills were referred to him for settlement (one for 7735 guilders in respect of arms sent to Weymouth), as Secretary of State this would have been normal, and there is no hard evidence that he traded independently. However Ormond warned George that he should establish proper procedures for payment, as he (Ormond) had been forced to pay for thirty casks of gunpowder out of his own pocket.[209] The War Council did, however, fully realise the importance of arms supplies from Ireland and George promised Ormond financial support even "were we to sell our shirts for it."[210]

On March 21 Rupert achieved a significant victory. Riding through the midlands in search of reinforcements he encountered Sir John Meldrum outside Newark. Meldrum, with an army of 7,000 was attempting to capture the town in order to secure the road to the north. Rupert charged without hesitation forcing the Roundheads across a bridge of boats on the river Trent. The garrison emerged from Newark and surrounded Meldrum. As Rupert's force was needed urgently elsewhere, he allowed the enemy to march off towards Hull without arms and ammunition. His success was haled by the Royalists as a great victory, and a potential turning point in the war.

Rupert was called back to Oxford to discuss the next move with the War Council. The majority of the council were now in favour of attacking the enemy in the vicinity of Oxford immediately, but Rupert argued in favour of moving north to confront the Scots. After heavy snowfall had prevented the Scots under Lord Leven from coming south in support of Parliament, late March brought kinder weather and they were able to move, crossing the Wear on March 25. Leaving a force to besiege Newcastle, they pushed the smaller Royalist forces they met across the Wear, and by April 8 they were within two miles of Durham, forcing the Earl of Newcastle, who had previously warned that the war in the north would resolve the fate of the realm, back towards York. The Fairfaxes had taken Selby and were advancing on York from the south. His army joined up with the Scots on April 20 near Wetherby, the combined force representing twenty thousand men, supported by heavy artillery. The Earl of Newcastle, heavily barricaded behind the formidable walls of York, settled down for a long siege. He felt that by rationing food, and with adequate ammunition, York could survive for a good while, but a relief force would be required to extricate him. On June 13, despairing of any help, Newcastle offered to negotiate surrender terms, but his demands that his army be allowed to leave with its baggage and that the clergy be permitted to continue the altar service at York Minster were rejected. An urgent request for help was sent to Rupert.

The usual shouting match developed in the council, with everyone having their own opinion. Wilmot argued with Rupert, the Prince responding aggressively and berating Percy and George. Culpeper, who considered himself a military expert, was loud in voicing his opinions. Lord Forth pretended to be deaf during these debates, while Astley also was reluctant to take sides. But virtually all of them opposed Rupert.[211] Some councillors were in favour of marching north to support Rupert while others advocated attacking the Eastern Alliance and so drawing the Earl of Manchester back from York. A third idea was to attack London, which appeared to be virtually undefended. No decisions were made, and in frustration Rupert responded by blaming the council, and particularly George, for the blunders and losses they had experienced. Increasingly the council was becoming a two-headed affair, with Rupert and George dominating proceedings. Sir Jacob Astley, who had once been Rupert's tutor, was manifestly awed by him and tried to avoid displaying his ignorance, while the king vacillated between sides as the argument raged.

After the victory at Newark Rupert had quickly returned to Shrewsbury where he was training recruits from Wales and Ireland and George now responded by saying that had his advice been accepted, Rupert would have stayed longer at Newark and would have been in a position to resist the Fairfax advance from the south before it reached York. Rupert argued that the force he had assembled for the attack on Newark was urgently needed from whence they came, the midlands and Welsh borders.

Despite their differences, George could see that he would have to work together with Rupert in the campaigns that followed. He thus set out to persuade Rupert of his good intentions, professing great admiration for Rupert's military ability. He had written to him from Oxford on February 12 assuring him that "noe man living shall bring more industry or more affection to the execution of all your commands, than I shall doe, whenever your honour shall wish them."[212] Now, as Rupert travelled north, George kept him well informed with the latest news, congratulating him on successes and assuring him at the end of orders that "these are onlye discourses wholye submitted to your judgement."[213] Rupert still distrusted George, however, and Arthur Trevor wrote from Shrewsbury that Rupert "hath no present kindnesse" towards George.[214]

Preoccupied with the northern campaign, the Council at Oxford now found they had a more immediate threat with which to deal. Essex had gathered his forces at Aylesbury, and was threatening Oxford. The Royalist commanders were eager to confront them but Rupert, aware of how thinly the Royalist resources were stretched, urged caution. He advised strengthening garrisons in the Thames valley and preparing to defend Oxford, thus conserving his army for deployment in the north. With Waller and Essex combining in a two-pronged move, the king was in danger. His main forces were split. Rupert was anxious to pursue his northern campaign. Closer to home, nearby Abingdon had been taken by the Roundheads and was occupied by Major-General Sir Richard Browne, known as "faggot-monger" because he had sent firewood down the Thames in barges to London. He kept up a number of sniping raids on Oxford. It was time for the king to move. In a letter to Prince Rupert George recounted how with "...Essex lying from Islipp towards Abingdon, and Waller having gained the new bridge, and passed over his army towards us, we were then fain to recourse unto art, which was to draw our army close to the town of Oxford to whisper intentions of possessing Abingdon, to draw our cannon, and many of our men into the town, and a little before evening to march with a great part of the garrison of Oxford towards Abingdon, as if we meant to possess it, and just as it grew dark for the King, to march with two thousand five hundred musketeers, and all our horse, to Burford, and so to make our retreat either to Bristol or Evesham, according as we should find it practicable."[215] This suggests that Gardiner may have been mistaken in having given Lord Forth (Patrick Ruthven) sole credit for having planned the escape, which was carried out as George describes and was successful.[216] Undoubtedly it relied upon good intelligence (which George still controlled) and a degree of daring, which he had in abundance.

From Burford the king, with George at his side, struck out through the Cotswolds to Evesham and Worcester. Waller, hastening after him, was without Essex, who had orders to remain in the Thames Valley. But Essex had gone west, hoping to capture Devon and Cornwall and perhaps even the queen who had moved to Exeter in expectation of the birth of her fourth child. Waller, furious at Essex for leaving the Thames valley and encroaching upon his command, wrote to Parliament pressing for Essex to support him in pursuit of the king. Essex received his recall at Blandford on June 14, but refused to obey.

At Worcester, Waller commenced to press forward against the king, who was hoping the garrison at Oxford would survive while he kept Waller occupied. Rupert, having moved north from Shrewsbury had been joined by Lord Byron's forces from Chester, giving him a combined army of fourteen thousand. Rupert proceeded to take Stockport, Bolton, Wigan and Liverpool in quick succession, securing most of Lancashire for the Royalists. Rather surprisingly, at Liverpool Rupert tarried, interrupting his normal headlong progress. It was argued that he needed to consolidate his position and reinforce his army with the Northern Horse under Goring and arms from Ireland. But the real reason appears to have been the splits in the Royalist command. It was reported to Rupert that Wilmot had professed that it was a matter of indifference to him whether the Scots or Rupert prevailed in the north, and that Wilmot, Percy and George were "plotting his ruin."[217] Wilmot had declared openly in the War Council when the king was absent that the English nobility should not be beholden to a foreign prince and should negotiate an honourable end to the war.

A supporter of Rupert, Lord Lindsey, son of the general killed at Edgehill, reported this to the king. Charles accepted Wilmot's disloyalty, and planned to replace him with Goring. Percy he could do nothing about as he was immensely popular with the army, and he could not believe that George was involved as he had already alerted the king to some of these discussions. Rupert reacted explosively, threatening to resign his commission, and questioned whether there was any purpose in him relieving York if he was being undermined elsewhere. His friends continued to stoke the enmity, and Trevor wrote on June 29: "Prince Rupert, by letter from court, understands that the king growes dayly more and more jealous of him and his army; and that it is the common discourse...of the Lord Digbye, lord Percy, sir John Culpeper, and Willmot, that it is indifferent whither the parliament or prince Rupert doth prevayle; which did so highly jesuite prince Rupert, that he was once resolved to send the king his commission and gett to France."[218]

Whilst in Liverpool Rupert received an ambiguous letter from the king urging him to relieve York, but at the same time requesting that he turn south to help at Worcester. The key section read: "If York be lost, I shall esteeme my Crowne litle lesse, unlesse supported by your suddaine Marche to me, & a Miraculous Conquest in the South ...but if Yorke be relived, & you beate the Rebelles Armies of both Kingdomes...I may possiblie...spinn out tyme, untill you come to assist mee; Wherefor I ....conjure you...immediately march according to your first intention, with all your force to the relife of York; but if that be eather lost, or have fried themselfes from the besiegers, or that for want of pouder you cannot undertake that worke; that you immediately March, with your whole strength directly to Woster, to assist me & my Army."[219] Rupert took this as a command to accelerate his relief of York and to defeat the armies of Fairfax, Manchester and Leven. Clarendon interpreted it as "no less than a peremptory order to fight, upon any disadvantage soever."[220] Rupert immediately set out across the Pennines, marching his army twenty miles a day.

What was not known at that time was that the Earl of Manchester had captured Lincoln and freed up his army of six thousand infantry, one thousand cavalry and twelve cannon to join the siege of York. The three armies laying siege now numbered twenty-five thousand men. When on June 30th the Parliamentary generals heard that Rupert was at Knaresborough, fourteen miles due west of York, they prepared to resist his arrival. Expecting him to take the direct road east from Knaresborough they withdrew their forces from the north of York and blocked the road across the flat heath near Long Marston to the south of the city. But with the road north now open to the Royalists, Rupert switched direction and was able to approach York from the north, where the Roundheads did not expect him. Marching along the left bank of the Ouse, he seized a Roundhead bridge of boats at Overton, enabling him to cross the river and occupy Poppleton. Leaving most of his army there, he rode into York at the head of two thousand horse.

The Roundheads were forced to withdraw, and set up camp on Marston Moor, south-west of York, anticipating that Rupert would come south to rejoin the king. Unaware that the king had seen off Waller, Rupert was anxious to return to his sovereign's aid. To save time and leave for the south he was all for attacking the Roundheads immediately. Had he done so, the outcome of the battle would probably have been very different, for the Parliamentary army had decided to withdraw south towards Tadcaster. It was not prepared for battle and was strung out over several miles back from the front line. But the local Royalist commanders, Lord Eythin and the Marquess of Newcastle, were no friends of Rupert. Eythin had fought with Rupert in 1638 at Munster and had quarrelled with him; now he influenced Newcastle's view of the brash prince, whom

Eythin considered rash and inexperienced. Eythin was reluctant to fight his fellow-Scots, and his men were in no hurry to move until they were paid. When Newcastle finally marched out of York to join Rupert, he found his army drawn up in battle array, facing a significantly larger force which, threatened by Rupert's appearance, had turned round to face him and was only a few hundred yards away. Eythin was critical of Rupert's battle formation, and resisted the prince's inclination to attack that afternoon, reminding him that a similar tactic in Germany had led to his capture. For whatever reason, Rupert decided to delay until the following morning. Cromwell, seeing the enemy settling down for the night, charged, and caught the Royalst army totally unprepared. The details of this famous battle are well known, as are the consequences of the Parliamentarians ultimately decisive victory. York was abandoned, surrendering on July 16, and Rupert escaped to the west with six thousand men. The defection of Newcastle, who decamped overseas, caused many of the Royalist leaders in the north to lay down their arms and declare the war lost.

George was making a determined effort to patch up his differences with Rupert, and during this period can be seen keeping the volatile and paranoid prince appraised of ongoing events. His letters of this period show how assiduously he kept Rupert informed of the king's movements and the skirmishes in which they were engaged. On July 12 he sent a detailed despatch from Evesham describing a skirmish at Cropredy Bridge. After Marston Moor, seeking to remain in with Rupert and not to be seen to be blaming him for the defeat, on July 17 1644 he wrote to Rupert from Bath reassuring him: "Although there is no matter for congratulation in the battle in the North, since the success was not answerable to your Highness's virtue; yet there is matter of comfort in that (your Highness being disappointed of these seasonable aids which you expected [help from Newcastle] and had given order for) the event was no worse, but having done the work you came for, of relieving York, your highness yet remains in a condition to renew the dispute upon terms not unhopeful."[221] On July 27 George wrote from Exeter describing Goring's advance to Bristol. He informed Rupert that the king was marching to meet Prince Maurice the following day.[222] He also professed great admiration for Rupert, and praised him whenever there was good news to report. This surprised the prince, as he did not regard George as an ally but as a rival and was still seeking to depose him from his position of influence with the king. It is possible that George, seeing in Rupert the Royalists' only remaining hope, was intent on maintaining his morale and providing reassurance that he remained in favour.

Much has been made by George's critics of his part in the king's ambiguous letter to Rupert. It was said that the letter was "in the unfortunate pen of my Lord Digby" but signed by the king.[223] Warwick goes on to say: "Had not the Lord Digby this year given a fatal direction to that excellent Prince Rupert to have fought the Scotch army, surely that great Prince and soldier had never so precipitately fought them."[224] From the description above, however, it will be seen that Marston Moor was a much closer-run battle than the outcome portrays. Whether George was the prime instigator of the instruction to Rupert or it was the king's own work, an argument can be mounted in favour of the move. The Parliamentarians were in disarray following Rupert's sudden appearance at York and his easy entry to the city; had he attacked the Roundheads when he first arrived at Marston Moor rather than waiting, it could have resulted in a famous victory. Bearing in mind the constitution of the Parliamentarian force that day, and their extended lines, who can say it would not have swung the war the Royalists' way? Eythin and Newcastle, never happy to cooperate with Rupert, had delayed fatally.

Nevertheless Marston Moor was to prove a major turning point in the war. The Royalists were now struggling to remain united and in control of events, with support from the general public fading fast. George's role as chief adviser to the king had become crucial. The king did his best to patch up the differences among his council, reassuring Rupert of the continuing importance of his role and the trust in which he was held. He defended George to the prince: "And for Lord Digby upon my word you are mistaken, I have found him very sensible of your interests the right way."[225] But the fact was that Rupert's influence was still resented by his fellow generals and that they suspected him of plotting to usurp the king.

Chapter 10.

Things Fall Apart.

The accusations levelled at George need to be seen in the context of other moves at the time. A new French envoy, the Marquis de Sabran had been sent to Charles's court. His brief was to initiate peace negotiations, as the conflict was causing some alarm in France. He approached George as Secretary of State with some trepidation, for George had the reputation of being pro-Spanish, and a noted hawk as far as the war was concerned. Sabran was pleasantly surprised when, on July 4, George agreed to support his peace moves. He wrote a letter to Sabran requesting him to convey a peace proposal to Parliament. In Sabran's despatches back to Paris he notes: "....je me suis estonne que Msrs Germain et Digbye qui m'avoient fait les ouvertures de pouvoir parler avec eux comme Parlement, m'y ajent voulu engager sans estre bien assurex du consentment de sa Mte B (Brienne)."[226] Even at this latter stage of the war, therefore, far from being the ultra-hawk he has been portrayed as elsewhere, George continued to explore any possibilities of a negotiated peace.

Meanwhile the king had marched west in a hurry, hoping to reach Exeter in time for the birth of his latest child and to defend his wife against Essex, who had declared his intention of capturing her and bringing her before Parliament to answer for her crimes. Charles was too late: the child, a girl, Henrietta, was born on June 16. With the Parliamentarians closing in the queen, who was in poor health with puerperal sepsis, moved silently out of Exeter at night carried on a litter and accompanied by several ladies and the faithful Henry Jermyn, who had replaced George as the queen's closest adviser when

George was made Secretary of State. At Truro on July 9 she wrote a farewell letter to her husband and on July 14 sailed for France from Falmouth in a small Flemish fleet that had been anchored there. The fleet was pursued by three Parliamentary warships which fired at her ship without damaging it. Keeping ahead of the pursuers past the Channel Islands, they finally came within sight of some French ships, at which point the English warships turned back. She landed at Brest on July 16, journeying from there to Bourbon for revival from the mineral waters. Too late, Charles reached Exeter two weeks later. From there he was able to lay siege to Essex at Fowey.

The leadership of Cromwell at Marston Moor had made him a hero among the Parliamentary forces. As a successful military leader and as MP for Huntingdon, he was well placed to lead the campaign for a new force. The campaign, now gaining ground in Parliamentarian and military circles, was for a new professional army, more reliable and disciplined than local and regional forces had hitherto provided. But it was on the advice of Waller, who brought news of disastrous mutinies and desertions by elements of the London, Essex and Herts trained-bands, that on July 12 Parliament passed an ordinance directing the formation of a new force of 10,000 foot and 3,050 horse to be raised from the southern and eastern counties for permanent service in place of the trained-bands. This was to become the nucleus of the New Model Army.

Wilmot and George, once close friends, were now so much at odds with each other that they could not both remain at the king's side. Wilmot and Rupert were also bitter enemies, with Rupert opposing anything Wilmot suggested on principle, and Wilmot openly criticising Rupert's influence over the king. Wilmot, who had enjoyed considerable success as a general earlier in the war, had found himself eclipsed by Rupert, and resented the lack of advancement which he consequently experienced. Raised to the peerage earlier in the year, he had expected rewards to follow, both in terms of money and power. When these were not forthcoming he married a rich widow whose kinsmen supported the Roundheads, a liaison not looked on favourably by the king's advisers. To add further to his unpopularity he had been critical of the failure at Marston Moor and openly spoke of suing for peace, if necessary by replacing the king with the Prince of Wales. To his credit George put aside his personal differences and strongly supported Rupert, telling the king that he believed Rupert would soon recover the ground lost.

Throughout the summer there had been growing mistrust and bickering, which now came to a head. During his march to York as we know Rupert had heard that Wilmot, Culpeper and George considered it a matter of indifference to them whether Rupert or the Scots held the north. This had caused him to pause and consider resigning his commission. Wilmot was supported by Harry Percy, who had no cause to like Rupert either. Rupert in turn blamed Percy for failing to supply his forces. But Rupert needed allies if he was to be rid of Wilmot, his second-in-command, and the troublesome Percy. So he turned to George, who had no cause to like Percy.[227]

The argument between Wilmot and George reached crisis point in August when the king was camped at Boconnock. Charles had sent out rather vague overtures to the Earl of Essex for a negotiated peace. Wilmot was drinking heavily and not always in control of himself. It was during one of these bouts that he had talked of deposing Charles and replacing him with his son, the Prince of Wales. An intensely ambitious man, Wilmot was suspicious that George and Sir John Culpeper were conspiring against him. There may have been more than a grain of truth in this for George, having patched up his differences with Rupert, started to campaign against Wilmot. Rupert agreed with George's criticism of Wilmot and urged the king to get rid of him. When Wilmot attempted to have George and Culpeper removed on the basis that they continually dissuaded the king from considering peace or listening to the opinion of the people George turned the tables on him by accusing him of treachery. Clarendon remarked that Wilmot's "carriage and discourses were quickly represented in full magnitude to the King by the lord Digby."[228] That it was an orchestrated campaign against Wilmot is given weight by O'Neill: "My Lord Digby, seeing that he could not work him to his friendship, indeavoured to remove him from his power, and therefore accused him to his majuestie."[229]

It transpired that when Charles had written to Essex offering peace terms if he would come to an "understanding" with him, Wilmot had added a secret, personal message promising to support Essex's during any peace talks in the hope that his alliance would enable him to overthrow George. He also implied that he would help Essex take the king into "protection" in London.[230] This message was discovered and, on August 8, in front of the army, the king had Wilmot arrested and imprisoned in Exeter. He was exiled and went to France, where he sought to rebuild his position by ingratiating himself with the queen. He and George were to cross swords again, this time literally, much later.

George had prevailed, and was now pre-eminent with the king, although Wilmot's downfall caused outrage in the army, who put the blame on George. Lord Percy, a staunch supporter of Wilmot, immediately resigned much to the delight of Rupert. Rupert sent for Goring in Lancashire to replace Wilmot as Lieutenant-General of the Horse. A dissolute and untrustworthy man, Goring was also elegant, good company and generous. He presented an attractive contrast to the dour Wilmot, but the move came close to provoking mutiny. Wilmot had been a popular leader and was regarded by his officers as a successful commander. Goring was not regarded as a successful general and was also a heavy drinker. The king was forced to ride up and down the lines explaining the reasons for Wilmot's removal. George immediately wrote to Rupert in triumph: "I make no doubt but all the ill-humours in our army will be allayed, now that the two poles, upon which they moved, are taken away." He added: "....my actions, if rightly understood, might hitherto have preserved me in your favour."[231] In fact Rupert was disappointed. Daniel O'Neill reported to Ormond: "Prince Rupert, who is known to be the prime mobile off that mischiefes [is] strangely unsatisfied with Wilmot's resolutione for hee thought to make use of this occasion to ruin Digbye."[232]

Rupert remained wracked with doubts and suspicions. Despite appointing Goring, he was aware that by commanding the army in the west the new appointee provided a counterbalance to Rupert's command. He was also jealous of the council assembled round the young Prince of Wales in Bristol, whom he felt wielded too much influence with the king. He still distrusted George: in fact there was only one general, Sir Richard Grenville, whom he respected.[233] George sought to reassure him, writing on September 23 from Exeter that the king "hath endeavoured to make it (the army) more worthy of you by removing those from it against whom your Highness had too just a prejudice."[234]

At Fowey, Essex was in a tight corner. He appealed to Parliament to send help, and Manchester was ordered to march towards him. Three thousand pounds' worth of food was shipped to Fowey, but these moves were taking too long. On August 31 he despatched Balfour with the cavalry to cut through the Royalist ring under cover of darkness while Essex himself, abandoning his infantry and guns, was rowed out to one of Warwick's ships and escaped.[235]

As the king commenced the long journey back from Exeter in September, the irrepressible George showed great cheerfulness. Throughout this turbulent period, he had kept his nerve and sustained the Royalist war effort whilst others faltered, harboured doubts about the outcome, or simply bickered with colleagues. With Rupert in the north and Wilmot in disgrace he felt in charge of matters, and able to provide unfettered advice to the king. He was very optimistic about the way the war was going and wrote to Ormond that affairs were "…in the best posture they had been at any time since these unhappy wars."[236] There were rumours of rifts between the Independents and Presbyterians, and news of a Royalist uprising in Scotland. He reflected that recently "God hath blest his majestie's affairs even to miracle. We are now marching eastwards, victorious and strong…so that you may confidently esteem His Majesty's affairs here are in the best posture that they have been at any time since these unhappy wars."[237]

For once the news was good: on September 26 George learnt that the siege of Basing House had been relieved by Colonel Gage, thus retaining control of the road to London from the wool suppliers. The west country campaign was going well, with Essex forced away and much of Devon and Cornwall under Royalist control. With the removal of Wilmot and Percy, Rupert and George were dominant on the War Council.

Charles had intended to make Rupert Commander-in-Chief in succession to Patrick Ruthven, Lord Forth, recently appointed Earl of Brentford, who had been wounded, and who was considered to be lacking in energy and positive ideas. A man of few words but a career professional soldier, Brentford was nevertheless popular with his men. Then, just when the prince's star was high, his elder brother Charles Louis, Elector Palatine, arrived in London and immediately pleaded for an end to the war and pledged to use his best endeavours to end the differences between king and Parliament. He was known to have supported the Parliamentary cause in the past. He was given free board and lodging at Whitehall, and was so obviously in thrall to Parliament that the king felt he could not promote Rupert. It is possible that Charles Louis, the eldest son of Charles' sister and therefore next in line after the king's children, expected to be offered the king's crown, and it was rumoured that Sir Henry Vane had suggested Charles Louis should stand by to take the king's place. Parliament reacted indignantly to this proposal however, and suggested Charles Louis leave London, but the Elector stood his ground and would not leave.

On the return journey from the west country in October 1644 the king and his army lodged at Sherborne for several days, where George entertained him. There he appointed George's step-brother, Lewis Dyve, as Serjeant Major General of the County of Dorset, and left with him a force comprising 150 soldiers from his own regiment, 200 horse and 50 other infantry. Soon Dyve was imposing his will on the county by a series of raids which subdued Parliamentary resistance and secured all the main towns. George, through his Sherborne estates, had interests in several Dorset ports, which were used to bring in guns to support the Royalist cause.

Meanwhile Rupert had undertaken to muster four thousand men at Bristol and bring them to Sherborne. It appeared that he was enjoying himself at Bristol, for there was some indignation among Royalist circles at stories of debauchery there.[238] George spent some time at Bristol with Rupert, along with the other army leaders Hopton, Goring, Newport and Capell. O'Neill wrote that Rupert and George were now "reconcyled which is a great happiness to the King."[239] But despite the outward display of friendship Rupert remained strongly opposed to George. "Digby makes great professions and vows to Rupert, but it will do no good upon him."[240] George returned to Sherborne, but by the time he reached the castle the king had moved on.

With winter approaching, it was time to settle back into a well-provided stronghold, but before the king could reach Oxford he had one more barrier to overcome. With seventeen thousand men under their command, the Earl of Manchester, Waller and Philip Skippon, a veteran of the Dutch wars who had commanded the trained-bands in London with distinction, sat astride the road at Newbury. The king had originally agreed to rendezvous with Rupert at Sherborne where his forces were secure, but had changed his mind and moved on to Salisbury before setting out for Oxford. Not for the first time Rupert's advice was ignored, but this time it seems that George was not consulted. Anticipating Rupert's wrath, George wrote to him on October 20 from Whitchurch that he had "wondered as much as your Highness doth to finde the Kinge at Salesburye, soe farr advanct, contrary to all former resolutions."[241] By October 23 George had reached Newbury and been informed that the Parliamentarian army was in some disarray, with their forces split. He wrote to Rupert urging him to send reinforcements immediately, for if they could confront the enemy with a considerable force "in all probabilitye it will bee fatall to them."[242] The reinforcements failed to arrive. Fortunately for the king the reluctant Earl of Manchester wished he was not there, and his heart was not in the conflict. So he watched while the king, having reached Newbury and found the way blocked, threw up earthworks to the north of the town, close to Donnington Castle. There the Royalists prepared their defence, covered by the guns from the castle. From the Parliamentary camp the Royalist position looked formidably strong, and a direct frontal attack was almost certain to fail. It was here that Manchester made the famous comment: "If we beat the King ninety-nine times yet he is King still, and so will his posterity after him, but if the King beats us, we shall all be hanged and our posterity be made slaves." To which Cromwell, who was also present, replied: "My Lord, if this be so why did we take up arms at first?" Suspicions arose that Manchester was no longer loyal to Parliament, which did not help the prevailing mood in the Roundhead camp. On October 25 George wrote to Rupert again describing the Royalist position in front of "Dunnington Castle" in "so advantageous a post that if your Highness can suddenly advance to us any considerable force, we shall be likely to hold them play at the passe for a day or twoe till you come up, and then be able to beate them, for they are not much stronger than wee."[243]

In the battle that ensued, known as Newbury II (October 29) the Parliamentary forces struggled to make headway through the narrow muddy lanes under heavy fire from the Royalist stronghold of Donnington Castle. Their progress was seriously hindered by Manchester's reluctance to act swiftly. Despite this lack of support Skippon pressed forward successfully and disorderly retreat of the Royalist cavalry made the king's position precarious. The strategic high ground on Speen Hill was the focus of the conflict, but attempts to breach Donnington Castle, where the king's heavy artillery was based, were repulsed. The king slipped away by night to join up with Rupert near Bath before heading for Oxford. Finally, realising they could not win, the remaining Royalists withdrew towards Oxford, leaving the field to the Roundheads. Much of the artillery and ammunition was left at Donnington Castle, but the next day recovered by Rupert.

On November 23, 1644 to wild cheering Charles rode into Oxford in front of the reunited army. He knighted some of the heroes of the summer, having finally appointed Rupert as General on November 6 at Bullingdon Green. It was apparent that the Elector Palatine was in no position to claim the Crown, and did not have the support of the Parliamentary leaders. The king's younger son James, present at Newbury, was quick to blame George for the defeat: "The lord Digby ambitious of doing somewhat extraordinary in the absence of Prince Rupert," he wrote, "advised his Majesty to pursue his advantage and follow him (Waller) to Newberry...." and felt instead he should "have made a timely retreat to Oxford."[244] This is patently untrue, for as we have seen, instead of waiting at Sherborne for Rupert to join him, the king had moved on to Salisbury and shortly thereafter, Newbury. George was not present at Sherborne when the king made this move, and can be seen at Newbury to have been desperately calling for reinforcements, which Rupert did not provide. In fact the prince was still just outside Bath when the battle occurred, and had shown no inclination to react rapidly.

Chapter 11.

Endgame.

As Secretary of State George found his time much taken up by problems in Ireland. The king was ill-informed on Irish matters, with a poor intelligence service there, and many of his councillors, with Edward Hyde prominent, were strongly opposed to the Catholics. The burden of seeking progress in Ireland fell on the shoulders of Ormond and George; there is voluminous correspondence showing their exchange of views. They can be seen discussing various appointments in Ireland, from military commanders to consideration of the Earl of Cork as "Treasurer of Ireland."[245] But their main preoccupation was a permanent peace in Ireland so that troops could be freed up for England. Negotiations were not proceeding well, and the council in Oxford were sceptical. On May 9 George wrote to Ormond: "Every body is restrained in councell by apprehensions of the ill effects which any concession to the Irish Catholicks at this time may have upon the affections of the people here."[246] Ormond felt that he did not have clear directions from Oxford and guidance on the position he should take.[247] George responded that they (the Oxford council) were "not soe fitt judges as your excellence of what may be best."[248]

The situation was not made easier by Parliamentary ships blockading Dublin. It was unlikely that Ormond would be able to send another force to England. Ireland was still in a state of rebellion, with the Catholics seeking to take advantage of the conflict across the Irish Sea. The king showed signs of wishing to negotiate with the rebels, who again presented a list of grievances to Ormond. This time they offered the king ten thousand men if these grievances could be redressed, and the Catholic Church recognised as the establishment in Ireland. This was further than any Protestant would be prepared to go, and despite prolonged discussion Ormond could not make progress with the Irish Catholic leaders, who distrusted him as a Protestant and felt betrayed by the failure of the earlier venture.

The lack of progress by Ormond frustrated the king considerably. He judged Ormond to be far too scrupulous in his conduct[249] and too protective of Protestant interests. Charles therefore turned to an outrageous plan put forward by Henry Somerset, Lord Herbert. Herbert and his father had poured money into the king's empty coffers, and it was said that the king owed him the staggering sum of £250,000. Herbert was a devout Catholic, a staunch supporter of the king and something of an intellectual.. He had been an unsuccessful commander in the field, having lost most of his force in Wales and was said to be "incapable of executing a commission or conceiving of a viable plan."[250] He now offered to go to Kilkenny under the guise of doing private business, and enter into a treaty with the Confederate Irish without Ormond's knowledge.[251] As a devout Catholic with an Irish wife he believed he would command their trust. He promised ten thousand men from Ireland and ten thousand more from his family's estates in Wales. In addition he would procure from the pope and other eminent Catholics a monthly subsidy of thirty thousand pounds, and would use this to organise an invasion of East Anglia from the Spanish Netherlands.[252] Charles was by now desperate enough to try anything. In April 1644 he made Herbert Earl of Glamorgan and gave him the secret commission to head an Irish army augmented from Europe, under the clear understanding that should his mission be discovered the king would deny all knowledge of it. It is clear from the correspondence that George was ignorant of the terms of Glamorgan's commission, and would have been horrified had he known what a free hand the earl had been granted by the king. However for some reason Glamorgan was not to reach Dublin until the following year.

Repeatedly George wrote that he had persuaded the king not to appoint officers to Ireland without consulting Ormond, only to have to admit defeat as the king gave in to special interests. On February 20, 1644 he had complained to Ormond that "there are divers here who presse for command of forts and places in Ireland, and some of them such as the King cannot well deny."[253] Meanwhile Ormond remained in charge of negotiations with the Irish agents, but remained reluctant to criticise the orders he was given, or take the initiative. The politics in Ireland were so confused that it was proving impossible to gauge whether any help would be forthcoming from that direction.

One other special interest in particular caused Ormond great difficulty. Randall McDonnell, Lord Antrim, a Catholic nobleman who claimed to represent the Confederate Irish in Northern Ireland, turned up in Oxford offering the king a force to join Montrose in Scotland. In fact he had no authority to represent the Confederates. Antrim's cousins in Scotland were the powerful clan McDonell and his wife was the widow of the Duke of Buckingham. George told Ormond that Antrim wanted the title of "Generalissimo of all the Popish Party.... Of soe great a scandall to his majestie that your lordshipp must look to the prevention of it vigilantly."[254] He also saw the appointment as a rival to Ormond's authority. Here George came to the rescue, for he was a shrewd judge of character, and could see Antrim's flaws as well as Montrose's sterling worth. He turned to a good friend, Daniel O'Neill, nephew of Owen Roe O'Neill the confederate general in Ulster and a rich Irish landowner, who was close to both Antrim and Ormond. At George's prompting Daniel O'Neill appeared in front of the king to explain that Antrim and Ormond would never work together. Antrim was consequently kept at arm's length, and not promised any fancy titles.

Nevertheless, the king's susceptibility to special pleading was to have serious consequences. The presidency of Munster had been granted against George's advice to an English absentee landowner, Lord Portland. George had proposed Lord Inchiquin. The only important Irish chieftain to have supported the English cause since the start of the Irish revolt, Inchiquin felt considerably put out by the preferment of Portland. He indicated to Ormond that George had persuaded the king to make him president of Munster, and had that stood he would have remained loyal to the king. But he was a Protestant, and opposed the truce which Ormond had negotiated with the confederates. He viewed with some alarm Antrim's presence in Oxford, and feared that some deal was being hatched by the king. So Inchiquin declared for Parliament. George, closely involved in political manoeuvres in Ireland, was criticised for the mishandling of Inchiquin but, as he wrote to Ormond: "Concerninge the presidentship of Munster, it was too farr gone to be recalled or stayed."[255] It was even suggested that Portland's appointment had been promised by the king five years previously.[256]

Despite the major setback at Marston Moor, what looked then like imminent capitulation by the Royalists had not transpired. The successes in the west, the ineffectiveness of some of the Parliamentarian forces, and differences between Presbyterians and Independents at Westminster meant the outcome remained uncertain. It was apparent that Parliament was deperately short of funds: Sir Edmund Waller, incarcerated in the Tower the previous year after negotiating secretly with the Royalists and with some reason to fear a formal trial, agreed readily to a contribution of £10,000 in return for his freedom. Whilst Presbyterians and Independents bickered, it was possible the king could exploit their weakness to negotiate a reasonable settlement. Clarendon believed that George may still have been supporting a negotiated settlement at this stage[257] but Sabran wrote that he believed George had altered his position and opposed a settlement.[258] New peace feelers were sent out and negotiations between the king and Parliament went on throughout the winter

George entered into secret negotiations with General Browne, who still held Abingdon for Parliament and was proving a thorn in the flesh of the king's group in Oxford. His plan was to coax Browne over to the Royalists, and his usual optimism led him to believe that he would be successful, as it was known that Browne's men were mutinous and short of pay. Browne was also promised His Majesty's Commission as Governor of Abingdon, the command of a brigade in the King's Army and a Baronetcy. But Browne was merely stringing him along while reporting everything back to Parliament, and buying time while he strengthened his fortifications. When he received 1500 horse from London, strengthening his garrison of 2700 men, he felt strong enough to end the pretence. On December 19 he called off negotiations and mocked George by claiming his intention to "play with you at your own game, till our works (which once were not so strong as you have now made them, though at the weakest would have been lined with our lives) were strengthened and accommodated with men and provisions....and therefore I acquit your Lordship of all misfortune that may befall me."[259] George attempted to discredit Browne by publishing the full correspondence in Mercurius Aulicus, accusing Browne of duplicity and implying that he was plotting to move over to the Royalist side if he was bribed.[260] When this became known in London it merely served to increase the hatred felt for George. Rupert attempted a surprise attack on January 11 1645 with the Governor of Oxford, Sir Henry Gage, in support, but was beaten back with heavy losses, Gage being a notable casualty. As a consequence Rupert once again felt humiliated and angry with George, whom he felt had misled him to attempt a foolish manoeuvre.

The feelers which had been put out to sound the possibility of peace negotiations resulted in a meeting at Uxbridge on January 29, 1645. The Duke of Richmond and the Earl of Southampton represented the king, with instructions to deal on matters concerning religion, the militia and Ireland. The main proposal was that the original reason for the dispute between Parliament and the king, the power of the bishops, be resolved by curtailing their influence while retaining their positions. This was precisely what George had advocated in the Commons prior to the outbreak of war. In addition the king offered to modify his requirement to control the militia by suggesting command be shared between ten people appointed by Parliament and ten by the king. Finally, and optimistically, the king assured Parliament that peace was resolved in Ireland.

It rapidly became apparent that Parliament was unyielding in its demands on the church and militia, and the negotiations faltered. George commented on the failure in a letter to Ormond, supporting the king's position. Peace could only have been achieved at the cost of "a totall subversion of the church and religion itselfe, a resigninge of the regall power heere into the rebells hands, and an entire giving upp of that Kingdome to the Scotts."[261] George expressed the view to Hyde that the apparent divisions among the Parliamentary leaders still gave hope of a settlement, and Hyde noted that despite his stance George may still have supported a negotiated peace.[262] At the same time George showed his realism by discussing with Hyde the rather gloomy military position. He held the view that if Parliament could resolve their arguments, with a better supplied army they could sweep westward from London and defeat the king. In such an eventuality, on behalf of the king he asked Hyde to take responsibility for the Prince of Wales and conduct him to his mother in France. Hyde was alarmed at the prospect, believing the queen to wield an unhealthy influence over her son, and afraid that the young Charles would be persuaded to become a Catholic. He was suspicious of George, too, remarking that "Discourse from the Lord Digby proceeded rather from some Communication of Counsels He had with the Queen, than any Directions from the King."[263] At the same time he expressed the hope that a peaceful settlement could still be reached: "..the divisions at London would yet open some door for a good peace to enter at."[264] The queen continued to encourage George as best she could. Writing to him from Paris on April 7, 1645, she starts by reproaching him for not writing: "I fear you are as inconstant to your friends, as men are to their Mistresses....(but) I am too well acquainted with you. For my part, I only have this fault, to be a good Friend, and I believe you know it."[265]

Rupert was now de facto Commander-in-Chief and working alongside George, whose constant cheerfulness and optimism managed to keep the king buoyed up at a time when many of his advisers were "strangely impatient for peace" as he wrote to the queen.[266] George had also formed a most unlikely friendship with Goring, leader of the forces in the west. It was based, wrote Hyde, on mutual distrust, "...either of them believing that he could deceive the other and so with equal passion embracing the engagement."[267] George kept Goring's spirits up with a stream of cheerful news, promising help from overseas any day, while at the same time inserting sly messages of admonition. Goring's heavy drinking made him careless and he suffered several setbacks as a consequence. George wrote to him: "Dear General, I have nothing to add but to conjure you to be wary of debauches, there fly hither the reports of the liberty you give yourself much to your disadvantage, and you have enemies who are apt to make use of it."[268]

Rupert had gone to Wales from Oxford and from there to Hereford and Bristol in order to shore up the position in the west. With the commencement of spring Cromwell had started a slow squeeze on Oxford. Yet again the king, with George in attendance, slipped out of Oxford undetected, meeting Rupert and his brother Maurice at Stowe on May 8 1645. A council of war was held. Rupert was as active as ever in his efforts to turn the war. He had placed a garrison at Chipping Camden to cut the route to Gloucester from its trade in Cotswold wool, and in combination with the Royalist strongholds at Worcester and Cirencester had started to squeeze Massey, the commander at Gloucester. But he was becoming increasingly pessimistic about the outcome of the struggle and as a consequence was at odds once again with George, who strenuously objected to any suggestion that peace negotiations be resumed at a time when he felt that Royalist prospects were good and the enemy in some disarray. This was quite a shift from his previous stance, and it is possible that he took this position in order to oppose Rupert, with whom his relationship was deteriorating rapidly. Arthur Trevor wrote to Ormond: "All is governed by P. Rupert who grows a great Courtier...Certainly the Lord Digby loves him not."[269] Whilst Rupert was not advocating that they sue for peace, he was at a loss to know how they were going to win. He believed the Royalists retained enough strength to negotiate peace, but not enough to win the war.[270] George was full of positive cheer: the Royalist army, he wrote to Ormond, augmented by troops already in the west or to be raised there, were "equal to any the rebels have at this time."[271] What was more, the Parliamentarians were quarrelling among themselves, foreign aid was still a distinct possibility, the Royalists remained in control of the south-west and the key ports of Bristol and Exeter, and so forth.

Rupert and his followers argued that the disarray in Parliamentarian ranks and the territorial advantages the Royalists held merely strengthened their position in peace negotiations, but was an insufficient base from which the war could be won. They were worried that the Scots could come far enough south to meet the Roundheads, thus uniting the north for Parliament, yet they still had their hands full in the west, where Fairfax was strong and threatening to join up with Cromwell. George, full of brilliant suggestions, proposed that they go east, attacking the Eastern Association and destroying Cromwell's hitherto unthreatened power base in East Anglia. If he had been listened to this strategy may have ended the war, but it involved great risks and was an all-or-nothing attempt, neglecting maintenance of the Royalists' strong position in the west. It is possible that George was influenced by a piece of intelligence in a letter from Nicholas to the king dated June 8: "…whiles the rebels lay before Oxford all their chief officers whispered among themselves that they feared nothing so much as your Majesty's going to the Associated Counties before they had force to withstand you. And one colonel… said that if you went into the North, you would not get any considerable force to march with you out of that country, and that you would there spend all the summer fruitlessly. But if you should presently strike into the Associated Counties they were all undone."[272] The majority were in favour of going west to prevent Fairfax from relieving Taunton and meeting up with Cromwell in Somerset, but Rupert favoured the northern campaign.[273] Chester, currently under challenge by the enemy, must be preserved as it was the only sea-route to Ireland still open. More importantly, with Fairfax engaged far south and Montrose gaining ground in Scotland, there was a real possibility that the Royalists could regain the north, augment Montrose's stretched campaign and force the Covenanters out of the war.

Rupert had other reasons for wanting to go north. The Northern Horse, a formidable cavalry outfit under the command of Sir Marmaduke Langdale, were not happy, and had a strong desire to go home in order to defend their own county, Yorkshire. Rupert did not know how long he could depend on their loyalty outside of Yorkshire. He also had personal motivation: to revenge the humiliating defeat he had suffered at the hands of the Scots at Marston Moor. Thus his arguments for taking the king's army north were somewhat subjective. When news came that Taunton had been relieved Rupert's counsel prevailed, and for once George was in agreement, writing to Goring: "On my conscience it will be the last blow in the business."[274] This optimism was reinforced when news came that the Parliamentarians had abandoned the siege of Chester. Goring was recalled to the midlands to join the king, who had travelled on to Market Harborough. At Ashby they were reinforced by Langdale's Northern Horse and Lord Loughborough with several troops of horse.

Although the king was disposed to believe George's optimistic forecasts of success, he was realistic enough to be increasingly concerned at the direction the war was taking. Fearing for his son's future, on May 5, 1645, he sent him to the west accompanied by Edward Hyde and Culpeper. Charles, Prince of Wales, was three months short of his fifteenth birthday. The garrison at Bristol was not strong, and it was clear to the prince and his party that the city would not provide a safe haven. They moved on, originally intending to sail for France in reponse to the king's instructions that "Whensoever you find yourself in apparent danger of falling into the rebels' hands, you convey yourself into France, and there be under your mother's care, who is to have the absolute full power of your education in all things, except religion."[275] The king's advisers, notably Edward Hyde, were secretly appalled at this direction, as they feared that should the prince leave the country it would be seen as capitulation by royalty.[276] The idea that the young man should come under the influence of his strong-willed but erratic Catholic mother was anathema. But George expressed his pessimism to Hyde, believing that the Parliamentarian army, now superior in number, would sweep west from London. Although he still hoped for a negotiated settlement, he urged Hyde to escort the Prince out of the country.[277]

As it happened the prince was pursued to Cornwall from whence he sailed to the Scilly Isles only to be blockaded by two dozen Parliamentary ships. He was able eventually to slip away on the one hundred-and-sixty ton frigate, The Proud Black Eagle, to Jersey, using the cover of a storm to evade the Parliamentary fleet. He was well received on Jersey, and took up residence there.

In control of the midlands, Cromwell first set about denying Oxford provisions, and the city was soon feeling the pinch. Short of food, the inhabitants sent a despatch saying that they could not hold out for long. George remained unfailingly cheerful, however, writing on May 26 from Market Harborough to Nicholas in Oxford that "If Cromwell and Fairfax advance we shall endeavour to fight with them. I believe it will be about Leicester. I hope by this time Goring is about Oxford with his horse. If we can be so happy as that he comes in time, we shall infallibly crush them between us. For God's sake quicken his march all that's possible."[278] A second letter by George written on the orders of the king and Rupert assured Nicholas that in the case of necessity Oxford would be relieved, but urged Nicholas not to represent the wants of the garrison as more pressing than they were. "If the Governor of Oxford assure us that he is provided for six weeks or two months, we shall then, I make no question, relieve our northern garrisons, beat the Scots, or make them retreat, and march southwards with a gallant army indeed." If Oxford could not hold out the king would march south, joining Goring between Oxford and London, saving the city and cutting off the besiegers.[279] In another letter to Nicholas on May 25 from Uttoxeter, George wrote; "The best intelligence we can get of the rebels is that parties of a thousand horse have hovered these two last days between Lichfield and Tamworth, and that they draw all their forces, as well Cromwell's as Browne's and those which came from Fairfax and Rossiter about Lincoln...If we can fall on any of them before they join we will not neglect the advantage. If they be much too strong for us we shall retreat toward Leicester and Northamptonshire witherward Col. Goring had orders sent him from Newport to march with all the force of horse, foot and cannon he can make."[280]

Buoyed up by reinforcements, although there was no sign of Goring's three thousand men, on May 30 the Royalists besieged the prosperous town of Leicester. Within four hours a heavy artillery bombardment had breached the walls sufficiently for a general assault to take place. Twice they were repulsed with heavy losses by courageous and resolute defence and started to waver, but then from the other end of the town another assault party forced entry into the town. The skirmish continued throughout the night, but by morning the Royalist superiority in numbers told, and the governor and officers defending surrendered. The town was mercilessly ransacked and wagons piled high with loot moved on to Belvoir Castle, which was held by the Royalists. From Leicester George continued to press Nicholas in Oxford with anxious requests about Goring's movements, emphasising the urgent need the king had of Goring's men.

Hearing of the loss of Leicester, Parliament became alarmed and directed Fairfax to raise the siege of Oxford and set out in pursuit, arranging to meet Cromwell who was coming from Huntingdon. This was precisely what the king had hoped would happen, as Leicester was a good place to assemble the Royalist forces, but he needed the support of Goring to withstand the numerically superior Parliamentarian army. Rupert and the Council of War were in favour of marching towards Oxford to relieve it, but Goring had not yet appeared and Langdale refused to take his cavalry any further south. Instead he prepared to return north to Yorkshire. Not even a personal promise permitting him back to Yorkshire when the battle was finished would mollify him initially, although he finally relented, and the army moved to Daventry. There they learned that the siege of Oxford had been raised, and the New Model Army was marching towards them, so they withdrew to Market Harborough.

An inner council met there on July 13 at midnight to take stock of the Royalist position. Present were Rupert, George, and the peers Richmond, Bellasis, Lindsey, Carnwath and Astley. Ashburnham was also in attendance. George was all for seeking suitable ground and standing firm immediately, but Rupert was more cautious for once. He knew that the joint Parliamentary force would be superior in numbers and he would have preferred to stand on more favourable ground. Perhaps they could move further north where they had hopes of reinforcements, particularly from Scotland, where Montrose held out the promise of bringing his army south by the end of summer. In addition there were Royalist garrisons at Newark and nearby towns which could be drawn on. Without Goring the Royalists would be outnumbered nearly two to one, the Parliamentary army numbering 13,500 to the Royalists 7,500. Walker reports that George and Ashburnham held sway in the Council: "resolutions were taken to fight and rather to march back and seek him out, than be sought or pursued, contrary… to Prince Rupert's Opinion."[281]

George felt they should make a stand at Market Harborough. His counsel won the day and the Royalists moved out onto a ridge running from East Farndon to Oxendon, two miles south of Market Harborough facing marshy ground and large open fields. This provided them with a very favourable position. There was no sign of the enemy, and questions were raised about the intelligence reports that they were near. A scouting party could find no trace of them, so Rupert drew a group of musketeers and horse and marched forward, looking to engage the Roundheads. Within a mile he received a report that they were close, and soon they appeared on the hill facing the Royalists across the marsh. Their movement was such that

Rupert surmised they were retreating, although he may have actually seen a scouting party returning to Fairfax to report. Alternatively it is suggested that Fairfax was simply moving his men to higher ground, having realised how marshy the valley was. Another opinion is that Fairfax deliberately let Rupert see his manoeuvre in order to encourage a Royalist advance into a battle which would favour the Roundheads. Rupert immediately sent word back that the enemy were retreating and that the Royalist army should join him, thus causing it to quit its favourable position on the rise.[282]

This decision proved to be disastrous. The Royalist were forced to charge uphill against prepared positions, and although Rupert's cavalry succeeded, as usual, in cutting through the enemy, also as usual it pursued its quarry off the battlefield, leaving the infantry struggling against superior numbers from an inferior position. Cromwell cannily held back his reserves at the outset, and threw them into battle later to tilt the balance. By this time Rupert had returned, but too late: the field was lost. Casualties were heavy, several hundred infantry lying dead on the field and between four and five thousand Royalists captured. The name of this place was to become renowned as the scene of Cromwell's greatest victory, for it was Naseby.

The retreat soon turned into a complete rout. The Royalist army, struggling back towards Leicester, were pursued relentlessly by Cromwell's cavalry and cut down in the road. Those who attempted to escape by leaving the main road were either attacked by local villagers or cornered in fields and slaughtered. Nor was any quarter shown when the pursuers caught up with the baggage train. Soldiers' wives, camp-followers and mistresses were put to the sword, justified in Parliamentary eyes because many of the women were Irish, and the animosity between Protestants and Catholics was intense. George was able to escape with his own coach and possessions intact, but the most important conquest of all came from the Royal coaches, for in addition to valuable jewels they contained the king's correspondence. This included all his letters from the queen, showing the requests for funds and the plans to bring in foreigners from the Continent to help the king. The correspondence was damning, revealing his contacts with Denmark, France and Holland over the two past years. Most damaging of all, it left in no doubt his intention to reinforce the Royalists with a contingent of the Irish Confederate army, led and manned by Catholics. Once the import of these negotiations was realised and made public, the Royalists lost many supporters. Those Parliamentarians who still wished for a peace settlement turned their back on the king. George realised that hope was gone, and became set in his determination to salvage what he could through war. His reputation as a "hawk" can be seen to date from this time. Contrary to his many critics' comments, there are few signs that before this time he was opposed to peace negotiations.

More importantly, Naseby was to prove to be decisive militarily. When Leicester fell to the advancing Parliamentary force three days later, the king's infantry was totally destroyed or captured, with 5,000 prisoners being taken, including 500 officers. All the Royalist artillery, 40 barrels of powder and arms for 800 men were also lost. The king, accompanied by Rupert and George, retreated through Leicester, Ashby-de-la-Zouch and Lichfield to Hereford, where they stayed three days, attempting to recruit fresh troops. Before they reached Hereford George wrote to Ormond from Bewdley urgently pleading for any infantry he could send from Ireland. His optimism surfaced yet again: if he could have more men "the consequences of this disaster will have no great extent."[283]

Rupert left the king at Hereford to hurry back to Bristol, fearing it might be the next target for the enemy. Without Rupert at the king's side, George was able to make his feelings plain. As usual, he was both unrepentant and critical of his fellow officers, and particularly of Rupert. He raised questions of the battle, which he observed at first hand: "…(whether) having store and provision with us we should not rather have tried to bring them to our post than to have assaulted them constantly in theirs. That if it were resolved we must assail them...whether it had not been fit rather to have advanced to or gained some place where the cannon might have been of some use, than to have drawn up hill against them so as never to make use of our piece. And lastly that before we joined battle whether it would not have been convenient to have viewed the enemy's strength and posture, rather than to have left to this hour in dispute whether the enemy had not three thousand men in reserve than those we fought with...I make no doubt but you would also have asked some material questions concerning a reserve and a placing of the King's person first where it would not have been suddenly involved in the confusion."[284] Bearing in mind that it was he who had urged they stand and fight while Rupert was anxious to delay until their forces were stronger, this was an attempt to escape blame bordering on effrontery! Yet his analysis of both the relinquishing of the high ground and the danger which the king was exposed to, was echoed by other respected observers. There was some substance to the accusation that Rupert had not taken the trouble to ascertain the strength and disposition of the enemy, and had not called a council to decide how his own army would best be deployed. He had not followed Astly's advice, and had no adequate reserve.[285] But the king commanded the reserve, and if Rupert's view had prevailed they would not have fought this battle.

Rupert took most of the blame for the defeat despite his advice against the battle, and his irritable, undiplomatic demeanour did not help his cause. In the same letter George reopened the ill-feeling and jealousies which still rankled, and had been papered over temporarily: "I am sure that Prince Rupert hath so little kindness for me as daily I find he hath, it imports to both me and mine to be much the more cautious not to speak anything that may be wrested to his prejudice. I can but lament my misfortune that Prince Rupert is neither gainable nor tenable by me though I have endured it with all the industry and justness unto him in the world." He had finally given up hope of finding common ground with the prince, and the breach between them was complete. The king's two closest advisers were at each other's throats.

George's letter was written from Raglan Castle, where the king's entourage, defended by a meagre force of cavalry, had made its way after Hereford, arriving on July 3. They hoped to recruit a new army from among the king's many Welsh sympathisers, but this attempt failed. They remained at Raglan for two weeks, hoping to cross the Bristol Channel for safe haven in Cornwall. These hopes were dashed by news of the rout of Goring on July 13 at Langport, where his force outnumbered the enemy and held the higher ground, yet still lost to a resolute Fairfax. Having lost two thousand men and a thousand horse Goring fell back to Barnstaple. There his weakened army was set upon by local militia, and he was forced to retreat to Bridgwater. By July 22 he had abandoned this stronghold as well, and the town was in flames.

From Raglan on July 10 George reported to Henrietta Maria in Paris: "We live here in great disquiet till we hear how your Majesty hath digested our late misfortune (at Naseby); God be thanked we have already lost the sharp sense of it. We have had many little successes since, and we are likely to find ourselves now within one fortnight in a posture fit to have a day for all, which certainly the rebels will give us in the west, whither they have drawn all they have…..It will certainly be fit for your Majesty to consider and to give your advice how we should behave ourselves now as to the avowing of those foreign treaties, which can be no longer a secret [the King's papers having been captured] especially that of the Prince of Orange, in case our late disaster hath not cooled his affection to the alliance….I must not conclude without humbly acknowledging your Majesty's great justice in your contempt of those scandals which his Majesty's enemies have endeavoured to cast upon me, unto which I shall only say thus much more, that I have been so pure a virgin in point of my integrity to his and your Majesty's that I thank God nobody ever yet durst ask me a question as to muy own interests."[286]

On July 13 George had written to Rupert in Bristol, suggesting that if he wished to participate in discussions over the next moves he should come to Wales.[287] In view of the defeat of Goring the west was no longer defendable, but Wales was, and a concentration of forces there would help with recruiting. There were (unfounded) rumours that Glamorgan had landed in Anglesey with a large Irish force. On July 22 the king met Rupert at Creeke, attended by the Duke of Richmond, the Earls of Lichfield and Leicester, Astley and George.[288] News had recently been received that Montrose had beaten the Scots near Edinburgh. Rupert persuaded the king to travel to Bristol. The new Welsh recruits were assembling at Newport, and could be used to recover the west. However, within twenty-four hours of returning to Raglan to prepare for the crossing to Bristol the king had changed his mind, persuaded by his Welsh supporters to stay. Clarendon believed that "they who did not love prince Rupert, nor were loved by him, could not endure to think that the King would be so wholly within his power."[289] Yet there is ample evidence that George was quite prepared to see the king go to Bristol: on the contrary, he looked forward to joining up with the prince's council.[290]

It appears that Rupert was also trying to convince the king that the war was lost and that he had no alternative but to seek terms of surrender. George wrote to Jermyn on August 27, by which time they had left Wales: "[The king was] in great distress in Wales, upon occasion of [Rupert] declaring unto him that there was nothing left for him to do, but to seek conditions."[291] George's hopes were now focussed upon the possibility of linking up with the Scots. Montrose had reported some success, and could make his way south to join the king. But George was realistic: "Without a miracle from God there is no more to be hoped for but a languishing defence this yeare, with expectation of certaine ruine the next."[292]

George continued to work hard at raising support from abroad, expecting an army from Ireland and hoping for aid from Denmark and France. On August 7 he told Jermyn: "It is most true that, desperate as our condition seems, I have an apprehension but that having got thus far in the year we shall be safe till the next from any further great mischief; and that probably by helps from Denmark and Ireland and monies from you, that is from France – we may possibly have a fresh and hopeful resource the next Spring."[293] The queen wrote to him raising hopes that Cardinal Mazarin would provide funds for the hire of men from the Duke of Lorraine. A damaging war between Sweden and Denmark came to an end with the Baltic Peace agreement, leading George to have renewed optimism of aid from Denmark: "I thinke there is more probability in that of Denmark for man, now the peace is concluded with the Swedes. And for money from Rome, then any other way, the business of Ireland hath hung long in suspense, although the King hath long since given my Lord of Ormond power to conclude Peace there, upon the very utmost concession that can possibly be yielded unto without causing a revolt."[294]

The king, searching for solace in these difficult times, preferred the calm optimism of George to the despondency of other courtiers. He hoped that the Irish would soon be joining up with his diminished force, and good news from Montrose in Scotland led him to believe he would be receiving help from that direction as well. George, although becoming pessimistic about the outcome of the war, stood by him: "Truly I have great confidence in the Kings vertue & steddines, & I am much improved in it by this enclosed Letter wch he wrote in his great distress in Wales, upon occasion of declaring to him there was nothing left for him to do but to seek conditions."[295]

Privately he wrote to Nicholas: "such a torrent of misfortunes hath quite overbourne my sanguine complexion. Yet that is supported by faith that God will not wholly desert us nor so good a cause."[296]

Rupert was busy improving the fortifications of Bristol in order to provide the king with new headquarters, but when news came through that Fairfax had taken Bridgwater, thus cutting the line between Bristol and the king's Western Army in Cornwall, this plan had to be abandoned. Neither Lorraine nor Denmark were to come to the king's assistance.

The king set out to whip up support in the north. Rupert, hearing rumours that Charles intended to make for Scotland, became alarmed and wrote to him advising against such a move, as it meant abandoning what he still had in England. He urged the king to open peace negotiations but Charles remained incurably optimistic, continuing to believe the Irish would save him. He also showed some alarm that Rupert should be advocating a treaty, as this did not help his resolve to fight to the end. Indeed, this difference of opinion was to come back to haunt Rupert. He was furious that the king had chosen to leave Wales against his advice, feeling that he had been abandoned. Inevitably he blamed George, but it appears that the king made the decision to move north himself. Edward Hyde, who was usually the first to blame George confirms this.[297] Certainly it would have been difficult and dangerous for the king to attempt to join Rupert in Bristol.

At first the king was successful, moving unhindered through Derbyshire into Yorkshire. By the time he reached Doncaster on August 11 he had added two thousand horse and felt more optimistic. This was as far as he could go however, for at Rotherham he was warned of a large Scottish force approaching. With its commander, Leslie, driving him back and General Sydenham Poyntz, a tough professional soldier and seasoned campaigner coming north he was in danger of being squeezed by a pincer movement. George wrote to General Leslie inviting him to a treaty of peace, and suggesting he join the Royalists, but the canny Scot would have none of his blandishments, and without breaking the seal sent the note on to Parliament.[298] The king once again turned south, at Stilton dispersing a small force which attempted to stop him, and on August 25 capturing Huntingdon, when the Roundhead garrison fled. There news reached them of a victory for Montrose at Kilsyth.[299] They moved on to Oxford, arriving there on August 29. George was depressed by their experiences as they moved through the country, and wrote to Jermyn more frankly about their prospects than he had previously made public: "...But alas, my Lord! ....there is such a universal wearinesse of the warre, dispaire of a possibility for the King to recover, and so much of private Interests growne from these upon every Body, that I protest to God, I do not know four persons living, besides my selfe and you, that have not already given clear demonstrations, that they will purchase their own...and the kingdom's quiet at any price to the King, to the Church, to the faithfullest of his Party. And to deal freely with you, I do not think it will be in the King's power to hinder himself from being forced to accept such Conditions as the Rebels will give him...I and those few others who may be thought by our Councels to fortifie the King's infirmness to his Principles, shall be forced or torn from him."[300]

Soon they were journeying west to Hereford, which was under heavy siege from the Scots army under Lord Leven. When Charles arrived there on September 4 Leven had gone. The Scots were hated by the English villagers, and the soldiers, short of food and pay, could not be sustained. The king entered Hereford amid great rejoicing and George, who had accompanied the king throughout the journey, wrote to Jermyn that with Montrose winning in Scotland, Rupert about to defeat Fairfax at Bristol and the Irish army's arrival imminent, all was well!

The old enmity between George and Rupert resurfaced. Rupert, in characteristic fashion, had been vocal in his criticism of the decisions made to send the Prince of Wales abroad, of the king's march to Oxford, of the leadership of the campaign.... in fact of everything. With George at the king's elbow, this was a direct criticism of him. George was kept fully aware of Rupert's criticism by his secretary Edward Walsingham, who remained at Oxford. Walsingham reported that Rupert wrote daily to Colonel William Legge, the governor of Oxford, and that Legge was outspoken in his animosity towards George. Legge was campaigning hard with Rupert's supporters to have George removed at all costs.[301] He was joined in this by the Duke of Portland, who still resented George's opposition to him as President of Munster. Walsingham felt that something extraordinary was going on, judging by the volume of correspondence between Rupert and Oxford, and that the Privy Council was meeting there to consider Rupert's views. George, influenced by Walsingham's alarm, expressed the view that Rupert and his soldiers wanted peace in order to preserve the profits they had made from the war.[302]

Walsingham felt that Rupert and Legge were generally unpopular, and that this would be a good time to take control of the king's council and force Rupert out: "Fancy when I came there [the garden of Christchurch College}, I found Prince Rupert and Legg with the Lord (116 – in cypher) walking gravely betwixt them on the further side. I seemed to take no notice of the gentleman's meaning, but came away resenting to see the gentry and nobility stand there bare at a distance as if his Majesty had been present. ...I will tell your Lordship who commits none of the least errors in the Court, by his extraordinary conduct and compliances with the Hugants and believe I have information of the best it gives extreme distaste there {at Paris} and to be plain in none of the greatest furtherances of his Majesty's assistance there, but makes even (212 – in code) suspected for giving countenance to him...I give you notice of it, that you may think of some way to have him timely admonished lest, if he proceed, more hurt than good be done there."[303] Jermyn wrote to George imploring him to do something about the widening rift. George replied that he had done his best but Rupert was being impossible, and would only be satisfied with the position of sole adviser to the king. He even posed the suggestion that Rupert, the Elector Palatine his elder brother and his mother were in the pay of Parliament and seeking to replace the king with another branch of the Stuarts. In a letter to Jermyn he raised the possibility that there were people close to the king who were plotting to force the king to make peace. In the original letter the names are scratched out, but it is possible to identify Rupert, Legge and Culpeper.[304] This view was to gain ground later, when Rupert surrendered Bristol.

On September 14 George's wife also wrote from Oxford warning him of Rupert's animosity towards him, while Rupert went about saying he had been warned that George would ruin him.[305] He blamed George for keeping him from the king's side. Pressure was mounting on George, who found his position under attack, but then one of the decisive moments in the Civil War occurred to change the situation permanently.

Chapter 12.

Defeat.

Throughout the summer Lewis Dyve had struggled to hold Dorset against strong opposition. In March 1645 Fairfax and Cromwell turned their attention to that county, and although Dyve received support from Goring, this was far from ideal as the Royalist general was, as we have seen, inattentive to detail. Goring lost Weymouth on March 15 through drunken carelessness. He commanded 3,000 horse and 1,500 foot, yet was driven out of the town by a small band of rebels who had been coralled in the lower part of town and were considered virtual prisoners. Retreating across Dorset into Somerset, he yielded the entire county with the exception of isolated garrisons at Sherborne and the Isle of Portland defended by Dyve.[306] As a consequence Parliament occupied a strong position in the county. In July Colonel Pickering sent a brigade of Parliamentary horse and foot to Sherborne to reconnoitre, and on August 1 he was followed by Fairfax himself, who assessed that the castle could be stormed. Soon the castle was under full siege. Dyve built new earthworks to accommodate ordnance which could fire down on the assailants, who were able to hide in a haystack close to the castle walls. But most damage was done for the defenders by two park keepers with fouling pieces who picked off a number of Parliamentary officers from the walls and caused some alarm. Fairfax was hampered by lack of ammunition and the siege became bogged down as the castle's defenders, aided by local inhabitants, harrassed the enemy troops. The Clubmen, locally assembled militia, continually troubled Fairfax, cutting off his supplies and threatening to starve him out.

Charles Fleetwood and Cromwell arrived with a siege train to batter down the walls. First Cromwell decided to deal with the Clubmen. The bulk of their force was assembled at Shaftesbury, twenty miles to the east, and Fleetwood was sent to confront them. He surprised them in a meeting with representatives of the Royalists and succeeded in capturing forty of their leaders. The next day, with the remainder mustering their forces to attack the Parliamentarians and rescue their leaders, Cromwell appeared and persuaded them to disband. Other local pockets were similarly either persuaded to disband or were attacked and scattered. Back at Sherborne the defenders' cannon were finally stormed and dismantled while miners coming from Mendip set about burrowing under the walls. By August 14 Fairfax had heavy guns moved in by sea to a local port and the defenders could no longer withstand the barrage. At last artillery breached the thick castle walls, and a mine detonated under the fortifications. The starving garrison surrendered, despite Dyve's spirited vow never to yield. He was taken prisoner and transferred to the Tower, while orders were given to demolish the castle. The losses to the Royalists amounted to 400 men, 800 arms, 16 ordnance, 1 mortar and stores of ammunition.

The fall of Sherborne gave Fairfax a direct route to Bristol. Rupert, in charge of Bristol, was left exposed by Goring's collapse in the west and the city came under siege. He had been preparing for this event for over a month and was well stocked with powder, cannon and food. He had provided sufficient ammunition and stores to withstand a siege for four months, and wrote a cheerful letter to the king assuring him of this.[307] As the city was situated in a hollow, extensive fortifications were necessary some way out from the city, forming a ring four miles in length. This required substantial resources to defend adequately, and Rupert had fifteen hundred of his garrison of two thousand five hundred manning it daily. With wholesale desertion occurring he found this difficult to sustain.

The king was at that time marching to the relief of Hereford, and was relieved to hear that Rupert could resist the siege. George was optimistic: "..that place [Bristol] will be likely to destroy his [Fairfax's] army, and so leave the Prince of Wales in the West and Us in Wales free to make levies."[308] Nevertheless, having been received rapturously in Hereford, the king quickly turned towards Bristol. He informed Rupert that he intended to ford the Severn with three thousand infantry and three thousand horse, at the same time summoning Goring to approach Bristol from Somerset, hoping to attack Fairfax from both sides. The day before Bristol fell George wrote to Lord Byron, commander at Chester, saying that all was going really well, with Rupert wearing Fairfax out with frequent sallies. "We shall have, by God's blessing, as quick a progress to happiness as we have had to the great extremities."[309] Without specific news from the West Country, George also reasonably hoped that Goring would be able to come to the relief of Bristol. He expressed the opinion that Poyntz and Rossiter, who had arrived at Tewkesbury in pursuit of the king, would be compelled to turn aside and support Fairfax.

Although Rupert's cavalry remained a potent force, his infantry were weak and inexperienced. Bristol, with its extensive outer wall, was notoriously difficult to defend, and with the Parliamentary navy controlling the Bristol channel and no sign of Goring, Rupert's plight was soon desperate. To avoid his army being completely annihilated he had no alternative but to sue for the best terms of surrender he could negotiate. By 8 am on September 10 he had agreed terms with Fairfax, surrendering the city in return for permission to march away with his men and horses, colours flying, towards Oxford. The king had only progressed as far as Raglan when he heard this terrible news: the promised four months resistance had lasted no more than four days. Angry and desperate, he returned to Hereford. George wrote to Nicholas from there on September 15: "Never was there soe sadd a relapse into desperate condition from soe happy a recovery of ye prodigious surrender of Bristoll has cast us into...and ye consequences which wee apprehend from ye strange manner of it weigh'd with preceeding advertisements looke more dismall if not timely prevented, then the thing itselfe."[310]

Rupert's position in the Royalist ranks was now perilous. George had suggested to the king that Rupert wanted peace at any price, and his rapid surrender appeared to support this. The Governor of Oxford, William Legge, was known to be one of Rupert's men, and there were rumours that he was prepared to make peace with Parliament. Sir Phillip Sydney, in his epic poem "Arcadia" alluded to Rupert leading the king a merry dance, and conspiring for him to lose the Crown. Most damaging to Rupert's position were the actions of his elder brother, Charles Louis, Elector Palatine, now living in London. Parliament had recently voted him a pension of eight thousand pounds and his support for the Parliamentary cause was well known. If Charles were to lose the crown and his children be barred, Charles Louis would be, next to his mother, first in line. George reminded the king of previous occasions when Rupert's trustworthiness and reliability had been questioned (mainly by him), and raised the possibility that Rupert may be planning a coup, particularly as the peace terms had allowed him to keep one thousand horse and fifteen hundred infantry.

When Rupert marched out of Bristol he was accorded every courtesy by Fairfax, and this had not gone unnoticed. George's wife, who was keeping her husband informed, reported an eye-witness at Bristol, now returned to Oxford, verifying this rumour. In a letter to George from Oxford on September 16 Walsingham reported that she was harshly critical of Rupert: "Lady Digby commanded me to give you an account of what passed betwixt her and the Lord Hawley, who upon his coming to town met with the most dejected man that may be, and who wishes a thousand times he had rather had no being than to have been upon this occasion at Bristol, where all things were carried so little to his satisfaction....Prince Rupert told him that he would make all the haste that could be to the King to induce him to a peace, which Prince Rupert says is the only thing his Majesty hath now to do. Observe but this popular and perilous design, which he is strongly encouraged by some here he hath disclosed himself to in that business....My Lady conjures you that you will not by any means permit his Majesty to be wrought upon to the utter destruction of himself and his party, by betraying all with a base and unworthy part. Surely there is no way left for his Majesty to recover, prosper and give life to his discouraged party but by expressing his high dislike and distrust to Prince Rupert..."[311]

Walsingham's intelligence from Oxford threw suspicion on Legge's loyalty. He reported that an informant claimed to have knowledge that Legge was preparing to hand over Oxford to Parliament. As Legge was one of Rupert's closest allies, this reflected badly on Rupert himself. Charles revoked Rupert's commission and ordered his immediate expulsion from the country and the dismissal of Legge. In an angry letter to his nephew he talked of Bristol as "The greatest trial of my constancy that hath yet befallen me" and went on: "You assured me that, if no mutiny happened, you would keep Bristol for four months. Did you keep it four days?"[312] The fall of Bristol led to the loss of Devizes, Winchester, Basing House and Chepstow, and materially affected the final outcome of the war.

Although most historians feel that Rupert was badly treated by the king over Bristol, many contemporaries felt differently. The queen, no friend of Rupert, spread the rumour that he was selling warships to raise cash. There were rumours that Rupert had been running a very slack regime at Bristol – "a great bawdy house." Walsingham's spies reported that he had been about to betray the city, and such stories were the talk of London. There it was rumoured that Rupert and

Fairfax had made peace and that Rupert would force the king to accept it.[313]

Rupert's disgrace left the field open for George, who was now unchallenged as the king's chief adviser. "The conduct of our military Affairs will perhaps fall into more fortunate hands," George informed Nicholas.[314] He was still full of optimistic schemes to win the war. A week after the loss of Bristol he wrote to Nicholas that he had two projects in hand which "if either succeed we shall not think our condition much impaired."[315] He believed it was still possible to agree a treaty in Ireland which would free up soldiers to reinforce the king's army, but the more hopeful prospect was help from Scotland. Montrose was still enjoying some success in the north, and George felt that if the king could win over the Scottish generals to his cause the day may yet be saved. He reasoned that if Montrose came south and Goring rejoined the king, the united army could attack London. He had still not given up hope of help from France either. With this in mind George composed a letter to Lord Leven in an attempt to persuade him to change his allegiance, promising that the Scottish state and religion, Presbyterianism, should remain "unassailed…whatever might be done in Engfland."[316] It seems that Leven did not receive this letter, for there was no response, and it is possible that his supporters may have suppressed it. It was rumoured that Montrose had entered England with twenty thousand men, encountering little resistance, and had advanced from Penrith to Kendal. The only realistic hope left Charles was some sort of pact with the Scots, so he was soon on the road again, marching north to join up with Montrose. This suited George, who wished to put the king as far away as possible from Rupert (who had still not left the country) fearing that a reconciliation would prejudice his own position.

At Chester, the vital stronghold which needed to be held if any relief was to be forthcoming from Ireland, the king found the garrison under renewed heavy siege. While he entered the city from the unblockaded west, his army took up a defensive position just to the south, at Rowton Heath. The Royalist cavalry under Sir Marmaduke Langdale faced the New Model Army under the command of Sydenham Poyntz. The fighting was fierce and prolonged, mainly involving cavalry, the advantage swaying first one way then the other. Finally a force of musketeers arrived in support of Poyntz, and with the superior discipline of the Roundheads prevailing the Cavaliers were put to flight, scattering into Wales. The king withdrew to Denbigh with 2,400 men while Lord Byron put up a spirited defence of Chester against heavy odds. Writing to Ormond on September 26 George almost represented Rowton Heath as a victory, expressing the opinion that Byron would have no problem in defending Chester, and that the "rebels" were in worse shape than the king's army and had retreated northwards.[317] Montrose was still victorious, and if only Charles could join him…Unfortunately, news came from Byron that Poyntz was actually preparing to follow the king across the Dee, and that Montrose, far from being victorious, had suffered a defeat.

Despite the king's desperate plight, "…as long as he had Digby at his side he was never likely to give himself completely up to despair."[318] George's unstoppable optimism surfaces time and again. In a letter to Henry Jermyn, who was in Paris, his hopes of foreign intervention are high: "….I have no apprehension, but that having gone thus farre in the yeare, we shall be safe till the next from any further great mischiefs, and that probably by helpes from Denmarke and Ireland, and moneys from you…we may possibly have a fresh and hopefull resource the next Spring."[319]

It is interesting to note that although George supported the peace negotiations in Ireland, he was concerned about English public opinion, and opposed unpopular concessions to the Irish Catholics. The king, writing to Ormond from Cardiff, sought to make progress in Ireland, hoping that peace there with the Catholics might lead to help becoming available in the form of an Irish army. He instructed Ormond to satisfy the Catholics although they were dissatisfied with what he had offered, namely the removal of penal laws. They were demanding the public exercise of religion and the free use of their churches, which the king dare not concede. "For," he wrote: "It is for the defence of His Religion principally, that he hath undergone the extremities of Warre here, and he will never redeeme His Crowne by sacrificing of it there…he will in that poynt joyne with them [the Irish], the Scots, or with any Protestant Profession, rather than doe the least act that may hazard that Religion, in whch, and for which, he will live or die."[320] Fine words, but not to be borne out by his actions, as we shall see.

As early as December 1644 George had written to Ormond that it would be "fatall to his majestye's affayres, and consequently though more remotely, even to themselves should his majestie draw upon himself at this time the scandall of such a concession to the Roman Catholicques there, as the repeal of the penal lawes would amount to."[321] This stance is in contrast to the crtiticism levelled against him by some historians that he would go to any lengths to avoid defeat, including offering major concessions to the Catholics. However the king's increasingly desperate plight as 1645 progressed forced him to promise the Irish Catholics more and more concessions if they would support him militarily. The correspondence between George and Ormond throughout the summer of 1645 shows him relaying the king's instructions to Ormond, which amounted to peace at any price, without enthusiasm. In one letter he laments: "..truly the King's necessitie of them [the Irish troops] is so pressing, that you must bee content rather to hazard much there by their absence, then to hazard all here by the want of them."[322]

With the route north now virtually cut off, the king contemplated returning to Worcester, but was dissuaded by

George. Prince Maurice was Governor of Worcester, and George was concerned he would intercede on his brother's behalf. So the party turned north again, going to Lichfield. It was reckoned that should Poyntz choose to follow, this would relieve the pressure on Chester. The final leg of the journey to Newark was hazardous as this was not secure Royalist territory, but the party finally reached Newark on October 4. There was still no sign of the Irish joining them and now even George began to worry, suggesting to Ormond that he arrange for the Irish to land in Scotland, and that he then return to England to take Rupert's place.

The general feeling in Newark was strongly in favour of Rupert, and there were rumours that he would soon be returning to assume his rightful position. Implicit criticism of the king was aggravated when he commenced reform of the Newark establishment, which was lax, by reducing some officers and cutting the pay of others. News arrived that Montrose had inflicted a defeat on Leslie, and George persuaded the king to continue the march north. In addition to the hope that the two armies could be united, George wanted to keep the king away from Rupert, who had set out from Oxford for Newark. No sooner were they on the road again than further news came that Montrose had been defeated on September 13 at Philiphaugh, that Leslie held Lothian and Montrose was retreating north of Stirling. His Irish infantry had been surrounded and destroyed, and many new recruits had defected. The Earls of Roxburgh and Home, Montrose's allies, had surrendered to Leslie, and were held prisoner at Berwick. It was evident now that Montrose had never succeeded in crossing into England, and if he was to be sustained as a force on the king's side, he would need help.

The king returned to Newark and on October 13 held a Council of War at Welbeck, just to the north of that town. George as usual made his views heard, adamant that the only course open was an immediate march north. Charles gave

Langdale orders to take his cavalry north to join up with Montrose, if needs be cutting his way through. Langdale expressed his willingness to take the risk, but added that he would be willing to serve under George as Commander-in-Chief. This caused some surprise but it was assumed that the king had sanctioned this appointment, and on October 16 he signed a commission appointing George Commander-in-Chief of Royal forces north off the Trent. Langdale had always expressed the wish to continue going north, taking his Northern Horse back home, but probably would not have wished to undertake the journey on his own. Hence his willingness to serve under George.

Many historians have expressed surprise at George's appointment, and his ready acceptance of the commission. After all, he was now principal adviser to the king, unchallenged by anyone. Was it prudent to leave his master in such an hour of need? With Rupert approaching Newark in a somewhat irate mood, there was bound to be confrontation if George stayed. Yet he had faced such challenges before, and demonstrated his ability to out-manoeuvre Rupert fairly easily. The king showed no sign of relenting over Rupert's banishment, and was showing considerable annoyance at his nephew's persistence and refusal to go abroad. Edward Hyde's memoirs, and George's letters themselves, perhaps throw some light on this move. George recognised that he remained very unpopular with the general populace, and was regarded as a traitor by Parliament. In the latter stages of the war he had taken a hard-line approach to the continuance of the war, and he felt that the combination of these factors would count against the king in any peace negotiations. He clear-sightedly saw the need for some sort of peace negotiations now, but feared that his presence would hinder that process.[323]

In an interesting letter to Hyde from George written on January 5, 1646, George explained the thinking behind his appointment and move northwards: – "…the King and I had long before (that is, ever since his affairs were made so desperate by the loss of Bristol) concluded it most for his service that I should absent myself from him for some time, in case I could find a fair and honourable pretence for it. I believe the accidents since befallen at Newark with P. Rupert and Gerard will have given you a sight of some reasons of my remove. The truth is, their violent designs were no secret to the Kingdom…if by my stay there I should give them and the rest of the discontented party at Newark a colour to do that with a personal pretence against me, which I having removed by my absence they durst not do with any aspect directly upon the King himself…I found the King likely to suffer much by my stay near him; the weariness of the war being so universal, and the despair of any improvement in his condition being so great in all about him, I found it almost every man's opinion that it would be best for him to submit, with the preservation of some that have been faithful to him…which being a kind of self policy that I could never concur in and those who had those aims believing that my interest with the King might hinder their compassing them, it was made their business to publish that I was the only hinderer of peace, and that the King, as low as he was, might obtain a good one but for my animosities…."[324]

So he packed his bags and took on the daunting task of joining up with the Royalist Scots. The army set out north, leaving the king at Newark. Soon thereafter Rupert approached the town to plead his case. Alarmed that the Prince may be planning a coup of some sort, the king instructed Rupert not to come any nearer. This command was disobeyed, and on October 16 he rode into Newark, accompanied by the Governor, Sir Richard Willis, to an enthusiastic reception. Still the king refused to speak to him, even when confronted by the angry prince. Willis was dismissed from the governorship of Newark when he dared to support Rupert. This dismissal, and the king's treatment of Rupert, caused uproar. With the enemy closing in on Newark Charles would soon need to retreat to Oxford, but was disturbed by the rebellious feelings evident among the garrison in Newark. On Sunday October 26, while the king was at dinner a number of senior officers led by Rupert and his brother burst in upon him to protest the dismissal of Willis. Inevitably they all blamed George, which the king denied. Charles Gerrard, who had recently been dismissed from his post as commander in South Wales replied: "I am sure, and can prove, that Digby was the cause that I was outed of my command in Wales." The king became angry: "Whosoever saies it lyes. Gentlemen I am but a child so you esteem of me: Digby can lead me where he will! What can the most desperate rebels say more?" When Rupert repeated his accusation that George had provoked the rift between him and the king, Charles again defended George:"…they are all rogues and rascals that say so, and in effect traitors, that seek to dishonour my best subject." Gerrard responded sadly: "Then we must be all traitors." He bowed and went out, followed by Rupert, who "showed no reverence, but went out prowdly with his hands at his side."[325]

Rupert had not helped his own case by being so dismissive of others' views, but there was a feeling at court that his treatment by the king over the fall of Bristol had been grossly unfair. The War Council met and, having heard Rupert speak, drew up a declaration which exonerated him of all blame for Bristol. The king would not bend. Although he reluctantly acknowledged that Rupert was not guilty of treason or disloyalty, he still placed the blame for the fall of Bristol squarely on his shoulders, and would not readmit him to his staff. When the king rode out on the Monday morning he faced a virtual mutiny, for the main bulk of the army sided with Rupert. Facing the army coldly that Monday morning, he suggested that if Rupert and his supporters could not accept his decision they should ride south and disband.

The campaign further north started well. At Doncaster, commanding 1,500 horse, George captured some infantry without a struggle. Continuing north, he forced his way past a small force at Ferrybridge. At Sherburn-in-Elmet he halted to rest his troops. Poyntz, marching to cut George off from the north, was unaware of his presence at Sherburn, and had not kept his force in a tight formation. On October 15 George, with one thousand two hundred horse, surprised a newly-recruited infantry force of two thousand men and forced them to surrender without striking a blow, taking at least eight hundred prisoners and capturing a considerable amount of arms and baggage, which they piled in a heap in the middle of the town until the carriages arrived to cart them away. George received notice that a force of 1,300 Roundhead cavalry under the command of Colonel Copley was preparing to mount a counter-attack. He immediately mustered his own cavalry and concealed them at the northern end of the town, planning to surprise the Roundheads when they appeared. Langdale rode out with a scouting party, and when he encountered Copley's cavalry misread his advance force of 2,000 for a small party numbering a quarter of that. Langdale immediately attacked. Copley was disadvantaged by having to approach Sherburn down a narrow lane, which Langdale swept with his cavalry. Routed, the Roundheads fled in various directions, a group galloping south through Sherburn. The Royalist troops thought these were attached to their own army, and joined their disorderly retreat. With only a handful of men left, George found himself fighting at close quarters and was wounded before escaping with Langdale to Skipton. Colonel Copley reported: "The Victory cleare, we kept the field, pursued the Enemy three miles, tooke above foure hundred prisoners, whereof many are escaped, by negligence of the Souldiers."[326]

Left behind was all the baggage including George's cabinet of papers, which was highly incriminating. It included details of the king's negotiations with the Prince of Orange to match the

Prince of Wales with his daughter. Dr Goffe wrote to Jermyn in Paris that in return for consent to marry the Princess, Orange would "declare in defence of the King." Negotiations included entering a League offensive and defensive against all enemies, a public declaration of dislike of the rebels later propositions to the King, the provision of arms and powder, an offer of the liberty of Dutch ports and a ban on Parliamentary agents in Holland. (This all came to nothing: Jermyn reported the Prince of Orange was not confident enough to act). However the Trasdunk was sent from Dunkirk "with four Frigots, 6040 Muskets, 2000 Pairs of Pistols, 1200 Carabines, Swords, 400 Shovels, 27000 pounds of Match, and 50000 pounds of Brimstone…The Queen hath sent 400 Barrels of Powder to Dartmouth" and "She gave order for 4000 pounds sterling to be sent to Falmouth.[327]

The cabinet contained pleas for aid to the King of Denmark, promises of help from France including an invasion force headed by the Duke of Lorraine, and the hopes of a liaison with the Scots. George's cousin Kenelm had been sent to Rome by the queen in a bid for financial support for the Royalists from the pope, and damaging reference was made in the papers to his arrival in Rome, his audience with the pope and hopes of money being forthcoming.[328] Eight letters related to George's appeals to the Irish for help and a number of messages from Edward Walsingham repeating the latest gossip there.

A letter (undated) written by the king to the queen, and discovered among the papers captured at Sherburn, must have given the Parliamentarians great encouragement: "By Sabrans conveyance…I hope before this can come to thee, thou wilt receive three Letters from me; who although hee Condemns the Rebells proceedings as much as any, yet he declares in his (French) Masters name a positive Neutrality, so that either he complies not with his instructions, or France is not so much our friend as wee hope for. Or rather thinke the latter, yet I doubt not but thy dexterity will cure that coldnesse of friendshp, which in my opinion will be the easier done, if thou make the chiefe Treatie for our affiliance, betwixt thee and the Q.R. in a familiar obliging way....As for the affaires here we are in so good state, that I am confident the Rebels (though all their strengths are now united) cannot affront us; and when my Nephew Rupert comes to mee (whom I certainely expect in few daies) I hope to be able to chuse fresh Winter Quarters, but where, I am not yet resolved, for which occasion and opportunitie must direct me."

George can also be seen to be pleading his cause with his greatest ally, the queen: "I must not conclude without humbly acknowledging you Majesties great Justice in your contempt of those scandalls whch his Majesties enemies have endeavoured to cast upon me; unto which I shall onely say thus much more, that I have been so pure a Virgin in point of my integrity to His and your Majestie, that I thanke God, no body yet ever durst ask me a question as to my own Interests, And as for any private negotiation, you may be sure I shall never proceeed in any, but with your Majesties preceding approbation, be it upon terms never so just, nor shall I though with your consent, ever vary from those principles which you have by you in a paper drawne by me, and presented to you, when you were pleased to engage certaine persons in the highest trust of the Kings and your service; this confidence I beg of you as to the publike....."[329]

Had he known it at the time, if George had held Sherburn he would have been able to threaten York and the control of the north, for there was no potent force of Roundheads remaining between him and this goal. The troops that confronted him at Sherburn were the bulk of the force defending this key city. With York under his control, the outcome of the war may have been very different. At Skipton the Royalists were able to reassemble most of their scattered army and once again set out north, only to meet Sir John Brown at Carlisle Sands and be soundly defeated. With their force drastically reduced George and Langdale pressed on to Dumfries, suffering heavy desertions along the way. They had news that Montrose was in Glasgow and on the offensive, but they could discover nothing of his movements there, and with no concrete prospect of making progress in Scotland they turned back with the objective of wintering in the mountains around Cartmel to await the Irish landing. But they were tracked by the Parliamentarians, and with no effective fighting force remaining the two finally sailed from Ravenglass for the Isle of Man on October 24 with a handful of officers. From there George wrote to the king justifying his action by explaining that there was no hope of reaching Montrose as the enemy stood in the way, and there was a better chance of obtaining help from Ireland. He assured Charles that in Ireland he expected to be able to organise such troops that were ready to come to England in support of the king.[330] After a month of waiting for favourable winds he continued to Dublin, staying there with Lord and Lady Derby, who had also escaped via the Isle of Man after putting up determined resistance under siege at their home, Lathom House by a strong Roundhead force.

Two armies, one English the other Scottish, were converging on Newark. Rupert's appearance and the subsequent unrest among the Royalist army weakened the king's position considerably and he was forced once more to decamp, returning to Oxford in two days of marching, arriving there on November 5. There for a brief while he found respite, indulging in his favourite sports and plotting feverishly to split the Parliamentarian alliance. He had not given up hope of foreign intervention and was rejoined by an apologetic Rupert, given a clear role now that George was absent. At first Rupert's overtures were rejected by the king, but finally he wrote acknowledging his errors in such an abject manner that the king accepted his return. George continued to correspond with the king from Ireland, attempting to keep his morale high with encouraging news of succesful negotiations and the hope of an Irish relief force. The king knew better. But he remained loyal to George, writing to his wife: "Assure Digby that he still stands high in my opinion."[331]

The Royalist cause was crumbling, as one after the other of their strongholds was stormed or surrendered. More and more of the country fell under Parliamentary control. The king's hopes of receiving help from abroad were fading. With Fairfax triumphant in the west and the Royalist army dwindling alarmingly as troops saw the signs of defeat and little hope left of external help, the king's plight was desperate. As the Parliamentary forces closed in on his headquarters at Oxford he disappeared, much to the alarm of his opponents. Was he heading for London? He was still king, still with popular appeal and ultimate sovereignty. Was he abroad? In fact on April 27, 1646 he slipped away disguised as a servant, with his beard and hair closely trimmed, attended only by his friend John Ashburnham and his chaplain Michael Hudson. They rode through Henley and Slough showing a pass bearing Fairfax's signature. He stopped at Hillingdon, hoping for a message from the Mayor and aldermen of London, which did not come. Recognising that he could not enter London uninvited, he turned north through Harrow and St Albans, stopping overnight at Wheathampstead. Hudson was despatched to Montreuil, the French emissary at Southwell to seek a written assurance from the Scots that they would receive the king on conditions satisfactory to him. While awaiting the reply, Charles rode on towards Lynn, ready to leave by sea if necessary, and reached Downham on April 30. When the Scots refused to provide assurances Charles moved on through Melton Mowbray and Stamford, heading for Montreuil's house. To everyone's astonishment on May 4, 1646, he rode into the Scots camp at Southwell, near Newark and gave himself up, relying upon a promise by Montreuil that the Scots would honour him and not persuade him to act against his conscience. Parliament immediately demanded that the Scots hand him over, but the Scots realised fully the value of their prize and marched off to the north with him, settling into accommodation at Newcastle. There they found him as slippery and unreliable as had the English. Attempts to come to a favourable agreement with him foundered as the ground shifted this way and that. Secretly he implored the queen to find a way of freeing him and conducting him to France. At the same time he wrote to Glamorgan in Ireland directing him to accept any treaty that Rinuccini would demand in exchange for troops.[332]

Chapter 13.

Ireland.

Whilst the king's position in England steadily worsened, in Ireland the situation appeared altogether more encouraging for the Royalists. Two years previously, in the "Cessation" of September 1643, the king had secured a truce by means of concessions to the Catholic rebels organised in the Confederation of Kilkenny. Later he commissioned Lord Antrim to use these forces against the Scottish Covenanters. Many of the king's Protestant subjects in Ireland regarded these moves with trepidation and as we have seen leading figures, notably Lord Inchquin, deserted the Royalist camp shortly afterwards. Overall, however, the balance of forces seemed favourable. Parliament might expect support from the new English settlers concentrated in the Pale around Dublin and in Munster, and perhaps from the Ulster Presbyterians of Scottish descent. But they faced the hostility of the bulk of the population, especially the native Irish and Catholics amongst the old English represented in the Confederation. Many Anglo-Irish Protestants were loyal to the king, and looked to the leadership of his lieutenant in Ireland, James Butler, twelfth Earl, and later Duke, of Ormond. If the Confederation and the king's supporters could unite, they would easily outweigh the Parliamentarian camp politically. For the moment the military forces at the disposal of Parliament were weak.

In 1645, however, there arrived in Ireland two figures whose intervention in this very volatile situation proved crucial for the Royalist cause there. These were the Papal Nuncio, Archbishop Giovanni Rinuccini and the king's special envoy, the Earl of Glamorgan, Catholic son of the Marquis of Worcester. It will be recalled that in 1644 Glamorgan had been granted a special commission by the king. He had been charged to reach agreement with the Confederates behind Ormond's back, in order to secure the long-promised Irish troops which might decisively shift the balance of the military forces in England. When Glamorgan finally reached Ireland at the end of June 1645 such an army, augmented by European forces, was all the more urgently required to stem the tide of Royalist defeat. Glamorgan proceeded to Kilkenny and there on August 25 he signed a treaty with the Confederates by which he conceded complete religious toleration and won a promise of 10,000 troops. Ormond, however, was kept in the dark.

Glamorgan had made considerable concessions, but they were not enough for the Papal Nuncio, Rinuccini, who arrived in Kerry on October 12. Rinuccini had alienated the queen by opposing her efforts to secure funds from the pope. Prominent in these efforts was her representative in Rome, George's cousin, Kenelm Digby. On his way to Ireland Rinuccini had stopped in Paris, where he was snubbed by both the queen and by Cardinal Mazarini. Affronted, he let it be known that he considered the queen to be a half-hearted Catholic surrounded by advisers who sought help from the Vatican but would not accept Vatican policy. This sally further alienated him from the English court,[333] though Mazarini provided him with 25,000 crowns.

Rinuccini brought supplies and large sums of money. His self-confidence stemmed in part from the influence these might confer, but it also owed much to papal backing. The Nuncio arrived at Kilkenny on November 12 armed with detailed instructions from the new pope, Innocent X, who was determined that a Protestant king should not be backed by the Vatican. But many amongst the Irish leaders were not so exercised by the King's religion, and thought him privately sympathetic to their aspirations. The Supreme Council of the Confederacy believed the English Parliament to be the most implacable enemy of Catholic Ireland and regarded with dismay the King's parlous position in England. Realising that without urgent Confederate assistance Chester, the main port of entry to England for the Irish, would be lost, they offered the Earl of Glamorgan three thousand troops as an advance guard, accepting his assurances that the king would make good his side of the bargain set out in the secret treaty.

But did Glamorgan have authority for his promises and assurances? Rinuccini was finding Irish politics more complicated than he had imagined. Impressed by Glamorgan's letter of commission from the king, he felt that the August treaty did not go nearly far enough, and set out to wring further concessions from Glamorgan, aiming to secure the abolition of penal laws, the right of Catholics to hold high office, and privileges for the church and its clergy. Ironically, it was an agreement signed by Kenelm Digby on behalf of the Queen at the Vatican on November 20 which embodied most of these far-reaching provisions, and which formed the basis for a second treaty, signed on 20 December, in which Glamorgan made a further promise that future Irish Lords Lieutenant would be Catholics.

The prospects for this agreement, and the military forces which might be made available as a result, depended crucially upon concealing it from the Protestant Anglo-Irish until its hoped-for ratification by the king. But concealment became impossible after the first August treaty was discovered in the coach of the Archbishop of Tuam, killed by Scottish soldiers in a skirmish near Sligo on October 17. When the terms of this secret treaty were eventually revealed to him on Christmas Eve, Ormond was horrified. The Lord Lieutenant now realised that he had been duped: his own recent efforts to negotiate with the Confederates had been pointless, serving only to provide a smokescreen for drastic concessions which he himself could never have contemplated. This realization came at a bad time for Glamorgan, who had just arrived in Dublin in the hope of getting Ormond to agree the open, political provisions of the treaty and to consent to his own appointment as military commander.

By now, George too had arrived in Dublin. Ormond was delighted to greet him, for although George had not been given authority to overrule Glamorgan, as Secretary of State he was able to speak in the king's name. Edward Hyde wryly observed that George now "..believed he was upon a stage where he could act wonders, and unite all the divided affections, and all the distinct interests, and make them all subservient to the King."[334] George was quick to become involved, and soon Hyde was reporting that "The noble person quickly took it on himself to say anything in the King's name, and the Lord-Lieutenant was steered by him."[335]

Thus, when on December 26 George accused Glamorgan of high treason, Ormond had every reason to cooperate. Glamorgan was brought before the Privy Council. He protested that he had done nothing without Ormond's foreknowledge, and cited in evidence a sealed envelope he had handed to the Lord Lieutenant when he first arrived in Ireland. This created a stir, as the Council was suspicious of Ormond and feared duplicity. For a while Ormond could not remember the letter, but then recalled having been told not to break the seal without fresh instructions from the king. The unopened letter was fetched and was revealed to be covered in meaningless squiggles circles and symbols. Red-faced, Glamorgan confessed it to be in cypher and that he had forgotten to provide the key! George immediately repeated his accusations and requested that Glamorgan be impeached, saying that he could not believe the king "…even to redeem his own life and the lives of the Queen and children, would….grant to the confederates the least piece of concession so destructive to his regality and religion." He confessed later that he was seriously concerned that if the Council had suspected he approved of the agreement they would have thrown him out of the window![336]

Whatever Glamorgan's secret brief from the king was, he accepted that his majesty was not bound by anything he had agreed, but he maintained that his conscience was clear. The king, now clearly embarrassed by the exposure of his double-dealing, wrote to Ormond: "I never intended that Glamorgan should treat anything without your approbation, much less without your knowledge. For besides the injury to you, I was always diffident of his judgement (though I could not think him so extremely weak), as now .....for which I have commanded Digby's service, desiring you to assist him. And albeit I have too just cause, for the clearing of my honour, to command (as I have done) to prosecute Glamorgan in a legal way; yet I will have you suspend the execution of any sentence against him until you inform me fully of all the proceedings."[337] He had previously, however, written to the pope: "So many and so great proofs of the fidelity and affection of our cousin the Earl of Glamorgan we have received, and such confidence do we deservedly repose in him, that Your Holiness may justly give faith and credence to him in any matter, whereupon he is to treat, in our name, with Your Holiness, either by himself in person or by any other. Moreover, whatever shall have been positively settled and determined by him, the same we promise to sanction and perform. In testimony whereof, we have written this very brief letter, confirmed by our own hand and seal ; and we have in our wishes and prayers nothing before this, that by your favour we may be restored into that state, in which we may openly avow ourself."[338]

George wrote to Secretary Nicholas on January 4, 1646 recounting something of what had occurred: "...I had by his Majesty's Command written to the Irish Commissioners a Letter...so diametrically opposite to the said Earl's Transactions." Glamorgan argued that he had secured 3,000 men, and this was becoming public, but:"...the Case being more strictly examined, we found, First, That by the Lord of Glamorgan's Oath, the Forces were not to be hazarded till his Majesty's Performance of the said Earl's Conditions, and Secondly, that the Supply was never intended by my Lord of Glamorgan and the Irish, till the Articles of Peace were consented; which the Lord Lieutenant durst in no wise do."[339]

The king, having quickly disowned Glamorgan, repeated that he had expected his emissary to consult with Ormond, and nothing to be agreed without the Lord-Lieutenant's approval. This left poor Glamorgan powerless and without influence, but when the king sent private instructions to Ormond that he was not to be harmed, he was released from custody and returned to Kilkenny. It was shown later that the king had indeed given Glamorgan an unrestricted brief to agree whatever terms were necessary to secure military assistance. The king's duplicity was revealed by a letter he wrote to his wife on March 27: "It is taken for granted the Lord of Glamorgan neither counterfeited my hand, nor that I have blamed him more than for not following his instructions."[340] Before that, on February 3 he had written to Glamorgan: "....you have been drawn to consent to conditions much beyond your instructions.... if you will trust my advice, which I have commanded Digby to give you freely, I will bring you so off that you may still be useful to me."[341]

The campaign to enlist Irish help was now in total confusion, and George, seen to be the senior negotiator, received the blame for the breakdown. Rupert continued to snipe at him, and other observers in England could not believe that Glamorgan would have risked so much, and gone so far in his concessions, without the acquiescence of the king, whose leading representative in Dublin was George. Archbishop Williams wrote to Ormond: "We be all lost in Wales by this business between you and my Lord of Glamorgan...Rupert is in great enmity with Digby. [Lord Astley] does likewise lay much blame on the said Lord because of Glamorgan his business....Sir Nicholas Byron reports Digby to be the cause of our misery, that Glamorgan has done nothing but with your consent and the King's"[342] Bitter that he was once again the one who was blamed, George wrote to Edward Hyde: "Let me ask you according to the laws of policy: have I not carried my body swimmingly, who before being so irreconcilably hated by the Puritan party have thus seasonably made myself as odious to the Papists? Well! My comfort is that the very few honest men in the world will love me the better, and while I do the part of a man of integrity and honour I am willing to trust God for the rest."[343] On January 17 he further defended his position to Edward Walsingham: "I believe the accident here of my Lord Glamorgan and my party on his prosecution, will at first have allayed me much with your friends...But when matters shall be rightly understood, you may assure them, That if His Majestys Service hath not obliged me to do it, yet in relation to their preservation, I ought to have done it, and without it, it would have been impossible for the King to favour them, or me to serve them, so far as a good and firm Protestant may do."[344]

It was agreed that George should go to Kilkenny and try his hand with the Catholics, who now felt betrayed and disillusioned by the turn of events. He wrote that Glamorgan left half an hour before he arrived, and that "..whate're the matter is, his lordship is in great indignation against me."[345] It does not seem to have occurred to him that he had recently been instrumental in destroying Glamorgan's position in Ireland. First George approached Lord Inchiquin, still leader of the Protestant Irish in Munster, with an appeal that he abandon his alliance with Parliament and return his allegiance to the king. Inchiquin remained alienated, however, and when this was met with a flat refusal, George attempted to win over the Catholics by joining Owen Roe O'Neill's army of over six thousand men in an attack on the Ulstermen. The Nuncio had encouraged an attack and supplied O'Neill's army. Unfortunately Lord Inchiquin commanded a superior force who managed to get amongst the rearguard and rout them.

George charged at the head of his troop but his horse was killed under him. He obtained another and narrowly escaped.[346]

Despite the unyielding opposition of Rinuccini, George's persuasive powers made some headway with the Catholics. The king once again denied that Glamorgan had his authority to make the concessions he had agreed, and George convinced the Catholic leaders that they could not rely upon this agreement. He persuaded them that unless they secured Anglesey the Parliamentary forces may mount an attack on Ireland from there. The moderate Irish leaders, Lord Muskerry and Thomas Preston, were becoming exasperated with Rinuccini and suspicious of his agenda. They had been convinced by George that their only hope was to join the king's party and face the prospect of all-out war between Ireland and England.[347] George wrote to Ormond on April 7 reporting that Muskerry pledged twenty ships of war, artillery, 10,000 muskets, 800 barrels of powder and 40,000 pounds in money.[348] He urged Ormond to provide 3,000 men for the invasion.

Meanwhile George had worries of his own, which he revealed in a letter to his wife dated January 19. When he left England she was pregnant, and he worried that "misapprehensions of grief might be of much danger to you; you can easily imagine my disquiet. God be praised for your safe delivery, and my Blessing upon my new Baby, and the rest; onely I take it very ill that you write nothing of them." He was anxious for her to send his son to him in Ireland "...if it were possible)...whence I will send him on to France." His wife and friends were pressing him to return to England, but he responded impatiently: "I cannot but very much wonder, how it is possible to be so blinded with kindnesse to me, as not to see, how destructive it must be to me and to His Majesty's Service, for me to return at this time without an Army to make me useful there...If the King should fail in firmnesse towards me, the losse would be His in His Honour." The feud with Rupert raged on, for he added: "And lastly, Sweetheart, whilst the Princes and Glemham are with the King, it is impossible for me to come there, without making such combustion as must overwhelm all the Majesties affairs by the disorder of it...besides that, although I am most assured, that the King's Justice and kindnesse will never fail me upon the private scene; who, if His Nephews should make the quarrel personal (as doubtless they will, if I come thither whilest they are there) I would not expect, nor would it profit the King to take my party against them." Then his natural optimism surfaced: "I make no question but by Gods blessing I shall ere long appear in England with so considerable a power to serve Him, as shall make my Enemies strike sail." And finally, mischievously: "In the mean while, if the Princes be received and remain with the King, it will not be amisse to give out some good while after this Despatch, That I am already in England in disguise, and will be such a day at Oxford, to try how it will work."[349] This letter is quoted at some length because it portrays so much of what made up George Digby's character. His self-justification for remaining in exile is obvious, but his concern for the king's cause and his ceaseless work at attempting to rescue that cause come through. His relentless argument with Rupert, and the struggle for influence are there too, as is George's love of intrigue, disguises and deception.

The Royalist cause by now looked hopeless, and the incentive of securing Chester appeared unattainable as Lord Byron's position there came under heavy pressure. On February 3 Chester surrendered to Sir William Brereton and the one port still able to receive Irish reinforcements was closed to the Royalists. A few garrisons still held out: Lichfield, Worcester, Wallingford and Conway. But they were isolated. In Wales Goodrich and Raglan Castles were still held by Royalists, Pendennis in Cornwall was defended by a garrison hoping for troops from abroad, and the Channel and Scilly Isles were still loyal to the king.[350]

What George now needed, he wrote, was the Prince of Wales to lead the Irish Army and he felt sure Catholics and Protestants would unite behind him in the proposed invasion of England. News that the Prince of Wales had left England the previous year did not help his cause: now he had to find him. About the same time a message arrived from the Scilly Isles, written by the Prince of Wales, saying that he was resident there, but because the island was so poor and had few men, he needed a hundred men.[351] So George went to Waterford and managed to secure two frigates, some money and three hundred men to take to the Scillies. He set sail on April 18.

When George reached the Scilly Isles he learnt that the Prince was in Jersey, and he followed him there, brimming with enthusiasm. Twelve thousand men stood ready to sail for England from Ireland, he declared, and if the prince would lead them the kingdom could be saved.[352] The prince was unconvinced, and having sent Jermyn, Capel and Culpeper to confer with his mother in Paris, said he would await their return. George, feeling time was of the essence and not regarding the emissaries very highly, offered to convince the queen by letter. He suggested to the prince's Council that he kidnap the prince, explaining how he could invite the prince on board a frigate for consultations and then hoist sails and set off for Ireland.[353] The Council, dominated by Hyde, was shocked and angry at this outrageous plan and told him so. Later, from Paris, George wrote to Ormond about this confrontation, still convinced his plan was a good one, but "There being such an invincible aversion in the Prince's Council against that design that nothing could have overcome but the....force which I had not power to apply in Jersey."[354]

The king was unhappy about his son's sojourn in Jersey, fearing the Channel Islands were no longer safe. He wrote to his wife requesting that she summon him to Paris "...with all speed - for his preservation is the greatest hope for my safety. And in God's name let him stay there till it be seen what ply my business will take."[355] George argued that all would be lost if he made such a move, as England would see him on foreign territory under the influence of Catholics. The prince told George that he was settled in Jersey and had no inclination to move on. Undeterred, George immediately changed tack and resolved to go to Paris to see the queen, arguing that he could be of most use to Ormond there, campaigning for funds and persuading the French of the Royalist cause. He believed that he could persuade Henrietta Maria to use her influence with Prince Charles to take up his proposal of a move to Ireland.

In Paris George could make no headway with the queen. He promised her that the treaty with the Irish was concluded, and that twelve thousand men were available to help Montrose in Scotland(!) While she was sympathetic to the Irish cause and could see advantage in the scheme being proposed by George, she was adamant that her son was not to be risked in such a madcap and dangerous venture. She believed he could be used to much greater effect as a figurehead of the English Crown in exile, feeding upon the alarm and concern that other crowned heads in Europe felt towards the Parliamentary challenge. Harry Jermyn was despatched to the French court at Fontainebleau to inform them of events, as a result of which Cardinal Mazarin, the effective ruler of France, summoned George there to put forward his ideas.

George knew the cardinal well, having negotiated with him in Charles' name and later as Secretary of State, and had always been treated cordially. Now however the situation had changed. George learnt for the first time of the king's surrender to the Scots. Undeterred, he pressed forward with his plan to take the prince to Ireland, arguing that this would unite everyone in opposition to Parliament and extend French influence. He argued that the only way to obtain peace in Ireland was to persuade the prince to move there and for sufficient money to be provided to finance the army. Mazarin agreed that it was important to dissuade the Scots from reaching any agreement with the king that did not include the Irish. However he recognised that Charles was left with no power or influence, and that the French needed to come to terms with Parliament. He must not do anything which would excite their animosity at this stage, but he could see advantage in helping in Ireland, where France may gain some influence, and George represented the Lord-Lieutenant. Mazarin was also prepared to accommodate the Prince of Wales in Paris, where he could continue to exercise some control. George wrote to Ormond promising to return soon with money, arms and ammunition pledged by Mazarin, "…such fruits of my journey as shall make you think it well employed."[356] Far from regretting his actions in Jersey, he continued to hope that he could persuade the queen to allow the prince to lead the Irish force in an invasion of England.

George took another tack. He and the queen drew up a memorandum in which concessions would be made by the king to the Scots, among them recognition of Presbyterianism, control of the militia to pass to Parliament to allay the fears of the rebels and agreement that Parliament would not be dissolved without its own consent, in return for government being restored to Charles. George reckoned that the Parliamentary factions, with their history of bickering, would not be able to live in peace with each other, and that the Presbyterians and Independants would clash.[357] Once their differences surfaced the French would be able to exploit the situation by intervening, and by supporting the king would allow him to reign in peace. This appealed to Mazarin, who had plans to annex the Spanish Netherlands and wanted a weak England, as he feared a strong Parliament would resist his moves.

There is evidence that the Scots received these proposals seriously, and had they been implemented the future course of English history may have taken a very different course to what actually occurred. It was said that the involvement of the French had united the Scots behind the king, and that a combined force of Scots and Irish would rally round the standard of the Prince of Wales. It was rumoured that the French clergy had contributed £40,000 to the queen's petition.[358] But in June Parliament received news of these negotiations, and the Scots, embarrassed at being caught in intrigue, denied everything.

So George sailed back to Jersey with Jermyn, Wilmot and a group of eighty gentlemen to bring the prince to Paris. He had not yet given up his plan to take the prince to Ireland, and told Hyde of his proposals to negotiate with the Irish and the Scots. Hyde was horrified, arguing that any deal the king did with the Scots and Irish on such terms would be a fatal blow to his acceptance in England. There was a rumour that Parliament may attempt to kidnap the prince and return him to London, so there was some urgency in securing his safety. This suspicion was reinforced by a letter from Mazarin to the Prince of Condé, who in turn communicated its contents to Henrietta Maria, warning that he had received information from England that some of the Prince of Wales' entourage had undertaken to deliver him to Parliament for twenty thousand pistoles. The situation was not helped by Hyde's antipathy to George and his allies. Hyde was later to write about Henry Jermyn; "He was not mischievous in his nature or inclinations, yet did more mischief than any man of the age he lived in, being the occasion of more prejudice to the King and to the Crown than any man of his condition ever was, and took more pains to lessen the King's reputation, and to make his person undervalued, than any other man did; and all this without the least purpose of infidelity, or desire of abating his prerogative, which he wished should be as high as any King's ever was, and desired only that they might prevail over it over whom he could prevail, and in that regard he cared not how low his reputation came to be."[359]

The neighbouring island of Guernsey had come under threat from a Parliamentary invasion, fortunately abandoned when the sailors mutinied. The prince's council was split over the wisdom of his move to Paris, where the influence of the queen would be all-powerful. Edward Hyde, the wise and conservative Chancellor, saw only risk and danger in any course other than the prince remaining on Jersey, and consistently opposed the silver-tongued arguments put forward by George. Jermyn argued that the queen's instructions were absolute and Culpeper agreed, producing in evidence the letters from the king to his wife requesting her to bring the prince to France. The queen wrote directly to the prince repeating his father's instructions and adding: "Considering of what high importance your safety is…I must positively require you to give immediate obedience to his majesty's commands."[360] It was not known at that stage that the king had written secretly to Parliament offering to send the prince back to London. A new arrival from England, John Ashburnham, a close friend of the king, depressed the Council with news of the king's predicament, pointing out he was now powerless in the hands of the Scots, and supporting Hyde's view that the prince would be better off staying clear of French influence. Five out of the six official counsellors to the prince supported the proposal that he stay in Jersey and await orders from the king. The prince asserted himself at this point. He was bored with Jersey and longed for action and some wider social contact. He announced his plans to sail for France, declaring that "he conceived it a command from the King and Queen, and resolved to obey it as soon as might be."[361] With the exception of Culpeper, the counsellors declared that they were thereby dismissed and would remain in Jersey.

To the last, George and Jermyn had been concerned that Hyde's opposition would sway the prince, and they accompanied the prince to the shore, one on either side. Unfortunately there was no sign of a ship, the seamen having refused to carry him to France. Charles was forced to appeal to the governor, Sir Philip Carteret, to overcome the problem, but by the time a ship was procured the winds had changed and the party could not get away. By now impatient and anxious to be gone, Charles was forced to wait three days by contrary winds, and then when he eventually started out his ship was driven back by a storm. All the time he remained on shore the councillors who had opted to remain in Jersey, Hyde, Capel and Culpeper, tried to persuade him to change his mind. This led to bad feeling between them and Jermyn and George, the two factions not being on speaking terms and only meeting for meals. At last, having resolved to row all the way if he had to, Charles boarded a small shallop with George and Jermyn each firmly holding an arm, to the great consternation of the councillors. The winds finally shifted and they transferred to a frigate, landing at Containville at eleven in the evening.

Back in England, the king was following developments closely. He had mixed feelings about the reunion of his son with Henrietta Maria, as his letter to Prince Charles indicates: "Hoping that this will find you safe with your mother, I think fit to write this short but necessary letter to you. Then know, that your being where you are, safe from the power of the rebels, is, under God, either my greatest security, or my certain ruin. For, your constancy to religion, obedience to me, and to the rules of honour, will make these insolent men begin to hearken to reason, when they shall see their injustice not like to be crowned with quiet. But, if you depart from those grounds, for which I have all this time fought, then your leaving this kingdom will be (with too much probability) called sufficient proofs for many of the slanders heretofore laid upon me. Wherefore, once again I command you, upon my blessing, to be constant to your religion, neither hearkening to Roman superstitions nor the seditious and schismatical doctrines of the Presbyterians and Independents. For I know that a persecuted Church is not thereby less pure, though less fortunate. For all other things, I command you to be totally directed by your mother; and, as subordinate to her, by the remainder of that council which I put to you at your parting from hence."[362]

With no promises of help for the king forthcoming from France, George once more boarded his frigate for Ireland, leaving Hyde in Jersey, there to write his famous History of the Great Rebellion and await the call of Royalty when and if it came. Ironically, in view of the harsh criticism meted out to George in this epic work, Hyde suggested that George help him, and that his two secretaries write from his dictation and supply Hyde with copy.[363] George took with him what was left of the money granted by Mazarin – eight thousand pistoles, "..towards the Supply of the King's Service there"[364]– landing at Waterford in July 1646. As Ormond received less than one thousand pistoles, a considerable sum went missing en route! Nevertheless Ormond was pleased to see his old friend again. George's wife, still in Oxford, requested permission to join him but this was denied by Fairfax.

Immediately upon his arrival George threw himself into fresh negotiations with the Irish as though nothing had happened since he had been away. He and Ormond returned to Kilkenny to talk to the Catholic leaders, pointing out that with the king defeated in England nothing now stood in the way of a Parliamentary attack on them. But the Nuncio had a separate agenda and cared little for the cause of the Royalists. He was supported by fanatics such as Owen O'Neill, who in Ormond's absence was threatening Dublin, and this made sensible discussion remote. Despite his roots in that part of the country, Ormond was no longer welcome, and little progress was made.

The Royalist cause in Ireland was doomed, and on September 26 Ormond wrote to Parliament offering to serve under them or resign his position. The Parliamentary involvement in Ireland was growing, and there was a strong Roundhead force close to Dublin. George was now in great danger and could not reside in Dublin, remaining in Kilkenny.

On a visit to Ormond he was recognised by a Parliamentary soldier who shouted: "Seize the traitor Digby," and was forced to ride for his life.[365] Frustrated by lack of progress in his negotiations with the Irish, though he continued to try all manner of bright schemes on them, George suggested that he kidnap the Nuncio! Ormond wearily agreed to lend support, writing to his commander at Carlow to assist, but the plot could not be implemented.

Ormond warned George of the peril of his position, wishing him safe somewhere else. The Parliamentary fleet were blockading Dublin harbour, their troops ready to besiege Dublin itself. Undaunted, George persisted with his negotiations in Kilkenny and wrote to Ormond on November 18 in triumph, announcing that the Nuncio's forces were in disarray, and that he had concluded a new agreement with the influential leaders, Preston and the Earl of Clanricarde, a close ally of Ormond. Ormond, involved in tortuous negotiations with the English Parliamentarians, to whose side he was increasingly inclined, met requests for support coldly and with great scepticism. A torrent of correspondence followed, George trying desperately to persuade Ormond to send troops, using every argument he could think of, including the suggestion that he was only treating with the Irish in order to give Ormond a fall-back position if he failed in his dealings with the English. At last Ormond agreed, safeguarding his position by insisting that nowhere was his name to appear upon the documents to the agreement.

The clericalist followers of Rinuccini and the Royalist interest represented by Ormond were sharply divided on key questions of church and state. The former were strengthened by the military successes of O'Neill in Ulster, and controlled the Supreme Council of the Confederation. But their military commander in Leinster, Lieutenant-General Thomas Preston, sought negotiations with Ormond after failing to take Dublin from him during the months when the Parliamentary forces in Ireland were at their weakest. On July 28 Ormond handed over his commission to the Parliamentary Commissioners. Lieutenant-General Michael Jones had already assumed command in Dublin, and on August 8 he defeated Preston at Dungan Hill, thirty miles north-west of the capital.

By Christmas George was back in Dublin, appearing before the Council. He announced his intention to return to France, where he believed substantial aid would be forthcoming. The problem was the blockade on Dublin harbour, and he was soon back south, writing from Ross on February 27 that he had met the French envoy, M. de Moulin there, and that there was the prospect of five thousand troops being sent from Rochelle. Despite several attempts to sail from other ports using French ships for safe passage he was frustrated by bad weather and concern by the French at the dangerous passenger they were carrying. In fact it was Ormond who was the first to leave, in the summer of 1647, with a safe conduct to England, the fruit of his negotiations with Parliament. There he had several meetings with the king before retiring to Caen in France with his family.

The tide against King Charles was gathering speed. On February 11, 1647 Parliament issued the crucial tract "A Declaration of the Commons of England" which was a resolution to have no further communication with the king, thus effectively refusing to recognise his position as reigning over the citizens. The first Earl of Bristol, George's father, exiled in Caen, on receiving this news from Ormond, responded by drafting "The Royal Apologie" which purported to put the king's case but in reality was more of a defence of his own actions and position. This did not surface until some time later in a much amended form, which had all the hallmarks of George's style and was attributed to a past member of the House of Commons, which could not have referred to the Earl, but was more likely referring to George. This pamphlet gained wide notice and was championed by the king's supporters. George continued to encourage Irish resistance to the Parliamentary force, but when Preston marched on Dublin with a Catholic force he was soundly defeated by the new governor, Jones, at Dangan Hill.[366] With all hope dissipated, George prepared to set sail for France once again.

Chapter 14.

Exile In France.

George's journey from Ireland to France was not going to be easy. Parliament had sent a force to Ireland, and controlled Dublin and its immediate vicinity. He was wanted by the Parliamentary forces, who saw him as public enemy number one; and he could expect no help from Rinuccini and his Papists. He was offered a pass by Preston to carry him to the coast, but he was afraid that any assistance given to him in the form of a safe conduct or travel pass would land him in trouble if he was stopped by one of Preston's enemies, and possibly compromise him with the Royalists. In May 1647 he rode out from Dublin to the port, where he was recognised by some Parliamentary soldiers. They demanded to see his pass, at which he spurred his horse past them and fled to the river where he was able to cross with the assistance of Viscount Theobald Taafe, a Catholic Irish lord who had served with Rupert's cavalry and was now a Confederate general. George remained in Leixlip for a while where surprisingly the Parliamentary general, Michael Jones, assured him of safe conduct. There he tried to find a ship to carry him away, but the English captains would have gladly handed him over to Parliament or thrown him overboard. His chance came when the Supreme Council mounted an assault upon Leixlip. With various Irish factions and English soldiers from both Royalist and Parliamentary sides joining in, a free fight developed.[367] In the confusion George crept away and embarked in disguise upon a small open boat of eight tons. The captain was a Protestant and aware of who George was, but he was persuaded to carry him safely to France.

George took up residence in Caen with his father.[368] A number of English exiles had gathered there, including Wilmot, and it was not long before he and George were quarrelling over recollections of events in England, a duel only being prevented by the intervention of George's nephew, another George Digby, son of Kenelm Digby.[369] When Ormond left Ireland George had asked him to take care of his wife and children, who were still in England but destitute. He hoped that arrangements could be made for them to join him in France, but Anne Digby resolutely chose to remain where she was in the hope that after the war she could salvage something of the family's fortunes and provide a future for her children. In this she succeeded beyond expectations due to the fact that her siblings were on the side of the Parliamentarians, and the Sherborne estates had been let to her sister for £530 per annum. Anne later negotiated repossession. She also received income from rental of other family properties by concession of the government, although some were sold to pay off debts.[370]

The cautious Hyde, conscious of his dazzling friend's capacity for creating waves, wrote urging George to adopt a low profile: "Borrow or beg (it is very honest) so much as will keep you alive and cleanly for one year, and withdraw into a quiet corner where you are not known and where not above two or three friends may hear of you. If you can but live for one year without being spoken of at all, you shall find a strange resurrection in your fortunes."[371] Despite petty squabbles Caen was a relatively comfortable and peaceful retreat for the English Royalists, but the quiet life was never an option for George, who was soon on the road to Paris, looking for and finding trouble. With him went a guard which he had hired and Daniel O'Neill, who had decided that his fortunes were better served by following George and the prince to France rather than stay in his homeland which was now dominated by Cromwell's army. On September 27, 1647 William Smith wrote to Richard Levesen: "Lord Digby and O'Neal are arrived in France lately with great danger. Digby has gone for St Germains to the Queen, where he saw Prince Rupert (who is quite recovered from a shot in his head, and is now in great esteem there) and my Lord Gerard to fight with, if the Queen do not salve matters."[372] Wilmot, also in Paris, was quick to take up the cudgels again, accusing George of disparaging him to the queen.

Mazarin had appointed Rupert as a Marshal in the French army, empowering him to recruit the exiled English, and fourteen hundred had applied to serve with him. The supreme commander, Field-Marshal Gassion, was jealous of his status, and contrived to place Rupert in mortal danger when they were ambushed by Spanish forces near the Netherlands border. Isolated, Rupert fought his way out but in the process received a head wound which was to trouble him for the rest of his life.[373] It took several weeks for him to recover, but once he was fit again he resumed his feud with George. George's part in his dismissal following the surrender of Bristol still rankled, and he sent word to George by a French friend, M. de la Chapelle that "he expected him with his sword in his hand at the Cross of Poissy, a large league off in the forest with three in his company."[374] George replied that he would willingly meet Rupert, but having no horses and wishing to avoid suspicion he would have to go there on foot. Rupert arranged for horses to be sent to meet him half way. However word did get out, and the queen attempted to stop the duel, sending Jermyn to persuade George with orders confining him to his quarters, but he was sent away with a torrent of abuse ringing in his ears, although George also suggested Jermyn should act as one of his seconds. Jermyn replied that if he was to act for anyone, it would be for Rupert.[375] Fortunately for George, as they were crossing swords the Prince of Wales rode up with a troop of the queen's guards and placed Rupert and George under arrest. The queen ordered an immediate inquiry to be held by the Lords Culpeper, Gerard and Wentworth and Sir

Frederick Cornwallis. Rupert's anger appeared to have abated and he "most discreetly and most nobly declar'd, that he was far from making a quarrel with the Lord Digby upon any thing he had done against him as Secretary of State, tho' of never so much prejudice to him: but that this resentment was upon speeches that he was inform'd the Lord Digby had publish'd highly to his dishonour."[376] This gave George the opportunity to withdraw without loss of honour, and overnight these two bitterest of enemies became firm friends and allies!

Shortly after this the animosity between George and Wilmot resurfaced, with Wilmot citing criticisms of Rupert in George's cabinet papers, and George defending Rupert's honour![377] George declared that "the Lord Willmot had given his Lordship such ungentlemanlike provocations…which was the only ground upon which he could then fight with him, namely, that the Lord Willmot had been the author to the Lord Digby of so unworthy a scandal upon Prince Rupert, as to tell his Lordship that his Highness would not seek right of him in way of honour, but that he intended his Lordship foul play."[378] Yet another duel ensued, near Paris on October 9, but feelings were running so high that the seconds joined in and a free-for-all developed. At one stage John Digby, the portly son of Kenelm, who was defending George, fell on Wentworth and nearly suffocated him.[379] Wilmot was wounded in the hand. Thus Rupert was avenged by one of his previous enemies, and George could be seen to be acting nobly by defending Rupert's honour.

George found the capital in an extraordinary state of excitement. Following the death of Louis XIII in 1643, he had been succeeded by his five year-old son, Louis XIV. The real power lay with the first minister, Cardinal Mazarin. Paris at that time was a stark contrast of Renaissance splendour, conspicuous wealth among the arstocracy and appalling poverty. Close to the grand boulevards and elegance of the Tuileries and Palais Royal were narrow, dirty alleys where citizens dared not venture. An average of fifteen people was killed in the streets of Paris every night and it was estimated that fifty thousand thieves and cut-throats roamed the city in organised bands.

The appearance of the Prince of Wales, joining the resident Queen Henrietta Maria, was an unwelcome intrusion. Mazarin was faced with the dilemma of building bridges with Cromwell in England while not turning his back on a future monarch who may be very important to him, and his mother, who was the aunt of the new King of France. Despite increasingly strident assertions by the exiles that the monarchy would ultimately prevail in England, Mazarin was not so optimistic. For this reason the prince was not officially received by the eight year-old king, Louis XIV, for five weeks, even though he was the French king's first cousin through a shared grandfather. During this period tortuous negotiations took place between Cardinal Mazarin, the queen regent and their advisers in order to establish the protocol and future treatment of their English guest. When they did meet, it was as though by chance in the forest of Fontainebleau, although the encounter had been carefully planned.

Although Charles' position in France was therefore tenuous, and his mother regarded as something of a nuisance, he still represented the focal point for Royalist hopes and aspirations. The English exiles rapidly placed themselves at his disposal, hoping for positions of substance in his court in exile. Many of them had made great sacrifices to support him and had forfeited their positions in England and were now totally dependent upon his patronage. Unsurprisingly George was not to be found lagging in seeking favour with Charles, promising him the same service, duty and devotion he had shown to his father. Hyde tells us that Charles had no particular liking of George[380], and the prince's closest companion, Thomas Elliott, was George's enemy. So he answered vaguely, holding out no promise of preferment. The Earl of Bristol was equally cast aside. Back into the prince's life came two childhood friends, the eighteen-year-old Duke of Buckingham, George Villiers, and his brother. They were regarded as rather undisciplined tear-aways, and the prince's advisers, led by Hyde and Francis, Lord Cottington, were concerned that their influence would not be good. The duke immediately set about dominating the prince and deriding his serious-minded, rather elderly advisers. He also offered Charles light-hearted diversions in the glittering city of Paris.

George no longer represented any influence over English affairs, and his presence in Paris was likely to be an embarrassment to a French government attempting to come to terms with the new powers in England. Without resources, he was shunned by Parisian society, although his natural optimism meant that he did not remain down for long. He sought to use his acquaintance with Mazarin to establish himself, but Mazarin was extremely reluctant to see George. When the first minister did eventually grant him an audience he "gave (him) good words, promised him some command in the army…and in the meantime gave him a very mean supply for his present subsistence, nor did he find any better reception from those with whom he expected to be admitted as a full sharer of all they enjoyed."[381] In theory this spelt the end of George's hopes of re-establishing himself in the French capital. His assets were frozen, he had fled from Ireland, and his patron, Queen Maria Henrietta, was equally destitute. But his restless spirit and positive attitude once more came to his rescue. He wrote to Hyde that he was lucky not having to waste his time attending the king but could get on with his own life.[382]

Meanwhile back in England Cromwell had run into difficulties. Talks at hammering out a reconciliation with the king and forming a new, workable constitution had faltered, partly through the intransigence and deviousness of the king and partly through growing disenchantment with the strength of the army. An unlikely concurrence of views between remaining Royalists and Prebyterians, whose only rallying cry was "God save the King"[383] led to the Second Civil War in 1648, with the declared aim of extirpating the New Model Army. Revolts occurred in Pembroke in Wales on March 23, in Berwick and Carlisle where Royalists captured the towns, and in Kent in May. On May 27 part of the fleet in the Downs mutinied and declared for the king. To counteract this Warwick assumed the position of High Admiral on May 29.

The only real rebels in England were Presbyterians in Royalist strongholds and Cavaliers still sufficiently loyal to the king to take up arms again. There was little popular support. The Scots sent a large force south in support of the uprising, but they could not persuade the people to join them, and Cromwell swiftly and ruthlessly defeated them at Preston and Warrington on August 17 and 19. Royalist resistance was brought to a sudden end and the Scots retreated north again.

In the same month there began in France a complex series of civil wars known as the Frondes, which for five years threatened the monarchy and unity of the nation. George went where the excitement was. He managed to procure a horse and entered the French army opposing the Frondists as a volunteer. When the rebels threatened the security of Paris, he rode out with the army to meet them. What occurred on that occasion is described in Edward Hyde's famous memoirs: "A personage of the other side coming single out of the troops to change a pistol, as the phrase is, with any single man that should be willing to encounter him, without speaking he (George) moved his horse very leisurely towards him, the other seeming to stand still to expect him, but he did in truth dexterously retire so near his own troops that before the time he could come to charge him, the whole front of that squadron discharged their carbines on him, while the other retired into his place. By this dishonourable proceeding he received a shot in his thigh with a brace of bullets, and keeping still his horse needed no excuse for making what haste he could back when he could no longer sit his horse."[384] The king was present at the time, as was the Prince of Condé, and his daring and courage was noticed. Enquiries were made as to who the stranger was. "He was no sooner recovered of his wounds and went to make acknowledgment to the King and the Cardinal, but he found the Cardinal's countenance very serene towards him, and himself quickly possessed of an honourable command of Horse, with such liberal appointments as made his condition very easy, the Cardinal taking all occasions to do him honour, and he very well knowing how he was the discourse of the whole Court and had drawn the eyes of all men upon him..... His quality, his education, the handsomeness of his person and even the beauty of his countenance (being not at that time above thirty years of age and looking much younger), his softness and civility in all kinds of conversation, his profound knowledge in all kinds of learning and in all languages in which he enlarged or restrained himself as he saw occasion, and made him grateful to all kinds of persons."[385] Thus George achieved his aim, and this appointment was to bring him advantages which he foresaw would put him in good standing with the Prince of Wales.

As a commander of horse in the French army George was expected to raise his own troop, and he rapidly succeeded in doing this, gathering together the frustrated English exiles with promises of glory. These promises were difficult to realise in the circumstances, and his financial situation was such that he could not meet the exiles' pecuniary expectations, but he was able to keep them together with his unstoppable optimism and enthusiasm. The French Court was an uneasy place, with several warring factions, but George's readiness to take on the most unlikely tasks and his steadfast loyalty led the cardinal quickly to trust him, and admit him to his confidence.

George's real interest lay in securing a position close to the prince. Despite the friendship of Henrietta Maria, he was not included in the prince's circle. In August 1648 George's resentment at this treatment boiled over. Accusing Jermyn, who was also close to the queen (they were rumoured to be lovers) but did enjoy favour with Prince Charles, of misleading him and excluding him from important discussions, he sent his cousin Kenelm as his second to challenge Jermyn to a duel. They arranged to meet at Nanterre, between St Germaine and Paris, but Henrietta Maria became aware of the quarrel. A guard was sent out to apprehend George, who was commanded to attend the queen in Paris, where the matter was settled privately.[386]

Then came a heavy blow: on January 30 1649 news was received of the execution of Charles I. The story is well known: how he refused to acknowledge the rights of Parliament, how he staunchly defended the legitimate rights of kings, and how ultimately he was convicted of high treason and beheaded. Although the saga had seemed to stretch out interminably, the final act sent a shudder across Europe. The states on the Continent were left uncertain at how to react: were they to treat with the new, republican power in England, thus denying the rights of kings and perhaps putting in jeopardy their own crowned heads, or were they to declare hostilities towards Cromwell and his New Model Army?

Henrietta Maria wrote to her son summoning him to her side so that she could advise and guide him, but Charles was at last totally his own man, and swore in his new council. George was not included in this council, despite Henrietta Maria's strong urging that he, his father and Sir Edward Nicholas should be appointed. They were her nearest advisers. She expressed her anger, but Charles was short with her, merely saying that in future he intended to "obey his own reason and judgment" and that she was "not to trouble herself in his affairs."[387]

George still had hopes of advancement. In March Charles wrote to him assuring him of the "favour and esteem both of himself and his mother. There were few men from whom the

King promises himself so good service; and Digby can do no more for the King as he now is, although absent, than in any other condition in which he could be placed."[388] In May 1649 George developed a scheme to introduce a number of French officers to Charles. The young king was, at the time, staying with his mother in the palace of the Louvre, and George envisaged turning it into a fortress for the French king's troops. At the last moment his scheme fell through, causing great embarrassment and some irritation on the part of Charles that he had been "used" in the civil war. George was unabashed, explaining that he was obliged to undertake it in the service of the King of France.[389]

As the new King of England Charles was an increasing embarrassment to the French, who were attempting to maintain good relations with Cromwell. Charles felt he could not stay in Paris in the circumstances, and did not wish to suffer more humiliation at the hands of the French. He resolved to depart as soon as he could. Only in Jersey was Charles recognised as the legitimate king, and it was to there on September 27, 1649, that he and his court, including Hyde, sailed. Charles steered the flagship and was pursued by ships of the Parliamentary fleet, but landed safely in Jersey to a tumultuous welcome. George, still out of favour with Charles, was not included in the king's retinue, remaining in Paris, although Edward Hyde believed he was to be appointed Secretary of State, together with Edward Nicholas.[390] George remained unpopular with the new regime in England as well. Following the execution of the king, Oliver Cromwell had set about reconciling the opposing factions in England, offering the Royalists a free pardon for their part in the war. However he excluded four leaders who were to be banished for life and their goods sequestrated for three years. They were the Lords Newcastle, Worcester, Bristol and Digby.

Negotiations with the Scottish Covenanters were reopened in Jersey. Charles was persuaded to go to Scotland for further discussions, but after nearly being shipwrecked he returned to Breda. There the Prince of Orange strongly advised him to continue negotiating with the Scots, so on May 24, 1650 he set sail once again. His reception by the people of Scotland was extremely warm, but their leaders were intent on extracting the maximum advantage from Charles' plight. In return for installing him on the Scottish throne he was required to accept their demands for the establishment of a Presbyterian kirk and Scottish parliament. He was denied access to his subjects, and lectured tediously on religious matters. Cromwell, recognising the threat to his position in England, defeated the Scots at Dunbar, east of Edinburgh. Threatened with further incursions by the English, the Scots army marched south with their newly-crowned king. The expected spontaneous uprising in support of Charles failed to materialise, the old English antipathy towards the Scots prevailing, and the Scots were finally cornered and defeated at Worcester. Charles escaped in disguise, and for six weeks roamed England, evading his pursuers with the help of citizens still loyal to the crown. On October 15 he set sail from Shoreham and with a favourable wind behind the small ship, was soon back in France.

With France embroiled in the civil war of the Fronde, its rulers had little time or thought for the destitute king. By September 1652 Charles was reduced to taking his meals in taverns as his servants could no longer afford to provide food, and many of his followers were virtually at starvation level. In their frustration they quarrelled constantly. He was not popular with the general populace, either, as his brother James was serving in the French army under Turenne, opposed to the Duke of Condé who held the sympathy of the Parisiennes. Pleas to neighbouring states for financial help had fallen on deaf ears: English royalty was not good news to governments coming to terms with the powerful Cromwell. Hyde complained that he was so cold that winter that he could hardly hold his pen, not having three sous to buy a faggot. "I do not know that any man is yet dead for want of bread, which really I wonder at," he wrote in June 1653, "...I am sure the King himself owes for all he hath eaten since April, and I am not acquainted with one servant of his who hath a pistole in his pocket."[391]

George, excluded from Charles' council and although close to the queen did not receive any payment from her, was dependent upon the French government for a living. He accompanied Cardinal Mazarin when in December 1650 he seized the northern frontier town of Rethel from the Spanish, who occupied the Netherlands. A counterattack was resisted with heavy loss of life on both sides.[392] A favourite with the French king, George was awarded a knighthood and appointed a Lieutenant General of the French Army on August 15, 1651 by the Queen Regent of France in the king's name, "to imploy our said Army, either against Flanders, or any other service."[393] In the summer of 1652 he replaced the Governor of Mante (Nantes), the Duke of Sully: "My Lord Digby is made Governor of Mante, Pontoise, St Germains and all this country hereabouts, with power to raise one regiment of foot, another of horse consisting of ten troopes, and an allowance of 700 pistols for raisinge of every troope, and besides all this, he is to have a free company of one hundred maisters horsemen besodes their servants, which is counted better than a regiment."[394]

His position gave him command of a post controlling the approaches to Paris by the two rivers, Seine and Oise. Effectively this provided him with a monopoly of all the trade which passed along these busy waterways. He appointed Lewis Dyve Deputy Governor of the Isle Adam on the Oise, and with their new-found wealth in August 1651 the two stepbrothers set up a magnificent establishment in Paris, at which they entertained lavishly. "Mercurius Politicus," a sharply critical English paper, berated George for profiting from the oppression of the French people. His success also seems to have upset his relationship with Henrietta Maria, for on

March 29, 1652, Hyde reported to Nicholas: "The Queen and Lord Jermyn hate Digby more than they hate Nicholas."[395]

Queen Henrietta Maria continued to occupy chambers in the Louvre, but was still living in extremely straitened circumstances, with not enough money for food or fuel. English exiles still called upon her frequently, and in the absence of her son she provided a focal point for Royalist sympathies abroad. George had become one of her closest confidantes, and she trusted him above virtually everyone else. Inevitably, perhaps, George went too far when in February 1651 Cardinal Mazarin was forced by unpopularity over the Fronde affair to beat a diplomatic retreat to Italy.: "When the Cardinal was compelled to leave the Court and the Kingdom, he left this person [George} in great trust with the Queen, who took all occasions, by frequent conferences with him, and frequent testimonies of his parts and abilities, to express a very good and particular esteem of him, which he..interpreted to proceed from his own great merit and abilities...and thereupon began to delight himself with the contemplation of the glorious condition he should be possessed of, if he could now succeed the Cardinal in the Office of Primier Minister in France....he..bare-face took upon himself to advise the Queen not to affect it [the Cardinal's return], as a thing impossible to be brought to pass...which she no sooner perceived than she gave the Cardinal advertisement of it."[396]

The prominence and success which George enjoyed and which was noted caused Charles, who remained in Paris, to look more kindly towards him. In 1652 he sent Ormond to interview him at his new home in Paris, and that worthy requested Hyde to accompany him to "assist his own bad memory"[397] so it was clear that this was an important meeting. George was committed to his post in the French army however, and the war of the Fronde was still in full spate, making it impossible for him to leave his position. He seized the opportunity to request that he be made a Knight of the Garter, and it says much for the king's change of attitude towards him that by the end of January 1653 "he had been granted his wish, the king dispensing with the usual ceremonies."[398]

George was also befriended by the powerful Prince of Condé, who managed to obtain for him an extra two hundred pistoles a month to add to his pension of one hundred pistoles, together with a command of troops in Normandy and promise of higher command.[399] Much of this wealth he squandered on gambling and women. "he was very amorous; ...he...would procure letters of his wife's desperate sickness of some disease that could not be cured, nor supported above two, or three months, and thereupon make offers and promises of marriage with the same importunity as if the time were ready for contract."[400] He vied for the favours of Isabelle-Angelique de Montmorency, the dowager Duchess of Chatillon, a cousin of Condé, who was being pursued by a number of men, including the Prince of Condé himself. Clarendon reported that "George was always amorously inclined, and the more inclined by the difficulty of the attempt, was grown powerfully in love with this lady, and to have more power with her, communicated those secrets of state which concerned her safety"[401] When Charles first came to Paris he had flirted with the dowager duchess, and he had been seen frequently in her company. His pet name for her was Ballon. By 1652 she was his mistress, and he was reported to have proposed marriage to her. Noted for her great beauty and charm, she was also notorious for her avarice, and saw in her suitors opportunities to add to her wealth. Therefore she was careful not to commit herself to this penniless, exiled king when richer pickings could be available and the Prince of Condé was still interested. Besotted by her, George lost a large sum of money to her at cards. Condé, too, was persuaded to give her his country house at Merlou.

The Abbé Cambiac, also thought to be an admirer, in his position as her spiritual adviser took her to task for her flirtatiousness. When she complained to George about the abbé's insolence, he took matters into his own hands and sent five horse soldiers to arrest the abbé and deliver him to the countess, threatening to take action himself if the abbé did not apologise to the countess. Both the abbé and the countess were horrified by this action, and the countess offered her unwanted hostage profuse apologies and lavish hospitality, as she could ill afford to make an enemy of the influential clergyman. Strangely, the abbé's wrath centred on the countess and not George, whom he said had behaved in a most gentlemanly way towards him, even giving him dinner before sending him to the countess!

George, realising that he was unlikely to make the countess his mistress, decided that she should be Queen of England. He was either unaware that the king had already proposed to her, or was undeterred by the fact. He persuaded Charles to try again, but she remained non-committal. By this time Charles was having second thoughts about a permanent relationship, and the two parted on friendly terms.

The Earl of Bristrol was in ill health, and came to live with George in his splendid Paris house. In January 1653 he died. He was not buried in the Charenton Cemetery which was normally used for "persons of quality," but in a newly-established plot bought by Sir Richard Browne to establish an English cemetery. This had formerly been a cabbage patch in one of the meaner suburbs of Paris, and the funeral was attended by only a handful of people, among them Bristol's younger son, John, but not George. Mercurius Politicus commented that few had been invited by George so as to save money, and he was indeed by now deeply in debt as he was often not paid his pension. Correspondence between George and Lewis Dyve at the time confirms that in spite of his accumulation of wealth he was still struggling to make ends meet. He refers to jewels which were to be pawned for 2,500 pistoles in order that his daughter Diana could be provided with a settlement.[402] This does not explain his absence from the funeral ceremony, however, and his reputation took quite a knock as a result. He never referred to his father's funeral in his letters, and his absence remains a mystery. It is possible that he had quarrelled with his father, for Bristol's will (dated December 3, 1651 but not granted probate in England until after the Restoration) showed that he left his house in Great Queen Street to John, together with one thousand pistoles. No reference was made of George in the will. To repair his position he hosted a magnificent supper the next month to which Charles, his mother and grandmother came.

In June 1653 George, now Earl of Bristol, was sent into Guienne "to command the King's forces under the Duke of Candale, in hope that he may prevaile with those Irish who revolted from the Spaniard to continue their revolt and not to serve the Bourdelois upon the Spanish account."[403] He was no longer in favour at court, however, and this together with his recurring financial problems was causing his faithful stepbrother, Lewis Dyve, problems in Paris. On December 16 he wrote to George, who was stationed at Cahors, setting out the difficulties he was having in finding quarters for George's troops. In the same letter he warned George: "[I] wish from my soule that the cause were not more then happily you imagine it to bee, and that you would seriously consider how to recover the loss you are att in Court at present."[404]

Dyve was tireless in pursuing George's interests. A series of letters from him details his attempts to recover debts due to George, and to raise money by selling or pawning jewels. The money from the jewels disposed of in England could not be transferred out of the country. In reply George was his usual, irrepressible self. Writing from Villefranche on February 7, 1654, he reassured Dyve: "…the truth is, Brother, that seeinge that besides the payment of five and twenty hundred pistols debt which I have discharged….I am like to be Master of treble that summe ere this winter quarter be over….I am resolved… to see whither…I may be assured of such command the next sommer as I shall like, and…if I can gett such assignations in this Country as may be likely to replace what I shall disburse of my stock for the next Camp service; in that case I shall serve cheerefully and honourably, if not having where withall to subsist handsomely in a retreate for some yeares."[405]

George was not able to make his peace with Mazarin. The cardinal had returned to Paris in 1653, and in the spring of 1654 made it clear that George was not welcome in Paris. He did however give him the choice of where he was to serve abroad, and George chose Piedmont. He requested that Dyve be given the position of Mareschal de Camp and accompany him to Italy.[406] Dyve received his commission, but was refused permission to join George. Before he could go to Piedmont, however, George was taken seriously ill with kidney stones, and was nursed in the College of Jesuits at Albi, where for fifteen days he was close to death. He remained there until the summer of 1655 when he joined Dyve, who had nevertheless gone to Piedmont to keep an eye on George's troops. He participated in the siege of Pavia. On November 13 Dyve wrote to George: "I have had a particular account of all your Lordship's generous actions this Campagne and of the high esteeme you have gained thereby in the wholl Army."[407] Nevertheless, recognising that he was never going to regain Mazarin's favour, George formally requested the French king to release him from service, and went into exile.

Chapter 15.

Attempts To Regain The Throne.

In England radical elements, notably in the army fresh from its victory at Worcester, were impatient for more rapid and fundamental change than the cautious members of the Rump Parliament would sanction. Cromwell, by now the most powerful figure in the army and the nation, reflected this growing frustration. Backed by a detachment of soldiers he dissolved the Rump on April 20, 1653. A replacement assembly (the Little or Barebones Parliament) which it was hoped would show more commitment to the cause of godly reform, gathered on July 4. But the new body proved incapable of overcoming its own internal divisions, and the majority willingly acquiesced in its dispersal on December 12. A new constitution, "The Instrument of Government," was drafted by senior officers in which the country was proclaimed a Protectorate. Oliver Cromwell was appointed as Lord Protector.

Those Royalists who remained in England had not given up hope of overturning the new regime. Various plots surfaced, most notably a rebellion planned by the Sealed Knot, or Council Entrusted, a group of high-born young men. Security was very lax, however, and Cromwell's intelligence service efficient. The rebels were ruthlessly suppressed. The thwarted attempts at rebellion made even more plain the threat posed to Cromwell by Charles, and pressure on the French to refuse him sanctuary was increased. Eventually Mazarin offered Charles restoration of his French pension on condition that he left the country within ten days.

The Spanish Netherlands made it clear to Charles that he would not be welcome there, and he finally settled on

Cologne. Hyde and Ormond had been anxious that Charles would not be received well in Cologne, a staunchly Catholic city with a thriving wine trade with the English government. But his reception was warm, the city greeting his arrival with a salute of guns.[408] There he passed a pleasant two years hunting and flirting in a society which found his presence novel and diverting. But intrigue was never far away. The failed attempts at rebellion had forced Charles to turn as a last hope to Spain, who had a sizeable army in the Netherlands. Although they were initially unenthusiastic, it occurred to the Spanish that Charles might be able to help draw off the Irish mercenaries who were offering stout support to the French army opposing them. Eventually a deal was struck whereby Spain would offer Charles 6,000 soldiers once his followers had secured a Channel port, in return for a promise that he would suspend the penal laws against English Catholics, stop the harrassing of Spanish treasure fleets by privateers, and cede Jamaica to Spain. Charles moved on to Bruges, that much closer to the Channel, and was joined later by his entourage, many of whom had been jailed in Cologne for unpaid debts, which took many months to discharge. There he was provided by the Spanish with a pension of 3,000 ecus a month, his French pension having dried up. Charles found his band swelling as malcontents flocked to his standard, forming the nucleus of an army.

When in 1656 George was evicted from France he followed the king to Flanders. His correspondence with Lewis Dyve shows that he was desperately in need of money, for although he would never admit his urgent financial needs his letters are full of anxious questions about debts owed to him and whether Dyve can raise money for him. Dyve reflects this anxiety, for instance in a letter of November 13, 1655: "…I am to render your Lordship all possible thankes for remembering me at such a time when oure owne wants are in a manner unsupportable."[409] Heavily in debt, George sought every way he knew to raise money on his jewels and defer his creditors.

There is evidence that Charles intended to send George to Madrid as an extraordinary ambassador to help the negotiations along. Lewis Dyve referred to this in a letter to George dated May 6, 1656: "Your lordship's employment into Spayne being in quality of Extraordinary Ambassador it is likely your stay there will not be long and indeede your presence neere the King's Person will be necessary to his servis in his most important affayres."[410] In the same letter he assures George that: "The French Ambassador [to Milan, where Dyve was at the time] told me yesterday at dinner that he had received letters from Paris that assured you your free passage through France into Spayne was granted by the King, though there was some difficulty made of it at first for some politike reason, and rather for forme sake then any reall intention of refusing it to you."

Although George was heavily in debt he put on quite a show, arriving in Bruges in August 1656 with a considerable retinue and splended equipment; quite enough to dazzle the impoverished king in exile. Hyde drily observed that he "could always much better bear ill accidents than prevent them."[411] After two or three days there, realising that the exiles were without realistic expectations of returning to England, without leave from the king he approached the Spanish headquarters seeking employment, arguing that he spoke Spanish fluently and knew Spanish ways.

The Spanish had bitter memories of George. Whilst Secretary of State in England he had been no friend of Spain despite his childhood there, and this they resented. Moreover, he had two years previously fought for the French against the Spanish, and was remembered for what were conceived to be savage outrages of plunder and firing of towns, events still commemorated in Flanders by song and verse. Fortunately for him the Spanish general Don Alonsi had been replaced by a new commander, Don Juan Jose of Austria, illegitimate son of King Philip IV and the actress Maria Calderon, who had helped gain a victory against the French in Catalonia in 1652 during the Fronde. Don Juan was captivated by this amusing stranger. George attended the commander at meal times and entered spiritedly into discussions with his advisers, displaying mastery of the Spanish language and making acute observations. He showed great understanding of the position in England, which was of great value to the Spanish. He was also adept at composing horoscopes, a subject dear to Don Juan's heart, and he fed on this by hinting at crowns and sceptres, playing up to Don Juan's ambitions. This sealed their friendship. Among Don Juan's staff was a General Caricina, who had fought opposite George in Italy, and they spent many a happy hour refighting their battles and reminiscing. Within a month he was accepted as one of Don Juan's confidants, and invited to spend the winter with him in Brussels. Hyde, seeking to take advantage of George's new position of privilege, bombarded him with letters ordering him to obtain money from the Spaniards.

The Spanish were still interested in using Charles as a way of exerting lasting influence over England. They perceived that the general public was becoming steadily more disenchanted with Cromwell's regime, and might be persuaded to accept a king again. George therefore had appeared at a most opportune time. With great energy he set about recruiting exiles, and succeeded in setting up four regiments. He then found that they were unlikely to remain in readiness unless paid, and he experienced great difficulty in obtaining funds from the Spaniards. Reputed to be the most wealthy state in Europe, Spain was finding that the stream of income from the West Indies was drying up, and even Don Juan himself was short of funds.

Hyde became impatient at the lack of progress in recruiting new soldiers and persuading the Spanish to proceed with invasion plans. He blamed George for the delays, and a series of tart letters was exchanged, the Chancellor becoming pompous, demanding and crotchety while George replied with acerbity and sarcasm. A flavour of these exchanges can be obtained from the following. The frustrations of Spanish bureaucracy were also making George impatient, as he doubted whether he could hold the exiled regiments together for long. When Hyde criticised him for travelling to Mauberge seeking quarters for his men when he should have been badgering Don Juan, he replied sharply: "I know not whether my absence from the army may chance cost the King some few days' subsistence of his men, and consequently your fat sides some grunts and groans." He followed this letter with a gift: "I send you herewithal a noble present of a rare cheese, knowing that to preserve your favour at court it is necessary to bribe you." Hyde was unmoved: "It is the worst cheese in the world," he wrote on November 1 from Bruges.[412] When he persisted in calling George lazy for not obtaining what was needed, he again protested: "You are very much mistaken if you think these ministers are to be wrought upon to mend their pace much less their purse in anything, by tenderness to the King's uneasiness of life."

Although Don Juan had given an order for the immediate despatch of the resources requested, nothing had happened because his secretary had not executed the order, even though George had "persecuted him for it till midnight, and having had a gentleman at his door ever since six oclock this morning; it was not signed last night because Don Juan was playing at tennis."[413] Hyde wrote criticising George for not having clinched the agreement earlier than he did, to which George responded: "I believe you will think it a faulte that I demanded not the letter from the Secretary of the Chamber and that I carryed it not to him my selfe to signe with his racquet."[414] And "I pardon your anger, reasonable in the subject though wrong in the object. Let me take the liberty to tell you that if you will have business well despatched at a secretariat so ill served as this, you must get some little blade of the office, who upon gratification may make it his business to see such things as appear as nothing and yet perhaps are of great consequence, punctually and timely dispatched, according to the memorials given by those that have other things to do than wait whole days at an under-secretary's lodging making themselves too cheap to be able to do any business of a higher nature. I hope this letter will make you wise for the rest of your life. Your testy letter made me lose a whole day. In the meantime, God give you a better temper."[415]

George was unhappy that he was not included in the king's inner circle and blamed Hyde for this. On January 25, 1657 George wrote to Hyde from Brussels complaining that correspondence between the king and his brother, the Duke of York, had not been made known to him. As a result he must be made ridiculous to Don Juan when his advice is asked. But can he wonder at anything when, upon Ormond's writing to him that he had no money and Hyde telling him that the king has pawned his George to enable Ormond to make his journey, he represents to Don Juan the extremity to which Ormond is reduced and is told that the latter has a pension of 500 crowns a month "How a divell, if I bee thus used, is it possible that I can perswade him of our threes being in soe perfect an intelligence together?"[416]

It was fortunate that an opportunity arose in March 1657 for George to show his persuasive skills at their best, and gain some credit with the Spanish. The Spaniards were besieging the key fortress of St Ghislain, close to Brussels, which was defended by the Huguenot General Schomberg, commanding the French garrison with a corps of Irish troops. Most of the troops came from one family connected to Ormond's private secretary, George Lane, and they were eager to support Charles in any way they could. They secretly offered to surrender to the Spanish, and Ormond was asked to approach their officers. He refused indignantly, saying he would have no part of any plot to persuade the Irish to commit treason, so George was asked to take on the mission. He took one of the four regiments assembled, commanded by Lord Taaffe, consisting of Irishmen, and appeared before the walls of St Ghislain. Schomberg, who was an experienced and intelligent professional soldier, had already become concerned about the number of Irish desertions from the French army. He noticed officers whispering in corners, and feared the worst. His suspicions were confirmed by an intercepted message to his lieutenant-colonel which laid the plot bare, and he sentenced the man to death. The trumpet of Don Juan was then heard, and he was informed that the Spanish were confident they controlled the fortress. He was offered quarter if he spared the man's life. While he was considering this offer, George led his troops into an assault, scaling the earth works and shouting to the Irish defenders: "What, are ye mad to fight against your own King?"[417] Most of the soldiers threw down their arms to join the Spaniards, and Schomberg was left with no option but to leave with the few men who chose to follow him. George formed the Irish into a separate regiment, which he commanded for a short time before handing it over to Colonel Farrel.[418]

Hyde said he was liberally rewarded, but could not resist adding: "Besides the consideration he took himself out of the moneys assigned to the officers and soldiers."[419] More importantly it gave credence to the support George offered the young king, and improved Charles' standing immeasurably. The king was called upon by grandees, attended a series of celebrations and was seen increasingly in the company of Don Juan, dancing, playing tennis and fives.[420] George too was feted. He had an assured position as head of a regiment, and was no longer seen as an exile living on charity. He was invited to Brussels where, for the first time, he was treated with dignity by the authorities. He attended all the State balls, and was much admired.

George still had a burning desire to be restored as Secretary of State, arguing that his status with the Spanish would be considerably improved by such an appointment, but Charles still showed no inclination to do so. He was however admitted to the king's household: his name appears on a list drawn up in April 1657. By applying himself to the king's needs and showing his value as a contact with the Spanish commanders, George finally attained his wish and was made Secretary of State.

Charles' younger brother, James, Duke of York, was a commander in the French army, and enjoying himself hugely under the tutelage of the great soldier Turenne. It was important to Charles that James was seen to be in support of the move towards restoration of the crown in England, and his cause was helped by Cromwell's insistence that members of the Royal family not be encouraged by France. He had little option, therefore, but to join his brother in Flanders, bringing with him a force of English exiles. But James was put out to find that he had exchanged the comforts and luxury of the well-endowed French army, where he was happy, successful and well paid, for a destitute court short of money and short of hope of winning back England. He was treated with little affection or ceremony.

With him came Sir John Berkeley, a professional soldier who had fought in the Civil War in the west with Hopton. He had fallen out then with Goring and refused to accept his orders; subsequently he had proved himself awkward and quarrelsome. The king had sent him as an envoy to Sweden where he had acquitted himself well, and on his return he became an attendant to Henrietta Maria. He had been sent by Henrietta Maria to James in order to protect him against unscrupulous intriguers such as Colonel Joseph Bamfield, who had attempted to ruin Hyde by testifying that he was in correspondence with Cromwell. Bamfield had become the young prince's principal adviser. He was said to exercise great influence over the fourteen year-old prince, and to be forever telling him he was unfairly treated by the king. He was even said to be plotting to usurp Charles' position and put James in his place. The king did not approve of Berkeley, primarily as he was an ally of Henrietta Maria. His nephew, Charles Berkeley, was also a close companion of James. George had warned Don Juan that the Berkeleys were a bad influence. Charles attempted to counterbalance their influence by forcing James to include in his household Henry Bennet, George's secretary. James was incensed, particularly as he detested Bennet, and saw him as a spy. He resisted all attempts to have the Berkeleys removed from his service, blaming George for being prejudiced against them.

Worse was to come. George told the Spanish that James should command one of their armies. In return James was informed that before assuming command of troops enlisted in the name of the English king, he was required to pledge allegiance to Spain. George persuaded the king to enforce this reqirement, but James heard of the arrangement through a third party and confronted George. When James protested George flew into a rage and berated the duke for his doubts. He also demanded to know who had told the Duke of the requirement. He spoke so loudly that it attracted the king to the room, but when James appealed to his brother, George's words were supported by Charles. James reacted by running away to Utrecht, blaming "the interference of violent persons" for his desertion. There followed a stream of letters from James complaining of George's bad behaviour and lack of sense.[421] This defection was a severe blow to the English cause, creating great embarrassment and loss of face with the Spanish and looking potentially fatal in the attempt to restore Charles' crown.

So every effort was made to persuade James to return, with Charles offering to agree to all his demands, and Ormond was sent to bring him back. James defended his action in a spirited way. He sent word to the king that he had not imagined his departure would given such an adverse impression, adding that "if the Lord of Bristol had had the same persuasion as his Majesty hath, he would not have pressed me so hard with his Majesty's authority, nor fortified it with that of Don John, in a matter of no public concernment." He then embarked upon a prolonged defence of his actions, blaming Bennet for misleading him, that he could not fight against Turenne "...it was not enough to serve the Spaniards in general, unless I consented immediately before there was any occasion or men to command against the army under Mons. Turenne, who is one of the men in the world I am the most obliged to and have the greatest value for." He explained himself further: "I having accidentally told my Lord Bristol I heard his Majesty's new Levies of his Subjects were to enter into a promise or engagement of fidelity to the King of Spain, and asked whether it were so or no; his Lordship [G]..forgetting all duty to his Majesty and respect to me, expressed a most exorbitant passion and rudeness, railing in the most unbeseeming manner against the dangerous author and reporter; which ceased not until I had declared that Sir John Berkley neither was, nor could be the author....the Lord of Bristol said to Sir John Berkley in my presence that if I concurred not with his Majesty's sense in all things it would be imputed unto him, which was to tell me fairly to my face, that I had no sense of my own."[422]

Finally, after much cajoling, James agreed to return and came back to Bruges to assume command of all the exile regiments with a bodyguard of fifty horse and an allowance of £200 per month from the Spanish. Berkeley, the person who was said to have informed James of the requirement to pledge allegiance, having apologised, was ennobled as Lord Berkeley of Stratton and Henry Bennet, who had remained in Bruges as George's secretary, was sent to Madrid as ambassador. Although this was regarded initially as something of a sinecure, with the new Spanish alliance it was a very important post. Bennet was well-read, worldly and experienced. He had come to prominence as George's secretary, and was master of several languages.

Within a few months George was writing to Ormond that he was working closely with Berkeley in great amity, although he complained that he could not keep pace with "the thousand projects in which there was neither head nor tail." This was rather rich, coming from George. He also appears to have made his peace with the Duke of York, for he reported on August 30: "The Duke of York's gracious usage of me continues and improves daily so far as to have removed all shiness of employing me in business of his particular interest, and truly Sir John Berkley carries himself towards me very handsomely and generously, and as well by the discourses he hath held with me as by divers of much freedom that I have had both with Don John and the Marquis de Caracena upon the Duke of York's subject."[423]

George complained that he was being maligned by a rather shadowy adviser to the king, Father Talbot: "I must tell you that your spiritual director, Father Talbot, has in his relation of that matter to Don Alonzo, employed all the malice imaginable, and personally against me. I believe you will think fit to take into consideration how to be rid of so troublesome a rascal."[424] He followed this on January 18 with another letter which suggested Hyde agreed with him: "...concerning our ghostly father, I conclude with you, that it is not a season for the King to appear in any thing against him; yet I hope I shall so order matters as to rid us finally of him for good of his soul, as well as the ease of his body, by having him sent to a more religious life...God forgive you your uncharitableness of wishing him in a well."[425]

Finances remained a severe problem. Hyde reported in September 1657 that every bit of meat, all the drink, firewood and candles were still owed for and there seemed little prospect of any aid being forthcoming. A further blow came with the defection of the Duke of Buckingham, one of Charles' staunchest supporters, who returned to England to marry an heiress, the daughter of Thomas Fairfax. It was apparent that he regarded the plight of the Royalists as hopeless.

The Spanish were refusing to help without hard evidence that an invasion would be supported, and Ormond was despatched to England to gauge general opinion. Rather ludicrously disguised with dyed hair which ran several colours, he was soon identified and barely escaped after being pursued from house to house. Ormond reported back that a rising would not be tenable. The only hope was external involvement. Encouraged by the moral support being provided by the Spanish, in January 1658 Charles resolved to send George to Madrid to seek more direct and tangible assistance. A passport enabling him to pass through France was thus again applied for but refused because so many Irish soldiers had defected from the French army to join Charles, presumably through the influence of George, who had formed a new Irish regiment. Cromwell had also made his feelings very clear to the French, and they preferred his friendship to that of Charles.

George continued to press the Spanish for help with money, troops and quarters, urged on by the testy Hyde. When Hyde again complained about lack of progress, and suggested George was not trying, he received a tart reply: "...you cannot possibly imagine I should return to Brussels without being able to say somewhat to Don John in the matter...what I shall produce...will neither require time nor much pains to be made use of; for you know I in three days do more business than such fat fellows as you in three months; Lo, you there, are you now contented with my excuse?"[426]

The English cause was helped by the defection of the Prince of Condé, idol of France, who had lost the power struggle with Mazarin and defected to the Spanish. He saw the prospective invasion as an opportunity to gain international influence, and offered his troops to James. However, all was not serene in the ranks, for petty jealousies and arguments broke out between the English and Irish. Money was scarce, and it was reported that they had no ammunition and bread only for a month. There were rumours that the army would be forced to disband.[427] The Spanish officers were also becoming resentful of the demands made upon them by the exiles. Then George had one of his brilliant ideas: to offer overall command to Condé, who would bring his French troops between the disaffected factions and by his presence weld the force together. This entailed persuading James to stand down and accept a subordinate position, which the strong-willed and independent young duke was reluctant to do. By refusing, James alienated Condé, and George ended up making more enemies and incurring further wrath.

Whilst attempting to establish himself with the Spanish, and at the same time regain his position with Charles, George's thoughts turned to his family, still marooned in England. Miraculously, and with great wit and resolution, his wife had managed to support his children although deprived of all George's property, which had been confiscated by the state. She was wealthy in her own right as the daughter of the Duke of Bedford, and by selling off most of her own property she saw to it that their eldest son, John, was well married and the younger son, Francis, educated at the Jesuit College. The two girls were more of a problem, and the elder, Diana, showed every sign of being rebellious and independent. In April 1657 she was sent to Flanders by her harrassed mother, and George arranged for her to be entered in the English convent at Ghent, close to where he was living. The Abbess, Mary Knatchbull, was a close friend of the family, and could be relied upon to keep an eye on Diana, but the girl was very unhappy about being educated in a Papist establishment, steeped as she was in the Protestant tradition. She thus seized the opportunity to respond to the overtures of Baron Moll, a young nobleman. George saw him as the solution to his problems with his daughter, and Hyde says "Bristol did not even delay to find what the bridegroom's future really was," although friends warned him of the dangers. Unfortunately Moll did not possess as much money as would appear, and was somewhat simple-minded. Diana was a willing partner, notwithstanding the warnings. Although Moll was not a great catch, she judged marriage a small price to pay for escaping the horrors of the convent. Hyde says that George forced her to become a Catholic, "which was a condition without which the marriage could not be attained to, and then frankly gave her up to perpetual misery which she entered into from the day of her marriage."[428] The marriage was a disaster, and the strong-willed and intelligent girl was condemned to a life of misery. George was forced to mediate when the Baron's jealousy of his attractive wife led to blows, and she refused to ride in the same coach with her husband.

The next major episode in George's life has puzzled historians, for George converted to Catholicism. Having worked so hard to re-establish himself with Charles, why would such an intelligent and astute courtier throw it all away? He must have known that whatever Charles' personal convictions were, he was unlikely to look kindly on such a conversion. Yet George must have come close to despairing of the young king's situation, and must have felt his future lay elsewhere. It was not in George's nature to rest for long, and his eyes had turned to Spain, where his standing was high. What better way to impress the Spanish rulers, so one argument went, than to become a Catholic? He would have reasoned, it is argued, that the only possible hope of restoring Charles to the throne would have been through Catholic help and arms. Virtually every major European power was at that time Catholic, and Spain was the most likely ally. Hyde confirmed this: "his hopes under the King were now blasted...Religion was that which could only make a man shine in the Court of Spain."[429]

For several years George had been carrying on a protracted correspondence with his Catholic cousin Kenelm about faith, and had recognised the strength of the arguments in favour of Catholicism. While in France he had become seriously ill, and had been nursed in the Jesuit college at Albi. He had used his time there to study the Catholic doctrines, but at that time was not sufficiently convinced to embrace Catholicism, although as Hyde said: "the Jesuits courted him with wonderful application."[430] By 1658 his adherence to the Protestant faith was no longer crucial to his career. With the help of his friend the Abbess Mary Knatchbull he is said to have made overtures to the Jesuits, and when he was stricken with a violent fever a priest was summoned to his bedside. He later related how he made a pact that if God would save him he would become a Catholic.

Carte relates a different version of the event which throws doubt on George's true conversion. He writes that when George was stricken with fever in March 1658 and the physicians told him his case was desperate, his thoughts turned to the afterlife. A Jesuit was sent to press him to convert. Although George resisted, in his weakened state he was finally persuaded to convert on the basis that if he recovered through the Jesuit's prayers he would embrace the faith. He was said to be embarrassed by this promise, and, Carte goes on, "he was not only free in declaring against the Court of Rome, but he never had a Romish priest in his family after he came into England, not was one ever known to come near him. His daughter, the Countess of Sutherland, being one day asked about it, answered that he did not care to speak on the subject, but it was always her opinion that her father never was really in his judgment a Roman Catholic."[431]

When he did convert, in September 1658, and quickly recovered (perhaps suggesting that his illness had been contrived), he summoned Hyde and Ormond to tell them the good news. Hyde, who as we have seen was becoming steadily more disaffected from his old friend, refused to come. When he heard the news of George's conversion he expressed great anger, and let the king know that in his opinion George could no longer hold office as a member of the king's court. The king was inclined to be amused, knowing only too well George's sudden changes of direction, and believed it was merely a brief flirtation, but Hyde took it so seriously that he convinced the king that George must be dismissed. "This was a change he did not expect his conversion would have produced, but had promised himself more advantage from his character in his new religion than in his old; that there was no more hope now of the Protestant Interest, and therefore that the Catholick must be now wholly applied to....as the confidence of the Catholicks, should be able to asdvance the King's service."[432] Thus Charles demanded that George resign his post as Secretary of State. George blamed Hyde for having influenced the king, widening the gulf between himself and the Chancellor. He retired to Ghent, where it seems that his wife joined him, for on October 7 Abbess Knatchbull wrote that she does not know whether Lady Bristol has arrived yet.[433] However on October 6 Lord Newburgh wrote to Hyde informing him that he "is this day invited to a second wedding, Bristol's and his lady's; the good lady of this town [presumably Knatchbull] treats them with as much ceremony as any newly-married couple." It must be presumed that thay married again in order for the union to be blessed by the Catholic church. On October 31 George wrote to Hyde saying he will wait on the King in Brussels when his wife has left.[434] She was still in Ghent on November 10.

In fact there were already rumours that Charles himself was thinking of converting to Catholicism. There were good political arguments for him to do so, particularly if he was to rely upon Spain for the restoration and subsequent maintenance of his crown. Yet to declare such a conversion publicly would be highly dangerous and potentially lose him sympathy with the English populace, and he was very careful to keep any discussions he had with the Jesuits secret. It is probable that by 1659 he had embraced Catholic doctrines if not actually converted. With the knowledge of Charles' agreement with the Spanish to show tolerance towards Catholics, and his later conversion to Catholicism, perhaps George was entitled to feel he should have been shown more understanding. In his attempt to secure advancement with the Spanish he came to Brussels and was careful to be seen publicly at Mass when Don Juan and the other Spanish grandees were present, but his conversion did not have the desired effect. By alienating himself from the king and Hyde he had given up what influence he was perceived to have and the Spanish were cold towards him. Nor was he offered any lucrative positions in Spain.

Unexpectedly, on September 5, 1658, Cromwell suddenly died. The reaction of the general public was one of indifference, for he was not popular, and without the Protector anarchy threatened. Charles was welcomed back into Brussels society. Even Mazarin referred to Cromwell as "the dead monster." Yet to all appearances nothing much changed in England. Opposition to the Protectorate did not materialise. Cromwell's son Richard took over from his father and attempted to pursue similar policies. The hard realities of poverty and powerlessness returned to the king and his band of exiles with full force. The army now ruled in England in all but name, and Charles' advisers turned to studying the army leaders. There was evidence that they were not in sympathy with Parliament.

It was reported that as a consequence of Charles' treaty with the Spanish, he had mustered 2,500 men in the Netherlands, poised to move across the Channel. The Royalists still living in England prepared plans for an uprising men still true to the memory of Charles I. This group had as its kernel what remained of the Sealed Knot, and the date of August 1, 1659 was set for the uprising to occur. However shortly before the date a secret communication arrived from Samuel Morland, Thurloe's under-secretary, reporting that one of the plotters, Sir Richard Willis, had long been betraying the Royalists' schemes to the government. The king was on the point of embarking for Deal, where he was to have been seized and murdered, so the voyage was abandoned. Others were less lucky: the inability to warn everyone involved led to sporadic signs of rebellion which were rigorously repressed. In Cheshire at Winnington Bridge on August 19 one thousand men under the Presbyterian leader Booth were routed by Lambert, who had mustered four times that many.[435] Booth himself escaped, dressed as a woman, but was reported by an inkeeper in Buckinghamshire when he requested a razor.[436] He was committed to the tower for treason.

Once again there was no alternative but to request assistance from other countries. It was hoped that either Spain or France would help, but these two powers were still embroiled in their own war, and not paying much attention to the English king's plight. Neither wished to alienate the English government while they had their hands full fighting each other. Henrietta Maria's continuing presence in Paris made the French a better prospect for Charles, and he sent Jermyn secretly into France to open negotiations with Mazarin. Although the Cardinal could see some advantage in having Charles in his debt, he dare not alienate the English government at this time, and so he snubbed Jermyn sharply when he appeared. In anticipation of French help, on August 11 1659 Charles left Brussels in great secrecy with a minimum of attendants and made for Calais, the port closest to England, hoping to gain support from the English fleet. The rest of his entourage, including George, who in spite of having fallen from his coach and bruised himself on July 30.[437] saw this as an adventure too good to miss, left Brussels by a different road and joined him later. Hyde was left in Brussels to cover Charles' absence. Jermyn's mission was to obtain fifteen hundred troops and a French ship to carry the king to England, but when this failed the Royal party was forced to rethink their plans. Intelligence from England indicated that the eastern counties, Kent and East Anglia, remained loyal to Parliament. Thus the king planned to sail for Wales, which was reported to be more likely to support him. Charles sent instructions to Bennet, who was in San Sebastian, to secure a ship, and the party moved on south into Brittany. With Charles went George, adopting an unusually low profile as he was still not welcome in France. The plan was to sail from St Malo in any ship they could find, and if that failed, to continue to San Sebastian where Bennet awaited them. Ormond was to join the party at St Malo, but first he went to see Mazarin and explain what was happening, apologising for the journey through France unannounced and without passports. Mazarin advised Charles strongly against going to San Sebastian, refusing to grant him safe conduct through France. Without French support and the vigorous suppression of Booth's uprising any immediate hope of returning to England was lost.

Charles decided that his only course of action was to go on to San Sebastian and seek Spanish support, even if this alienated the French. He first attempted to sail from Nantes to San Sebastian, but the winds were adverse, and the party was forced to make a hazardous trip overland. It was rumoured that the French court was sitting at Bordeaux, directly on their route, and this was particularly dangerous for George, who would doubtless be imprisoned if he was discovered to be in France.

A conference was being held between the French and Spanish on the Isle of Pheasants, on the river Bidassoa half way between Fuentarabia on the Spanish border and Hendaye on the French side, and Charles aimed to attend there to press his case. The meeting was being held in a building constructed for the purpose spanning a river separating the two countries, so that both parties could claim to be on home soil. Both France and Spain had repeatedly told Charles that only the war between them was impeding any assistance that they could afford him, and that once that war was over he could expect their cooperation. With the war coming to an end, and peace negotiations in train at this conference, the signs looked more hopeful.

Thus the English set forth. The party seems to have been in no hurry, and ambled through southern France via Lyons, the Languedoc and Toulouse, taking in all three months to reach their destination. George, so knowledgable about France, proved a delightful guide, and the king gave every appearance of thoroughly enjoying himself after the rigours of Brussels. Travelling in heavy disguise, it appears the party was not identified or harrassed and the authorities were either unaware of their presence, or willing to turn a blind eye in the interests of maintaining good diplomatic relations. As they approached Toulouse they learnt that the French court was sitting there, and on October 7 Ormond was sent on to enquire discreetly of progress at the Fuentarabia conference. He was informed that the conference was successfully completed and that Mazarin was expected in Toulouse any day, wrongly as it turned out, as Mazarin was still in Fuentarabia. It was reported that Don Luis, the chief Spanish negotiator, had returned to Madrid. Deciding that nothing could now be gained by going on to Fuentarabia, the Royal party turned for Madrid, slipping over the Pyrenees unnoticed and stopping at Zaragoza.

In fact, although all matters of substance had been settled in Fuentarabia, the agreement had not been finally concluded yet, and Don Luis remained in residence there. When the Royal party learnt this, Daniel O'Neill was sent post haste to the conference to see how matters stood. There he met Don Luis, who was very agitated to hear the king was in Spain and intending to move on to Madrid. He urged that Charles come to Fuentarabia as soon as possible, and held out the possibility of a meeting with Cardinal Mazarin. Unfortunately the English Parliamentary representative, Lockhart, had been there for some time, skilfully putting the English case to both sides and speaking against Charles. His organisation was such that he was able to intercept all Bennet's mail and therefore was fully familiar with what was planned. Bennet, who had been waiting for the Royal party in San Sebastian in some frustration, was sent to the cardinal's lodgings at St Jean de Luz, fifteen kilometers north of Fuentarabia, to prepare the ground for Charles' arrival. He was turned back on the stairs and informed by the Captain of the Guard that the cardinal could only see him with the permission of the King of France. Don Luis was much more accommodating, and Lockhart had as much difficulty gaining an audience with him as Bennet had with Mazarin. Don Luis told Bennet that all Lockhart wanted was that the war between France and Spain should continue.

Inevitably, George was blamed for encouraging the king to tarry and enjoy himself instead of pressing on to the conference in time to meet the negotiators there. "In this particular my good Lord of Bristol (who is not thought to do any thing by chance) bears the full weight, as if the design were to make Don Juan the instrument of doing the King's business, without the administration of Don Louis, but as I am sure the ground of the Journey to Saragosa was the opinion that Don Louis, was returned to Madrid, so I cannot but hope that before he passed the Pyrenees he was informed that the Ministers were not parted, and then it may be his Majesty came to them in the very conjuncture that was to be wished."[438]

On the same day that Hyde wrote this letter, Charles rode into Fuentarabia on a wet and stormy night in a coach provided by Don Luis, who showed him every courtesy. Mazarin was still refusing to see the English party. However, the king's party suspected that despite his hospitality Don Luis was in collusion with the French. The main priority for the French and Spanish was a marriage settlement between the young king of France and a Spanish princess which would seal the peace, and Charles' presence was nothing more than a nuisance. Ormond was sent out to meet Mazarin "by accident" on the road near the Isle of Pheasants, but although Don Luis cooperated by making sure Ormond had time alone with the cardinal, he could make no headway. Mazarin explained curtly that he could do nothing until after the Royal wedding. When this was reported back to Charles, he suggested that he should marry Mazarin's niece, the twelve-year-old Hortense Mancini but this, too, received an icy response. News reached the Netherlands that the king had attended Catholic mass in one of the private chapels with George, alarming the exiles. Hyde worked hard to reassure the Royalists in England that this was merely malicious slander, knowing very well that if the king was thought to have converted to Catholicism his chances of regaining the throne would be nil.[439]

Charles suggested that he go to Madrid. Don Luis produced 7,000 pistoles as pension money due from the Spanish under the agreement Charles had reached in the Netherlands, but it was made clear that this was to pay for his return journey to Brussels. So when Mazarin moved on at the end of the conference to Dax, near Bayonne, Charles followed but without success. The Cardinal remained out of reach. Thus the king was forced to travel on to Bordeaux, intending to return to Brussels via Paris. He took the opportunity on his way back to visit his young sister, Henrietta, at Colombe. She was his favourite sister and the two were very close. Finally Charles returned to Brussels on December 24, 1659.

George remained behind. Don Luis, in spite of vexation at what he saw to be George's deviousness, had been much impressed by this irrepressible Englishman who spoke faultless Spanish, and offered him three hundred pistoles and suggested he accompany him back to Madrid. George suggested he go as Ambassador Extraordinary, to give him an official role, but there can be little doubt that he had hopes of persuading the Spanish to offer him a good position. The Spanish king received him graciously, remembering his father fondly, and it was arranged that he would stay at the English residence. Uncharacteristically he spent considerable time at his devotions, leading to the suspicion among observers back in Brussels that he was attempting to establish his Catholic credentials with the Spanish court,[440] although ostensibly he was there to obtain financial help for Charles.

As soon as George was gone the Royal party fell to blaming him for the failure of the trip, and the inability to make progress with the French. Even his erstwhile friends turned against him. He was blamed for the failure of the king to sail from St Malo to England, even though that expedition would certainly have been a disaster. In particular O'Neill, previously one of his closest allies, now wrote scathingly about him. He did not believe that George remained in Don Luis' good books, and was extremely sceptical that his stay in Madrid would come to anything. He accused him of meddling in Spanish affairs, attempting to mediate between Don Luis and Don Juan, and not being serious about securing Spanish help for the king. It was also suggested that this was all a devious Spanish trick to prevent Charles coming to terms with Mazarin, who had not welcomed George's appearance at Fuentarabia. The fact that all this was reported by Clarendon in his "Life" does rather question its veracity, bearing in mind Hyde's bitter animosity towards George when he wrote the words years later. Undoubtedly George had an eye, as always, to his own future, but of the Royal party at Fuentarabia he represented by far the best chance of making progress with the

Spanish in view of his good relations with both Don Luis and Don Juan.

It seems that George was actually well thought of in Madrid. The Venetian ambassador there, Quirini, reported on March 11, 1661: "They [the Spanish] express themselves as very well pleased with the Earl of Bristol who supports and explains the claims of the Catholic king."[441] It is interesting that Quirini was in no doubt that Charles had converted to Catholicism. Although well treated by the Spanish, George was denied any meaningful role in Spanish society, and was reduced to gaining what goodwill and promises of help he could for the Royalist cause. Don Luis was generous in his gifts of money, which George seems to have kept for himself. The main sufferer was his wife, who had no idea where he was and what he was doing, and was attempting to subsist on a pittance, all the property having been sold off. She wrote several letters in code to Brussels through various people, but mainly the Abbess Mary Knatchbull. News of George's conversion to Catholicism had not been well received in England, and despite her staunch Protestant credentials she suffered much opprobrium and prejudice as a result.

George's greatest critic was Hyde, who fretted and fumed from Brussels, loosing a barrage of acid letters on him, to which George replied with spirit. To Hyde's accusation that he was looking to his own fortunes and had abandoned any thought of helping the king's cause, George replied with wit: "I had liked to have said, the devil take my Lord Chancellor, but I do say it with all my heart, the Devil take his letter of the 30th Dec., which I received just now as I was making up my packets and thinking to burn it after I saw there was nothing of moment in it, instead thereof I burnt a letter of four sides of paper I had newly finished to you. You must therefore be content with a short and sharp one tasting of the humour I am in."[442]

The uncertain political situation in England had not yet been resolved, and without any progress to report on that front, George was left without any negotiating tools. He also complained that he received no word from the king, and this left him lacking knowledge of the political situation. Finally he took his leave, returning to Brussels with "a thousand pistoles in three perfumed purses"[443] given to him by Don Luis, who promised he stood by to help in any way he could.

Chapter 16.

Restoration.

At last events in England were moving in favour of the king. The downfall of Richard Cromwell, who did not possess his father's talents and had been unable to reconcile the disparate factions of government, had been followed by a period of near-anarchy. The Rump Parliament and the Army officers bickered over army status, finance, constitutional arrangements and the direction of politics, whilst in the country ministers and gentry worried about the threat to religion and the social order posed by the Quakers. In the autumn of 1659, with the army again in control, there were growing refusals to pay taxes. This undermined the state's capacity to borrow and its ability to pay the troops.

The Royalists had identified the commander of the army in Scotland, General Monck, as someone they could look to, although at this time they did not know what his attitude was towards the crisis in the country. He was a professional soldier who had served against the Irish rebels in 1642, then served the king during the Civil War. Unlike the charismatic Lambert, a dashing cavalry officer, he had risen through the infantry, a blunt, hard-working, no-nonsense warrior. He had played a leading part in forcing the Scots to submit in 1650-1, and was made military governor of Scotland in 1654. He managed to retain the loyalty of his troops by a judicious combination of concessions and purges of open dissidents. He also managed to prevent the clamour in England for payment of arrears spreading to Scotland.

It is difficult to know what Monck's intentions were when he finally acted; perhaps he did not know himself. Certainly he was alarmed by the aggressiveness of the army leaders. When he did finally act, he first moved to secure the strongholds of Scotland and disarm his Baptist officers. He then announced to his troops that they were about to march into England to assert "the freedom and rights of three kingdoms from arbitrary and tyrannical usurpations."[444] On December 5, 1659 he entered Berwick with seven thousand men and prepared to face Lambert, who had reacted to this new threat to army supremacy by marching north to meet him. They never confronted each other The rank and file in the army had not been paid for some time and now mutinied, leaving their officers powerless. As Lambert marched through York, heading for Newcastle, news came of similar defections in other parts of the country. By the time Lambert reached Newcastle he had no more than one hundred horse, the remainder of his army melting away.

Monck's own chief political demand was for the restoration of the Rump Parliament. Following mutinies in the Portsmouth garrison and the fleet it was reconvened on December 26, 1659. Monck then commenced a triumphal march down England, crossing the Tweed on January 1, 1660. He made no new demands, and kept his intentions to himself, and certainly he could not afford to declare in favour of the restoration of the king while other sections of the army leadership remained loyal to Parliament. But the Rump Parliament remained divided and impotent. Any resistance to Monck's march crumbled away as he proceeded. Spontaneously the people of England expressed their disillusionment with the old regime.

Monck finally entered London on February 2, 1660. On February 6 he met Parliament, repledging his complete loyalty to the House and stating "that he would live and die in their service"[445] He used the occasion to warn the House against Royalists and fanatics, and urged fresh elections in order that the pressing issues before Parliament could be accelerated.[446]

Parliament attempted to pit him against the city of London, but was in such disarray that he easily defeated their attempts and secured the backing he needed. Only then did he urge admission of secluded members as a way of breaking the deadlock. Under his protection they were admitted on February 21.

Despite overtures from Royalists Monck refused to speak to the king, and the party waiting anxiously in Brussels was no wiser as to his ultimate intentions. However George's wife, now back in England, appears to have played a significant part as a go-between. On March 23 she reported via Slingsby to Hyde that a Junto of Presbyterians of the Council of State and others had resolved to engage the King with their propositions before the new Parliament met. This group included Anne Digby's brother, the Duke of Bedford, as well as the Duke of Manchester, Pierpoint, Popham, Waller and St John. No doubt the line of communication was through Anne's brother. Monck was reported to abhor the impudence of the Presbyterian proposals, but, she added, "...the King may openly send a messenger to Monck and should set out a plausible declaration, for the people are on his side."[447] On March 30 Anne wrote to Hyde that the king should be prepared for whatever may happen.[448] On April 6 she wrote again to Hyde, telling him that a member of the Rump Parliament had told her that, during their sitting, overtures were made to them for a treaty with the king; he would not name the agents but said they desired the Rump to insist on the banishment of some of those at present with the king.[449] Then on April 11 Slingsby wrote to Hyde: "Lady Bristol says the Presbyterians are dissatisfied; they foment divisions underhand...Monck by an express from Scotland is told the Scottish nation will submit to the King without capitulations...She says that Browne expresses great zeal to the King's service, reproaches the Presbyterians with imposing conditions on the King, and says the City will turn the scales."[450] Finally on April 27 Anne wrote to Hyde that during proceedings in Parliament on April 25 and 26: "The General persuaded some lords, in particular Oxford, to forbear sitting for three days; it might have been better if others had forborne. In both Houses there are guilty persons who endeavour to impose conditions on their King." She feared "the subtle party may overreach the honest party in both Houses" and looked for "no good except what is inspired by Monck." "But," she warned, "the King should not neglect any aid that is offered to him; it is good to treat with a sword drawn."[451]

As the mood of the country became apparent, Monck was persuaded to receive the king's emissary, Sir John Grenville. Still fearful of opposing factions and cautious to a fault, Monck indicated that if the king were to write an appropriate letter to him he would deliver it to Parliament. He added that he was concerned for the king's safety, and advised him to move out of Brussels so that he was out of the reach of the Spanish. This would also indicate to the English people that Charles was no longer allied to the hated Spanish.

On March 21 Charles secretly left Brussels in the middle of the night for Breda in order to place himself out of the reach of the Spanish. At Breda on April 4 he wrote his reply to Monck, the famous Declaration of Breda, promising tolerance and security of tenure to "all good men" and offering Monck the position of Captain-General of his forces. On May 1 Monck entered the House and announced that a servant of the king, Sir John Grenville, had brought him a letter from the king which he had not presumed to open without approval of the House, and was waiting outside. The time was ripe for the resoration of the monarchy. New elections in April had resulted in what was to be called the Convention Parliament. On May 5 both Houses declared that the government of England properly consisted of king, Lords and Commons, and voted to invite the king to return and rule them, granting him £50,000 immediately for his expenses. The country rejoiced.

On May 29, 1660, his thirtieth birthday, King Charles II entered London over London Bridge in a grand procession which was cheered by the huge crowd which had turned out. Hyde accompanied the king, although there were some who advised the king to leave him in Holland. Hyde was said to be "very much in the Prejudice of the Presbyterian Party,"[452] and the king was advised that it would be wise not to have him too close in the early days of his reign in England. Nevertheless Charles appointed him officially as Chancellor and the king's closest confidant. This made him the most powerful man in the land after the king, and the most influential in making appointments. The Chancellorship brought with it the Speakership of the House of Lords. The new king advised petitioners to apply to Hyde rather than other ministers. At court he was constantly seen to be advising the king privately, and increasingly took the stance of a faintly disapproving but avuncular elder statesman. This was to make him extremely unpopular in the country.

George did not accompany the king but moved to Paris, anxious to see how affairs developed in England before returning. After all that had occurred, he was still popular in Paris and obviously enjoyed his stay there, for he was reluctant to leave. He took up the position of Chancellor to Henrietta Maria. But affairs were proceeding apace in England, and if he was to secure himself a prestigious position in the new regime he needed to be back in his homeland. His long-suffering wife had already made a plea to Hyde that George not be forgotten, and that he help her secure for her husband the post which she recommended (this is unspecified in the correspondence).[453] George also wrote to Hyde seeking his support, but by now Hyde was Lord Chancellor and in a position to spurn the courtier of whom he was so critical. The first investiture ceremony of the Garter under Charles II took place at Windsor. Several of his staunchest supporters, who in exile had been granted the garter, had never formally received it. These included James, Duke of York, Prince Rupert, and George. At the ceremony George's investiture was received by Sir Richard Fanshawe.

By July 1660 George was back in England, sitting in the House of Lords. He was too late to pick up any of the plum offices awarded to the king's supporters, and whilst it would have been surprising in the circumstances for him to be favoured, he was nevertheless indignant. In an attempt to win back recognition and status, on August 31, despite the parlous state of his finances, George provided a huge feast for the king and his dukes.[454] The king, whilst not recognising George to a formal position, was nevertheless delighted to have him as a confidant, and continued to encourage him to meddle in affairs as he chose.[455]

Hyde's position had been considerably compromised by the actions of his daughter, Anne, who had been seduced by the king's brother, James. When she found herself pregnant, without consultation and in secret she married the Duke of York on September 3, 1660. James then denied that he was the father of the child and attempted to have the marriage annulled on the grounds that it was not legal, but it turned out that the ceremony had been carried out by the duke's chaplain in the presence of witnesses. The child was born on October 22 but subsequently died. Hyde was furious at the match, threatening to have the unfortunate girl sent to the Tower. He fully realised the potential harm it could do his position, which immediately became apparent when he was accused of attempting to make his daughter Queen of England. The king, although annoyed at the liaison, refused to grant the annulment. To show that he did not hold Hyde responsible for the mess, he insisted that he accept a peerage and a grant of £20,000. He was subsequently made the Earl of Clarendon. Anne was ultimately accepted back in court.

The bad blood which had existed between Clarendon and George in exile now took on a more tangible form. Clarendon showed no sign of helping his long-time friend, but launched a bitter and insulting attack on George's character. He wrote: "He [George] was in his nature very covetous and ready to embrace all ways that were offered to get money, whether honourable or no, for he had not a great power over himself and could not bear want which he could hardly avoid, for he was nothing provident in his expenses."[456] Clarendon used his new authority as Chancellor of Oxford University to dismiss George from its stewardship. Coming as this did after his lack of success in gaining high office, George blamed Clarendon for his misfortune, and the rift between the two became irreconcilable, a rift which was ultimately to destroy the careers of both of them. In August he petitioned the Court for the return of a post he had held under Charles 1, that of Surveyor of the Race at Tilbury, but even this minor position was denied him.

One of the Royal palaces, Theobald's Park, had been occupied during the 1650's by Baptists led by Major William Packer, and had been allowed to fall into disrepair. In September 1660 Anne petitioned for a lease on Theobald's Park as "the walls and tenements are so much out of repair that it is not likely to be again used for pleasure." She argued that she had previously given up her jointure to raise £30,000 imposed by the "rebels" for the redemption of confiscated estates at Sherborne. These estates had been settled on her eldest son, John, on his marriage to Alice Bourne. She added that her husband, "having lost all in his Majesty's service, was unable to settle anything on her."[457] Her request was refused, and the house granted to Monck and his heirs in 1661.[458]

George was certainly penniless in his own right, and in recognition of their past association the king awarded him £19,000, with which he immediately bought Wimbledon House, a prestigious manor house South-west of London, from Henrietta Maria. The dowager queen had been granted the manor by her husband in 1638, shortly before the Civil

War, as a haven of peace to which they could both retire from London as the pressures and troubles built. On her departure to France she had lost the ownership to Adam Baynes and Lambert, but it had reverted to her in 1660. As a token of his appreciation George sent Henrietta Maria a "table diamond" worth £500.[459] George and his wife entertained lavishly at Wimbledon House and, with the help of John Evelyn, set about redesigning the extensive gardens which had been originally laid out by the famous gardener to Charles I, John Tradescant. George described it to his brother as "the lovely solitudes of that place which exceede almost any place seene, being but five miles from the City."[460] Grottoes, fountains and statuary were added. Predictably, Clarendon criticised George for his extravagant gambling and for the money he spent on refurbishing Wimbledon House, "as much money …in building and gardening as the land is worth," although it is not clear where this money came from. George also received from the king land in Ashdown Forest and in Sussex.[461]

George's preoccupation with his new house did not prevent him from getting into trouble, however. Old enmities with the house of Buckingham surfaced. An argument with the Duke of Buckingham which would have led to a duel was stopped by the king who issued a strict ban on duels. George was consequently sacked from his post as Chamberlain to the queen.

George appears not to have enjoyed any income except £200 per annum from lettings at Sherborne, which estate was only valued at £600; plus Wimbledon which yielded £300 per annum "over and above the necessary charges of keeping the place in repaire." It was purchased for £11,000 "which his Mty was pleased to give him (with his Highness the Duke of Yorke's consent) out of the Henningham Estate. And it is all that the Countesse of Bristol his wife hath in joynture....And this being the sayd Earle's whole Estate, hee is out of it to make his family subsist, and to provide for his Daughter Anne, and for his Sonne Francis alsoe, untill such times as hee shall come to enjoy Sir Robert Long's place, which His Maty hath been graciously pleased to grant him under the great Seale in next in reversion. Out this poore revenue hee doth alsoe pay unto his Daughter Diana twoe hundred pounds a yeare, and Interest for three thousand pounds debt."[462]

George petitioned the king at some length in order to alleviate his financial woes. His claim fell under three headings: the first, recovery of money provided to Charles I during the Civil Wars by his father, which he valued at £10,000 plus accrued interest for the years he had been in exile; the second a pension which he argued was due for his many years of service to the Crown, valued at £2,000 per annum; and thirdly expenses incurred while he was Secretary of State in exile which he calculated at £8,125.[463] He also argued that he had not taken from the king £2,000 per annum rent upon the Court of Wards and Wardship of the Brookes estates, due since 1648. He argued that if he had received this it would have made him well off! It was soon apparent that, with the king assailed on all sides by petitioners seeking to restore their fortunes under his reign, it would be some time before George's petition would be addressed. He did not receive his full claim, but was granted a pension of £2,500 per annum.[464]

The position George most coveted, a seat on the king's council, was still closed to him, and he needed to find a role for himself. The country was undecided at this time on the question of which was the better ally to encourage, France or Spain. France was increasingly the dominant European power and an alliance with that country, which had so many connections with England, particularly through the Royal family, would be advantageous. But Charles could not forget the cold treatment he had received from Mazarin during his exile. In addition, there was a fear that this large, strong neighbour could be as much trouble as of assistance. Many favoured the Spanish, weaker and less aggressive than formerly, more conservative, less strident in their demands than the French. George, with his background and connections, was well placed to take advantage of any leaning towards that country, so he took the lead in the pro-Spanish party in the House.

Part of the deal struck between the king and Monck involved measures to be taken against opponents in the Civil War. Monck insisted that they be pardoned, with the exception of the regicides who had signed Charles I's death warrant. A proposed Act of Indemnity and Oblivion was presented to the Commons, who immediately set about lengthening the list of those exempt from pardon. As time dragged on, the new king had to apply considerable pressure before the Bill was passed up to the House of Lords. There it was delayed further by objections and detailed amendments, until George, back in his seat, made a brilliant speech which persuaded the peers to pass it back to the Commons with only minor changes. Of the forty-one living regicides identified, twelve were executed, the king staying the sentence on the others as he was "weary of hanging." An indication of the extent to which public opinion had switched to the king was exhibited when the corpses of Oliver Cromwell and Henry Ireton were exhumed and publicly hanged at Tyburn, with Cromwell's head publicly displayed on a post at Westminster. The date was January 30, 1661, exactly 12 years after the execution of Charles I, deliberately chosen to influence public opinion by showing what would happen to rebels and regicides.

The newly elected Cavalier Parliament sat for the first time on May 8, 1661, and immediately fell into old ways. Although Parliament had initially voted generous sums to the upkeep of the Court, it was not long before the old divisions appeared and members of the Commons started questioning the position of the king and resisting the voting of any further funds. The annual deficit was running at over a third of the total revenues, and the government was forced to borrow from City bankers. Corruption among petty officials was rife. Much of the religious tolerance shown by the king on his accession, and the pledges set out in the declaration of Breda, were rolled back by what came to be known as the Clarendon Code, after its architect. This was a series of measures addressing matters of state and church, aimed at tightening the screw against non-conformists. Clarendon was a staunch supporter of the Anglican Church, and he used his office to introduce measures which recognised the pre-eminence of the Anglican Church and barred from the Church's ministry and from the magistracy and state employment anyone who refused to take the sacrament according to the rites of the Church of England. It was as though nothing had changed since the reign of Elizabeth I. Clarendon, though widely regarded as friendly to Protestant non-conformists, regarded Catholics with suspicion and distaste, and attempted to block their advancement. The fact that the Catholics themselves were not united, split between secular and clergy, did not help their cause. In response, when Clarendon proposed a new prayer book, George opposed its introduction. Rather than answer Clarendon's strictures directly and in public, George complained to the king about the Chancellor's behaviour. Charles sharply told George that he "knew the Earl of Clarendon's virtues better than Bristol" and insisted upon a reconciliation between the two. It was not destined to last.[465]

It was not surprising that one of the main preoccupations of the new court was to find Charles a suitable wife, and this was much discussed. Mazarin offered Charles his niece Hortense together with a huge dowry, but the Cardinal's unfriendliness at St Jean de Luz was well remembered, and the king rejected her. Clarendon still favoured forming some liaison with the French, and when King Louis XIV suggested Catherine de Braganza of Portugal he supported this proposal. The Portuguese offered him three hundred thousand pounds in sterling, the port of Tangier, the island of Bombay and free trade with Brazil.[466] The Spanish ambassador took an aggressive line against this, insinuating that the Portuguese princess was underdeveloped sexually, and incapable of bearing children. As an alternative he offered to match the dowry promised by the Portuguese if Charles would consider a Spanish bride. George, although not admitted to court officially, spent a considerable amount of time with the king. Hyde wrote: "He had an excellent Talent in spreading the Leaf Gold very thin, that it might look much more than it was: and took Pains by being always in his Presence, and often whispered in his Ear....to have it believed that He was more than ordinarily acceptable to his Majesty. And the King, not wary enough against those Invasions, did communicate more to him of the Treaty with Portugal, than He had done to any other Person, except those who were immediately trusted in it."[467] George took the Spanish side, and derived great pleasure from opposing Clarendon. He advised the king that Portugal was poor, and would be unable to pay its portion, and that an alliance would provoke an attack on it by Spain, who would overrun it within a year.[468] His suggestion was the Princess of Parma, reported to be beautiful, witty and intelligent. Soon George was packing his bags for Italy to open negotiations, and telling Clarendon gleefully that the Portuguese match was off.

Furious, Clarendon enlisted the help of Ormond, and after prolonged argument with the king managed to persuade him that George's mission was ill-advised, and Catherine de Braganza was a much better choice. Clarendon pointed out how far negotiations with the Portuguese had proceeded, and therefore how deeply the king was already committed. If he reneged on the treaty now "...He would so far expose his Honour to Reproach, that all Princes would be afraid of entering into any Treaty with him."[469] The king of France, seeing considerable advantage in the avoidance of an English liaison with Spain, indicated he was in favour, and was supported in his opinion by Henrietta Maria, now back in

England. The die was cast. Kenelm Digby was sent hurrying after George to recall him.

In March 1661 George passed through Brussels, ignorant of the change of plans, and spent three days in Parma in April. There he learnt of his recall and travelled to Genoa, where he urgently sought a ship to take him home. He had not given up hope of matching the Princess of Parma with Charles, although he privately confessed he did not find her beautiful.[470] It was reported to Hyde that "Bristol said the elder Princess of Parma was very ugly and the younger monstrously big.."[471] The dowry offered was five hundred thousand gold crowns, only a quarter of that offered by Portugal, and included the proviso that England return Jamaica and Dunkirk to the Spanish. Little of this was known publicly, for it was reported at the time that it was thought England would break with Spain, "…and the Earl of Bristoll, who was going Embassador to the King of Spaigne, beeing passed over to Ostend, was recalled by his Majesty."[472] Once George reached London, he realised that the decision had been made, and the negotiations with Parma were abandoned.

Although Clarendon had won the argument over the king's wife, it did him no good. Catherine was neither beautiful nor intelligent, and was a Catholic. She was married by proxy to Charles, the faithful Bennet standing in, and landed in England in May 1662. The king was not taken with her appearance- she was said to be "swarthy…with a long nose" and her make-up and clothes in the Portuguese fashion were not to English tastes.[473] However for official consumption he wrote to Clarendon: "…her face is not so exact as to be called a beauty, though her eyes are excellent good, and not anything in her face that in the least can shock one. On the contrary, she has much agreeableness in her looks altogether as ever I saw; and, if I have any skill in physiognomy, which I think I have, she must be as good a woman as ever was born."[474] She in turn was horrified at Charles' open association with Barbara

Palmer, his mistress. Catherine had lived a very secluded life, having been educated in a convent, and was not skilled in the ways of society, which put her at a disadvantage. She was certainly not used to the notion that a husband, if sufficiently eminent, had the right to flaunt his adulterous relationships. When she made her displeasure at the king's mistress known, the king created Barbara Palmer Countess of Castlemaine, and there were angry scenes between him and his wife. Clarendon attempted to mediate, and scolded them both, to no effect. Catherine was not well received in England, and the king never showed her any affection.

With the feud between George and Clarendon intensifying, George approached Barbara Palmer and asked whether the Patent creating her Countess of Castlemaine had been signed. When she said it had not, he warned her that Clarendon would block it by talking to the king, and that if she did not reassert herself the Chancellor would make life difficult for her. She then produced the Patent, signed by the king; it had been sealed in Ireland (where the title resided) to bypass Clarendon, whom she said had no knowledge of it, and she was already fully empowered to use the title. The king was annoyed by George's interference, and although the new Countess saw that George was trying to use her in his battle against Clarendon, she was no friend of the Chancellor and, content with having had her jest, she willingly entered into an alliance with George to ruin Clarendon.[475]

The profligacy of the new court ensured that the coffers remained empty, and funds were desperately needed. Kenelm Digby hatched a scheme whereby sympathisers would raise a £100,000 loan for the king that "would produce 30,000*l* a year at least" but, although Charles showed vague interest and promised to consider the idea, Kenelm became "weary of waiting for the fulfilment of the king's written promise."[476] Clarendon proposed that to raise funds Dunkirk should be sold. It was costing £321,000 per annum to maintain, was not easily defensible and had questionable value as an aid to trade. The natural acquiror was France, and after hard bargaining lasting five months the sale was agreed for five million livres in October 1662. This deal was very unpopular both with the merchant community, who were sceptical about a French promise to keep Dunkirk clear of privateers, and the general public, who had enjoyed the possession of a Continental territory. There was a sense that a conquest obtained at heavy cost should have been preserved, augmented by a strong antipathy towards the French.[477]

George wasted no opportunity in reporting the unfavourable reaction to the king, and pointed out that this was seen as an act of provocation by Spain. It was actually a good deal, as the possession had not conferred any strategic advantage on England and the cost of maintaining it was considerable. A groundswell of Francophobia arose, causing Clarendon, the architect of the deal, to receive widespread criticism. George, enjoying the Chancellor's discomfort, took every opportunity to point out Clarendon's mistakes. When Clarendon subsequently built a vast palace in the fields north of Piccadilly, now known as Clarendon House, he attracted further considerable criticism. It was popularly rumoured that he had financed this costly edifice at the expense of the Exchequer, and the building was dubbed "Dunkirk House."

The stage was set for a battle of wills. The king increasingly used George as his agent in Parliament, preaching toleration. Charles was interested in reaching some sort of rapprochement with Rome, and sent two representatives secretly to the Pope to enquire whether it would be possible to maintain the independence of the Anglican Church while acknowledging the Pope as the head of Christendom. George seized this shift in Royal attitude to further his ambition to champion the English Catholics. He called a meeting of leading Catholics at his house and declared that the time was ripe to seek indulgence for Catholics and non-conformists. Parliament remained opposed to any relaxation or tolerance of Catholics, believing that another Gunpowder Plot was always a strong possibility. Nevertheless George pressed ahead, representing the Catholics. Robartes, who stood for the Presbyterians, and Lord Ashley, Anthony Ashley Cooper, a former MP and member of the Council of State under Cromwell who was a moderate and tolerant Anglican opposed to the Clarendon Code, joined George in suggesting to the king that a formal Declaration of Indulgence be drawn up to implement the promises he had made to his many Catholic friends. To his annoyance this proposal caused disquiet in the House of Lords, which took particular exception to the tolerance offered to Catholics, and to the fact that the Declaration had not been referred to Parliament before being issued. George was thought to have been the architect, but it is unlikely that he would have dared suggest the king issue it on his own authority, and Bennet believed the king to have decided to bypass Parliament. It was known that Clarendon had opposed the declaration strongly in Council but had been defeated by George and Buckingham acting together. The king was reported to be very displeased with Clarendon, and to have considered withdrawing his seals of office.

George knew that the chief obstacle was still the bishops. Indulgence had already been blocked by Archbishop Sheldon and his clerical and lay allies following the passing of the Act of Uniformity, because they believed that indulgence would undermine the bishops' position. There were proposals to reinstate them to the House of Lords, where they would be in a position to block the Declaration, so George suggested their reintroduction be delayed. As he had been one of those pressing for their reinstatement initially, the king was very surprised but could see the sense in what he was saying.[478] However Clarendon accused the king of reneging on his commitment to the bishops, to which Charles replied that it was all George's doing. Clarendon warned him that if it was known that the delay was the doing of the Catholics, any toleration towards them could be forgotten. Faced with this challenge, the king agreed to the Bill proceeding immediately. It was quickly passed by both Houses. Clarendon rose from his sick bed to support it. Sharp words were again exchanged between Clarendon and George as a result, but the bishops were reintroduced to the House of Lords.

Despite the known opposition of the bishops, the Declaration of Indulgence was again advanced. But it was doomed, and Clarendon spoke strongly against it in the Lords. His cause was helped by lack of solidarity among Catholics, and the reluctance of non-conformists to be bracketed with Papists. Catholic gentry were suspicious and afraid of the Jesuits, and had learnt from experience that the best way to prosper in England was to maintain a low profile. They were reluctant to be seen supporting such a risky move. Clarendon made the most of these fears, and when the Declaration failed he followed it quickly with a Bill making it a criminal offence to say the king was a Papist. This proved immensely popular in Parliament: Clarendon's victory was complete.

George had been busy in the property market. The money he had lavished on Wimbledon House had caused raised eyebrows, but not content with this fine country retreat, he used the remains of his £19,000 grant from the king to acquire a town house in Queen Street, Lincoln's Inn, with a fine long gallery and enough space to entertain on a grand scale. His daughter Anne, who inherited much of his brilliance, good looks and wit, but also much of his waywardness, presided as hostess. Indeed, his entertainment was noted for its brilliance. The Countess of Castlemaine and queen mother were among regular attendees and a pro-George set built up around him, including the keeper of the Privy Purse, Sir Henry Bennet, later to become the Earl of Arlington, who was made Secretary of State in October 1662, replacing Edward Nicholas, Clarendon's closest ally.

Clarendon was without any friends at court, and unpopular with Parliament in spite of his success with the anti-Papist legislation, for he reminded them of the conflicts of the past. George was once again in favour. Although still excluded from the king's Council, he was regarded by Charles as a most pleasant and amusing companion, and was consulted on a number of issues. The Venetian ambassador, Vico, reported: "...the earl of Bristol was the king's chief intimate the one to whom he confides his most secret thoughts and interests, and to whom he has referred the most important affairs, and since his return to the throne he has also kept him constantly informed of his plans, as a man of great capacity and prudence, although not yet of very mature age."[479] He was seen as the resident authority on Spain and was referred to on any question relating to that country. He maintained his contacts, and was close friends with the Spanish ambassador. He continued to take an active interest in affairs and spoke frequently in Parliament. When he argued the Catholic case in the Lords, he managed to water down a proposal to exile priests to only the most tactless among the clergy.

Clarendon, in an attempt to regain some ground by ingratiating himself with the king, on March 12 1663 spoke strongly in favour of Royalist Catholics and moderate priests, but this merely lost him the support of the Episcopalians.[480] George attempted to capitalise on the Chancellor's troubles by proposing that two of his friends, Ashley and Robartes, the non-conformists who had supported the Indulgence Bill, be admitted to the king's Council, from which Clarendon was now excluded. Charles was not ready to abandon his Chancellor despite his displeasure, and urged Clarendon and George to reconcile their differences.[481] The two continued to argue heatedly, however, mainly about the Declaration of Indulgence, and when George appeared to be winning the argument Clarendon retired diplomatically to bed with gout.

George would not surrender so easily. He was approached by a member of the Commons, Sir Richard Temple, who felt he could guide the Declaration of Indulgence through Parliament if it were amended. Temple had become prominent by advocating severe treatment for Catholics, and had actually proposed the exclusion of the Duke of York from the succession. He was a most unreliable man with twelve thousand pounds of inherited debts, which he thought could be paid off from the fruits of office.[482] He was someone with whom George would not have cared to associate himself, but he was prepared to try anything to get revenge on Clarendon. He carried a message from Temple to the king suggesting the Declaration be resurrected, but this created such a storm of protest that the king immediately disowned it. Temple, desperate for funds, decided that his best course was to make himself such a nuisance to Parliament that they would buy him off, but this tactic merely enraged Charles. When Parliament demanded to know who the author of this intrigue was, Charles identified Temple. Temple denied his part in it, and absolutely denied that he had sent a message to the king. Inevitably George was blamed. On June 26, 1663 a report on Parliamentary proceedings cited: "Mr Secretary Morris did acquaint the House…that the Earl of Bristol was the person that did deliver the Message from Sir Richard Temple to his Majesty." An answer from George was requested.[483]

On July 1 1663 he was summoned to appear in front of the Commons. A chair was set at the bar of the House for him, but he hardly used it. Strutting backwards and forwards bareheaded, he put on a bravura performance. Temple had denied sending any messages and the king denied having received any. Very well then, he would admit that it had been his advice to Charles that Parliament did not feel antagonistic towards the king or his plans, and that he should not ask them for money but rather advise them to press ahead with making the laws which the country needed. This was obviously where the misunderstanding had arisen. He confirmed that Temple had not sent the message, and took the entire blame upon himself. Desiring their pardon, he claimed that he had acted as he did, not to wrong a fellow member of Parliament, but out of zeal to the king. As for his Catholicism, ... "why, I have been pointed out unto you for an inflamer of His Majesty against his Parliament; for an enemy of the Church of England, and for a dangerous driver-on of the Papistical interest. It is true, Mr Speaker, I am a Catholic of the Church of Rome, but not of the Court of Rome, no negotiator then for Cardinals' caps for His Majesty's subjects and domestics; a true Roman Catholic as to the other world, but a true Englishman as to this; such a one as had we a King inclined to that profession (as on the contrary we have one of the most firm and constant to the Protestant religion that ever sat upon the throne), I would tell him.....that if he meant to be a King, he must be a constant professor and maintainer of the Religion established in his dominions...I do clearly profess that should the Pope himself invade that ecclesiastical right of his, I should as readily draw my sword against him as against the late Usurper."[484] If only his famous cousin, Kenelm, had been so eloquent he may well have avoided many of the misfortunes which he encountered! His skilful affirmation of the king's Protestantism while at the same time suggesting that "if" the king were Catholic he would still have a clear conscience and not be subjugate to the Pope (knowing that the king probably **was** a Catholic) is particularly masterly.

The House absolved George of any wrong-doing, ruling that he had carried himself with all dutifulness to the king, and that Temple had not broken any privilege. The House of Lords censured him, however, vexed that he should have appeared before the Commons without their leave. Seeing the hand of Clarendon in his misfortune, George devised a new plan. The king had always showed interest in astrology, and George drew up his horoscope predicting that he would fall by the hand of his brother. As the Duke of York was married to Clarendon's daughter this was only a little short of accusing the Chancellor of plotting to overthrow the king, but instead of causing the king to distance himself even further from his Chancellor, it put him in some fear of his brother, whom he did not like. George let it be known that he believed Clarendon had attempted, by championing the Portuguese match, to pervert the king through marriage to Catholicism so that it would be invalid and Clarendon's daughter, wife of the Duke of York would later accede to the throne.[485] This was not his belief alone, for on March 11, 1661, the Venetian ambassador to London had reported: (There) "are the private interests of the chancellor, seeing that Bristol, a man of wit and finesse, has gone to Parma....he may ingratiate himself with the future queen to unseat him...He fears and foresees his fall; ...he has now changed his mind and supports the other (the Portuguese princess) to confuse the business and drag it out, not because he wishes either that the king should marry her....but because he would like to see his Majesty wifeless."[486]

George now carried his feud with Clarendon into the House of Lords. In July 1663, in a speech criticising the Lord Chancellor, he implied that Clarendon had committed treasonable acts, and was not fit to occupy the position. The king, having heard reports of George's speech to Parliament, called him to give an account of it. This he did, rereading the speech with great passion and drama. The king reacted badly, calling it "vain, mutinous, seditious and false." In anger and frustration, George turned on the king. Accusing him of unwisely tolerating the Chancellor, he criticised the many excesses of the court, of whom the main perpetrator was the king himself. (Even Clarendon observed "He said many Truths which ought to have been more modestly and decently mentioned."[487]). He told the king that he "knew well the Cause of his withdrawing his Favour from him; that it proceeded only from the Chancellor, who governed him and managed all his Affairs, whilst himself spent his Time only in Pleasures and Debauchery."[488] Moreover, he went on, if he was to fall from grace he would reveal matters which "would trouble his peace and the prosperity of others." The king asked whether he was threatening him, but George deflected the challenge by saying he was accusing Clarendon of high treason, and had the document of impeachment in his pocket. Charles enquired the grounds for the charge, but George replied that he intended to accuse him in Parliament. The king replied: "My Lord, you should have done it without my leave." It was clear from the start that this move by George, out of pique and in high temper, was ill-advised: no peer could impeach another by law.[489]

Nevertheless the next day, July 10, he moved to impeach Clarendon formally on seven grounds. First, that he had made peace with the Dutch on disadvantageous terms, and had been bribed to do so; second, that Dunkirk had been sold on his advice to the detriment of England; third, that he had been given £6,000 for promoting the division of lands in Ireland; fourth, that he had arranged the Portuguese match knowing that the queen was incapable of bearing children; fifth, that by allowing his daughter to marry the Duke of York he was advancing his family's interests; sixth, that he was responsible for breaking off the match with Parma; and seventh, that he had promoted Popery, campaigning for a cardinal's cap for the Duke of Aubigny and replacing Sir Edward Nicholas, a good Protestant Secretary, with Sir Henry Bennet, a Catholic. In his speech to the House, delivered with great passion, he claimed that attempts had been made to intimidate him. "... Your Petitioner further Informe your Lordsps, that when he exhibited the Sayed Articles, he was forced to reserve others of a far higher Natur till a Conjuncture of More Safety, he having bin highly threatened with violence on his Person, In case he should accuse the sayed Earle of some Certaine things... .(Clarendon) hath by many fals and mallicious aspersions, cast upon your Petitioner, soe far prevailed with his maty…to apprehend your Petitioner in his owne house during the dayes of Priviledge of Parliament."

The charge against Clarendon of high treason was heard in the House of Commons. Parliament ordered the judges to consider the charges as detailed previously and report back to them. The judges returned a formal verdict that even if they were true none of the charges amounted to high treason. The king showed his displeasure by telling the House of Lords that he looked upon the charges more as a libel against him than against his Chancellor. Charles was particularly incensed at the attack on his marriage. George had gone too far, and a warrant was issued for his arrest. Orders were sent to all the ports to stop him if he attempted to leave the country. It seems that although he continued to live in his house at Wimbledon and was seen in public, no action was actually taken against him. The problem was that England did not have a police force, and Clarendon was anyway deeply unpopular. So George remained at large. Finally he sent word that he was seriously ill, and petitioned to seek medical treatment in London.

This may have been a "diplomatic" illness. In order to pursue his argument with Clarendon, George made an approach to Parliament to be admitted to his seat, but it was resolved that without the king's sanction he could not be recognised there. The king actually placed sergeants with their maces at all the doors to the House of Lords with instructions to detain him if he should attempt to enter. This caused some grumbling in the Lords, but Charles was determined to impose his will. In April 1664 the Venetian Ambassador noted: "The Earl of Bristol, who is more active than ever against the Chancellor, will afford occasion for close observation, for while he is ostracised by the King, not to say hated and menaced, he is correspondingly backed by secret but powerful support."[490] It was rumoured that the Spanish were involved. In the same month the Earl of Northumberland wrote to the Lords in support of George. His wife also petitioned Parliament, and he himself wrote to the House requesting guidance as he did not know how a member should proceed legally if he was disbarred. This simply served to anger the king even further.

Pepys recorded in his diary that he had been told "That my Lord Digby did send to Lisbon a couple of priests, to search out what they could against the Chancellor concerning the match, as to the point of his knowing before-hand that the Queene was not capable of bearing children, and that something was given her to make her so."[491] Pepys also reported that the King had been heard to say "that he would soon see whether he was King, or Digby."[492] In fact, it is arguable with hindsight that George's attempt to have Clarendon impeached did him a favour in the short term: J.R.Jones claims that "Only Bristol's folly in launching an ill-timed and maliciously inspired attempt at an impeachment in July saved Clarendon from the consequences of mismanagement."[493] There is no evidence that Clarendon plotted against the king; it would have been out of character for him to do so. However in his latter years it is questionable whether he was the most competent of Chancellors, and his pompous, over-bearing attitude must have grated with the young king.

Clarendon wrote that the king was so stunned by George's insolence that he had it in mind to incarcerate him in the Tower. George was banned from court. A report at the time recorded that "....after the recesse the King first issued a warrant to arrest and convey the Earle to the Tower, which he evadinge by hidinge himselfe, prohibitinge any to conceale or harbor him, as letters also to the ports, requiringe he were not suffered to transport himselfe, but if he came to imbarque to seise and secure him, notwithstanding all which he hath escaped us and som intelligence purports that he is gotte to Brussels."[494] George's house at Wimbledon was searched and troopers held his servants at gunpoint to discover where he was. Clarendon records : "He concealed himself in several Places for the Space of near Two Years; sending sometimes Letters and Petitions by his Wife to the King, who would not receive them."[495]

George had not left the country, but simply removed himself from public life. Once he had cooled down he sent his cousin, Kenelm, to offer an apology, saying he would not accuse the Chancellor and would go wherever the king wished. "The King replyed his insolence was too great to be easily pardoned and that his forbearing to charge the Ld. Chancelor he should never account an obligation upon him, and that he had soe little regard of what he did that he was not concerned where he lived."[496] Kenelm then sought help from the queen, who was sympathetic and promised to mediate, but Charles would not hear of it.

In December 1663 George made a rather curious attempt to rehabilitate himself by appearing in an Essex church to declare himself a Protestant. This move seems to have been designed to allow him to take his place in Parliament so that he could continue to accuse Clarendon. In February 1664 the Venetian Ambassador wrote: "….the party of the Earl of Bristol has strengthened itself in order to withstand the excessive authority (of Hyde)…not withstanding that the Earl was disgraced by the King. …No one can stop the Earl's access to Parliament now that he has conformed in religion."[497] Again in January 1664 he was seen at church in Wimbledon[498] and was reported in March to have turned Protestant and was attending church regularly.

On March 15, 1664 George wrote to Secretary Morris from Wimbledon, asking him to impart his version of his misfortunes to the Privy Council. He explained that he had withdrawn into strict retirement "since his excess of zeal for the King's service aroused his displeasure." He had begun a journey to London to make a statement to Parliament when he received a printed copy of the proclamation for his apprehension and news that the minister of the parish of Wimbledon and some of his servants were committed for not causing him to be arrested. He had been resolved to appear before the Council but "was seized with a sudden infirmity and prevented from continuing his journey." He was now in better health, and desired the Council's directions.[499]

On March 19 he sent a petition to the House of Lords alleging that Clarendon had prevented him from prosecuting his case, and complaining of the proclamation against him. He insisted that he had been prevented from presenting serious charges against Clarendon through fear of the Duke of York's guards. He also complained that when Parliament reassembled on March 16 there had been two sergeants at arms at each door to apprehend him if he should attempt to take his seat. That afternoon his houses in Wimbledon and Queen Street, London, were searched. He argued that all these proceedings were contrary to law and the privileges of the House. He claimed that Clarendon should be brought to justice, pleaded that he be allowed to sit in the House, and requested that the House mediate for him with the king.[500]

On March 20 George wrote to the king, begging pardon for his indiscretion. He said that he had information which concerned the King's crown and life and which could be trusted to his ear alone. He went on to imply that if the king would not give him access he would be forced to make it known to Parliament. This seemed to involve Clarendon, for George complained that Clarendon prevented any letter of his from reaching the king because he knew that George had enough evidence to destroy the Chancellor.[501] Observers held their breath: was George about to make yet another come-back?

Chapter 17.

Final Days.

George's four children were still alive. Diana, as we have seen, was unhappily married to the Baron Mol, and his favourite, Anne, the youngest was about to marry. Francis was in the navy, serving with distinction, as we shall see later. The eldest boy, John, was dependent upon the family estate. Sherborne had been redeemed and settled on him, and his mother had arranged an early marriage for him with a rich heiress, Alice, daughter of Robert Bourne of Blackhall, Essex. She died young in 1656, and John married a second heiress, Rachel, daughter of Sir Hubert Windham in Dorset. With her he settled down to a sedate country life. He left no children, and on his death the bulk of his estate passed to his sister Anne. There is a curious story about a bet he took in 1670. "Your neighbour Digby did upon a wager of 50*l* undertake to walk (not to run a step) 5 miles on Newmarket Common in an hour, but he lost it by half a minute, but he had the honour of good company, the King and all his nobles to attend to see him do it stark naked and barefoot."[502]

George's wife, Anne, had lost patience with the delays in her husband's petition for financial relief, and made her own approach. Long-suffering as she was, the latest calamity of George's exclusion from court did not deter her, as a newsletter at the time reported: "The Countess of Bristol is much troubled with her lord's misfortune, but is not distracted."[503] She was much more practical than George, outlining the losses she and her family had suffered after the Civil War. Instead of asking for a grant, she requested farming rights in the parks of Theobalds, a Royal palace no longer used by the king. She offered initially £200 per annum rent,[504] for 41 years. Later, perhaps in an attempt to negotiate, she wrote to say that her attention had been drawn to the value of the property, and a fairer rent would be £500 per annum.[505] When this elicited no response, she petitioned again, arguing that her eldest son John had all his estates confiscated during the Civil War and that neither she nor George had the means to redeem them. She wanted her son John and his heirs to have property but could not see how her family could endow him, so she would offer £400 per annum for the right of John to farm the parks.

George's fall from grace at the Royal court dealt him and his family a heavy blow in relation to any claims he should make and it was evident that the main claim, £10,000 of recompense for his father's losses, would not be forthcoming. This was serious, for George's daughter Anne, was preparing to marry the Earl of Sunderland, a nobleman of substantial wealth but undistinguished ancestry,[506] and the £10,000 had been pledged as her settlement. This misfortune caused the groom to take fright. He left his lodgings, sending her a brief note releasing her from his rights and claims to her without giving a reason and begging that no one ask him why he had acted so. George and his wife, by mortgaging belongings and importuning friends, finally scraped the £10,000 together. There is some doubt as to how long the rift with Sunderland remained, but the couple were finally married on June 10, 1665, and seem to have lived happily together. Letters from Anne to her husband show genuine feeling to exist, and it was popularly considered to be a love match. Princess Anne, formerly Anne Hyde, wrote: "Never was a couple so well matched as she and her good husband," then added: "for she is the greatest jade that ever lived, so he is the subtellest working villain on the face of the earth."[507]

The diarist, John Evelyn, was a friend of the Countess of Sunderland, and visited her home frequently. The family name of the Count was Spencer and the family seat was Althorp.

Evelyn describes the house and gardens in some detail.[508] He also heaped praise on Anne: "And what is above all this, govern'd by a lady, who without any shew of sollicitude, keepes every thing in such admirable order, both within and without, from the garret to the cellar, that I do not believe there is any in this nation, or any other, that exceedes her in such exact order, without ostentation, but substantially greate and noble." His good opinion did not extend to her family however: "I wish from my soul the Lord her husband…was as worthy of her, as by a fatal apostacy and court ambition he has made himself unworthy." In fact the entire Spencer family at this time seems to have been regarded with some disfavour. Anne's son, Charles Spencer, was to become highly regarded however. In 1686 he married Lady Arabella Cavendish, heiress to a huge fortune, and when she died of smallpox in 1698 he lost no time in courting Lady Anne Churchill, the second daughter of the first Duke of Marlborough, who built Blenheim. They were married in January 1700. When the Duke's two sons died before reaching marriageable age, the title devolved to the male heirs of his daughters. The eldest daughter, Harriet, had no sons, and thus Anne's grandson inherited the title, which has remained in the family ever since. Of course, the Marlboroughs' family name was Churchill, and the name Spencer has survived in the Churchill line ever since.

George's youngest son Francis now petitioned the king. As the Digby family had not received the £10,000, he devised a scheme to follow his famous uncle, Kenelm, into privateering. He enquired whether the king could lend him 3 frigates, one of fourth rate, two fifth and a fire ship, "manned victualled and set out from 1st February to 15th May next and that thereafter he be employed in the navy as his Maty shall think fit." He and the king would share the prizes in accord with previous practice.[509] There is no evidence that this request was granted.

Around this time George can be seen trying to curry favour with the king and his brother James, Duke of York. His brother-in-law, Edward Russell, the fourth son of the Earl of Bedford, had married Penelope Hill, the widow of William Brooke. She had three adult daughters of whom the younger two, Frances and Margaret, were heiresses to a substantial fortune in their own right. George offered Penelope, Lady Russell his assistance in introducing them to court circles, and hosted dazzling dinner parties which the king attended, and at which the girls were present. George hoped that the king would be attracted to one of the girls, but Lady Castlemaine got wind of what was happening and insisted on attending these events. This effectively ended any attention the king may pay to the girls. The Duke of York, who had been watching the manoeuvres with some amusement, now took the king's place, paying court to the younger sister, Margaret. She responded positively. Her mother, concerned at the implications of an affair with the Duke, a married man, swiftly found her a socially acceptable husband, Sir John Denham. However the groom was in his fifties and Margaret twenty-three. Her marriage simply increased the Duke of York's fascination in her, and he pursued her everywhere. Within a year of her marriage in May 1665 she was his mistress, and the affair was public knowledge. They were frequently seen in public together, and Denham was said to be intensely jealous. Margaret repaid the man who had introduced her to the court, George Digby, by becoming an enthusiastic advocate of his schemes. Unfortunately this only annoyed the Duke, who did not react kindly to his mistress championing George. James attempted to introduce her to his household as Lady of the Bedchamber but his wife, Anne, strongly resisted this move. Shortly thereafter Margaret died in painful and rather mysterious circumstances. It was rumoured that her husband had put poison in her cup of chocolate, others said the Duchess of York had placed powdered diamonds in the chocolate, but an autopsy showed no trace of poison.[510]

War with Holland now threatened. English merchantmen were harrassed off the cost of Guinea by the Dutch after seizing the fort at Cape Verde. The Dutch and English were vying to dominate world trade on the high seas, and their fleets were well-matched in power and size. Charles still remembered with resentment the poor treatment he had received from the Dutch while in exile, and did not need much persuading to open hostilities. The war started well for the English with a resounding victory off the coast of Lowestoft on June 13, 1665, but excellent Dutch seamanship in smaller, more manoeuvrable ships gradually began to tell as the war continued unabated, culminating in triumph by Admiral De Ruyter in June 1666 in what became known as the Four Days Battle. Eight English ships were sunk and nine captured, with six thousand men killed. The coffers were empty, and further war effort was financially impossible for both sides. The stalemate led to negotiations towards a peace treaty. When these stalled, in June 1667 the Dutch admiral De Witt led a daring raid on the Medway at Chatham, attacking the English fleet at anchorage. The surprise was complete, and the Dutch were able to tow away the English flagship, The Royal Charles, causing panic in London. The peace treaty was speedily completed to England's disadvantage.

George, denied an active role in court, took to the arts. He wrote two plays, "'Tis Better than it Was," and "Worse and Worse," although neither has survived under these titles. They were performed at Davenant's Theatre between 1662 and 1667, and Pepys called the latter "very pleasant." In collaboration with Samuel Tuke he wrote a further play, "The Adventure of Five Hours," which was very popular at the time and which Pepys preferred to Shakespeare's "Othello!" A play which was clearly written by him still exists in print. It is titled "Elvira, or The Worst Not always True." Which of the two plays mentioned above this is cannot be ascertained.

With Lady Castlemaine's assistance, George gradually returned to the king's favour. She persuaded the king to see him in private, but he was not readmitted to court and seems not to have been noticed during his period of disgrace. Finally in July 1667 he slid back into the House of Lords, not wearing his robes and retiring tactfully when the king appeared.

Clarendon's lack of popularity finally told against him. While he was useful and fulfilling an important role in government, Charles could tolerate this, but his stiff, censorious attitude and crusty ideas were at odds with the pleasure-seekers at court. Nor could he look to Parliament for support: the Cavaliers resented him for his legalistic caution and tendency to temporise with the Presbyterians, whose influence was waning. When the Lord Treasurer, his protégé Southampton, died in May 1667 he lost his last powerful ally. Clarendon saw himself as the elder statesman, advising the king on a range of affairs, as he had in exile. But Charles was now his own person and in command. He had tolerated Clarendon's criticism for long enough, and did not enjoy being lectured like a child. With the ground swell of opposition now mounting against his Chancellor, he felt it was time for a change. Clarendon, dragged unwillingly into recriminations over the Dutch war, was afterwards blamed for the debacle, and this proved the final straw. Public feeling finally overwhelmed him, the king withdrew his support and he was dismissed from all offices in disgrace on August 30 1667. Albemarle and James - Clarendon's son-in-law - were sent to demand the surrender of the Chancellor's Great Seal, but he would listen to nobody other than the king, and was finally summoned to court to be dismissed. He was persuaded that England was no longer a safe place for him so, old and ill, he moved to Montpelier in France, there to live out the rest of his life in exile and to write his epic opus, The History of the Rebellion. The man who, perhaps more than anyone else, had remained at the centre of court affairs, loyal and diligent, was in disgrace. Who can blame him for the bitterness which poured from his pen thereafter?

The removal of Clarendon helped George regain the favour of the king. Pepys wrote in November of that year: "The King who not long ago did say of Bristol that he was a man able in three years to get himself a fortune in any kingdom in the world and lose it again inn three months, do now hug him and commend his parts everywhere above all the world."[511] His presence was once again felt in the House of Lords.

The Corporation Act, passed in December 1661, stipulated that anyone refusing the Oath of Allegiance should be barred from military or civil employment. In March 1673, bowing to further public demands that Catholics not be permitted to grow in influence, the king agreed to the introduction of a Test Act stipulating that in addition to taking the Oath of Allegiance all candidates for public office should take the sacraments according to the 39 Articles of the Church of England, and should repudiate the doctrine of transubstantiation. James, Duke of York resigned as Lord Admiral as a direct result. As the Catholics generally refused to swear the Oath, pledging their allegiance instead to the pope, these Acts would test their loyalty to the Crown to the limit. It would have been expected that George, as a converted Catholic, would oppose the Test Act, but he spoke in favour of it. Catholics, he argued, were not prevented from exercising their religion and there were no penal provisions or threats of banishment. He warned the Catholic Members of Parliament that "they ought not to speak as Roman Catholics but as members of a Protestant Parliament." This sensible, mature speech was to be his last in the House of Lords.

Shortly thereafter he retired finally from politics, selling his houses in Wimbledon and St Martin's Lane and settling at Chenies Walk in Chelsea in the house previously owned by Sir Thomas More. This house had been sold to Charles I in 1625 by the Earl of Middlesex, and subsequently given to George Villiers, Duke of Buckingham, Charles I's favourite. George bought it from the second Duke of Buckingham, who was forced to sell the property to pay his debts. He spent £2,000 installing an orangery, a billiards room and an ice house. His remaining house in Queen Street passed into the hands of the Commissioners of Trade and Plantations in 1671.

George's second son and favourite, Francis, had entered the navy. England was again at war with the Dutch, this time with the backing of the French. By May 1673 Francis had risen to command a ship of his own after serving as a lieutenant on the Royal Charles, and had been given the governorship of Deal Castle. In May of that year George was visiting his son at Deal when news came that the Dutch were not far off the coast of East Anglia. George would have loved to have joined the action, but was forced to be content with accompanying him up the coast on his ship, the Royal James. He was put ashore in a pleasure boat at Great Yarmouth, and watched his son set sail to seek out the Dutch, and to engage them. Unfortunately the English fleet, who had joined a French squadron, were surprised while at anchor off Southwold by the Dutch who had not waited for them to come out into the open sea. Crowded together, the English ships found it difficult to fire effectively. The Royal James, having destroyed two fire ships, was set alight, and Francis was killed by a single shot to the breast. He was carried back to his mother's home and buried among the Russells in the family chapel at Chenies.

There is evidence that even in his last years George provoked extreme feelings in others. On April 27, 1676 a court case in Dorsetshire found against him and awarded £1,000 in damages to Lord Shaftesbury "for the scandalous words" he had used about the lord. But his days in the public spotlight were over. By now in poor health, he lived out the rest of his life in retirement at his house in Chenies Walk. He died there peacefully on March 16, 1677 and was buried beside his much-loved son, Francis, in Chenies Chapel. The house was bequeathed to his wife.

Epilogue.

The picture of George Digby which commentators on the seventeenth century have given us is one of a rash, headstrong man who overreached his position in the court and created considerable mischief. He is described as unreliable, impulsive, and the architect of many of the misfortunes which the Royalists suffered before, during and after the Civil Wars. His two sternest critics and opponents were Edward Hyde, Earl of Clarendon, and Prince Rupert. In many ways the picture we have of George is formed in reference to these two important figures. Yet we have seen how they had their failings, and should share the responsibility for errors and failures. George was never a man to shirk confrontation, and his brushes with Clarendon and Rupert led to considerable bitterness, which surfaced in Clarendon's recollections as a resentful old man in exile, and in critics who saw Rupert as an heroic figure, and anyone opposed to him as wrong.

If we examine George's career, a rather different picture emerges to the one presented by his critics. He was hardworking, loyal and assiduous; no one could criticise him for lack of effort. Nor can it be said that, in any of the advice he gave Royalty, or the efforts that he made on their behalf, he acted in any way other than with the intention of serving their cause. A non-military man, he acquitted himself well on the battlefield during the first Civil War and built a considerable reputation among the French and Spanish as a military leader once he was exiled. As a Parliamentary performer he was outstanding. Not only did his persuasive powers sway fellow members on countless occasions, but many of his speeches stand even today as models in the defence of Parliamentary freedom.

The essence of the criticism levelled against him is that he repeatedly gave the king poor advice during the Civil War, betrayed his fellow Parliamentarians over the impeachment of Strafford, and worked at bringing foreign forces to England in defence of the Crown. He has been criticised for pursuing the Civil War to its bitter conclusion at all costs, and rejecting any peace proposals. Hopefully this book has countered at least some of these criticisms. Rupert, although undoubtedly a brave and dashing commander, imperilled the Royalist army on more than one occasion by his rash excursions. As an adviser to King Charles I Rupert does not emerge as a wise and balanced counsellor. In fact, few of those surrounding the king match George in this area, and none stayed with the king from start to finish as George did. Much of the advice given by George, which superficially looks reprehensible, when examined in depth shows a rationale and a logic not previously remarked upon. As we have seen, on several occasions he instigated peace moves, and would have settled if the terms had been right. Too often these moves were thwarted by Parliament, who for their own reasons did not wish to settle with a king who, back in power, would be able to do them considerable harm. Even when George was wrong, one can see the thought processes which led him to the conclusions he drew. This was a man who thought deeply and untiringly about his job.

George's part in the attempted arrest of the five Parliamentarians has led to accusations that he was responsible for starting the Civil War. This is plainly nonsense. King and Parliament had for some time been on a collision course before this incident, with Pym and his followers intent on eroding the king's authority and the king being inflexible in his belief that he had an absolute right to rule. Whatever the rights and wrongs, the country was dangerously close to anarchy at the end of 1641, with mobs besieging Parliament in an attempt to influence their decisions and the king's position seriously threatened. George's advice to the king may have been rash and provocative, but it was not unconsidered. His was the voice in Parliament raising serious concern about the mobs and the inability of Parliament to conduct its business, and the suspicion that the riots had been orchestrated by members of the Commons attempting to prosecute their own aims is not ridiculous. Thus attempts to arrest them, when they themselves were attacking the king's supporters, were not totally mad. Following George's volte face over Strafford, he was reviled by the Commons, and anything the king's followers did to thwart Parliament's aims was automatically placed at the door of George. Undoubtedly he became the whipping-boy. Hyde, who favoured moderation and negotiation, despite its obvious failure in these testing times, was already a critic of George.

King Charles I was notorious for his inconsistency. Time and again he confounded his supporters by changing his mind, and infuriated his adversaries by proving untrustworthy. He was highly susceptible to blandishment, and often took the easy course by conceding favours to his followers unwisely. There is considerable evidence to indicate that the king was his own man, making his own decisions. Many of the decisions which were criticised were his own, often against the advice of his Council. It may therefore be unfair to lay at George's door many of the misjudgements and errors which disadvantaged the Royalists during the Civil War.

His love of intrigue led George into more trouble. He is accused of being the prime mover in the removal of Waller and Percy, and the exile of Rupert after his defeat at Bristol. No doubt he was pleased to see the back of Rupert, but the king steadfastly refuted accusations that he had acted on George's advice in despatching his nephew. The dismissal of Waller and Percy was subsequently seen to have been justified. In fact, much of the correspondence during this period shows George desperately trying to keep the Royalist commanders together, even to the extent of attempting to make peace with Rupert and Goring.

Once George landed in Ireland, he not only found himself involved in difficult and tortuous negotiations, but as usual blamed for anything that went wrong. We have seen how the king gave instructions to Glamorgan which would have resulted in a disastrous treaty with the Irish Catholics. Almost certainly, George and Ormond were kept in total ignorance. George can be seen to be trying everything he can to muster an effective Irish force to rescue the king. His attempts to persuade the Prince of Wales to lead such a force, his appeal to the French for help, his attempt at a deal between the Scots, Irish and French were all done with such an aim in mind. If any of these had succeeded, it is just possible that the king could have been saved and the history of England changed. Both the Scots and the Irish were extremely wary of Parliament, and not disinclined to side with the king if the conditions were right. It is just possible that a United Kingdom could have followed from George's efforts. Above all, he dared to lift his eyes and contemplate the ambitious, the almost unthinkable, when other courtiers accepted defeat. Most notably, Hyde can be seen to adopt a cautious and conservative stance that was of no help to the king, while Rupert was quick – perhaps too quick – to believe that the Royalists should sue for peace on disadvantageous terms.

In his personal life George was less than perfect by today's standards and he can be criticised in particular for the way he treated his long-suffering wife. However he should be seen in the context of the times when such behaviour was the norm. He was not faithful to her, and too often left her to defend the family estate in England without any support or resources from him. But he was regarded as Public Enemy Number One in England by the Parliamentarians, which made it difficult for him to achieve anything in his home country. It seems in this regard that George was too often the scapegoat for the misfortunes that beset the king, and the problems encountered by Parliament. Yet it will be seen that from 1640 onwards

Parliament was determined upon a collision course with the king, and Pym in particular would brook no deterrence in his objective of bringing the monarch to heel.

Whatever one's opinion of George may be finally, there can be little doubt that he did have considerable influence upon the momentous affairs of the seventeenth century. Yes, in the light of his prodigious talents and ability, he did underachieve. By his actions, often rash and impulsive, he alienated Parliament and ensured he would be excluded from the forum where he could have exercised most influence, for much of his life. When he was present, what he was able to achieve in the Commons and Lords through his intellect and powers of oratory provide a tantalising glimpse of what would have been possible had he exercised more moderation and pragmatism. Despite his occasional duplicity and actions of self-interest, his aim was to further the interests of the reigning monarch as well as his own. It is tempting to speculate what the consequences would have been had his ideas and proposals been listened to more often.

Even his bitterest critic, Hyde, writing after he had been exiled, could not help admitting George's merits: "It is a pity that his whole life should not be exactly and carefully written, and it would be as much pity that any body else should do it but himself…and make the truest description of all his faculties, and passions, and appetites, and the full operation of them; and he would do it with as much ingenuity and integrity as any man would do, and expose himself as much to the censure and reproach of other men, as the malice of his greatest enemy could do; for in truth he does believe many of those particular actions which severe and rigid men do look upon as disfigurings of the other beautiful part of his life, to be great lustre and ornament to it…to believe that a very ill thing subtilly and warily designed, and well and bravely executed, is much worthier of a great spirit, than a faint acquiescence…..
and yet if any man concludes from hence that he is of a fierce

and impetuous disposition, and prepared to undertake the worst enterprise, he will find cause enough to believe himself mistaken, and that he hath a softness and tenderness enough about him to restrain him, not only from ill, but even from unkind and ill-natured actions."[512]

It is interesting that many authorative books on the Civil Wars and the monarchies of the first half of the seventeenth century make only passing reference to George Digby. Love him or loathe him, George Digby was undeniably a major figure in seventeenth-century England. That he did not receive more favourable recognition, or be regarded as an influential figure of that time, owes much to the adverse comment of his contemporaries who were also his enemies. It is hoped that this biography has gone at least part of the way towards providing a more balanced view of him.

Appendix.

Evidence of social pleasures is shown by a curious incident during George's journey through the Pyrenees in October 1659 with Charles before they reached Furtenarabia. Staying overnight in a small village where there was a religious order, their curiosity was attracted by a girl's voice singing beautifully in the mountains. George wrote a poem of the occasion, which describes the event better than prose:[513]

> "Downe from those Extended Mountaines
> Whose Threatnenge prints of frozen Snowe
> Give terror to the Fires Above
> And Bounds, for Empires here belowe.
>
> In disguize a Kinge descended
> Believinge such a Southern Course
> His readiest way to Northern Crownes.
> By a Romantick Count Attended
> The Station on Iberian Soyle
> Where first these Weary Adventurers
> Almost quite spent with heate and Toil
> Succor and refreshment found.
>
> Hiacea was of Olde a Court
> To Kings of the Abarea'es Race
> But now (god Will) a sorry Place
> To veile a mighty Monarck Pleasure.
>
> After a Savorye Repast
> They both walkt out, to see a Towne
> Where Rocks, Seemed into houses growne
> To entertaine so greate a Guest.

The Structure of an Ancient Portick
Invitinge them to Stopp a while
There eares were on the Sudderne Ravisht
With Accounts of a Voice Angelick.

Both quick of Sense, but not Content
With Musick of a Second hand,
Gently unto the Temple Went
Whence eccoes of divine were sent.
But to their Cost, they quickly found
Charmes to the Eye transformed in Flames,
Farr more dangerous than those
Conveyed before to the Eare, in Sound.

Dona Teresa Abarea, was,
The Vestal maide, Enchantinge, All
With heavenly Notes, But with a face
In more Excess, Angelicall.
The Amorouse Count struck to the heart
Now Leanes against the Grate, & Gates
Whilest the Soveraigne Acts his part
Keepinge a respectfull distance

The Gallant now accosts the Dame
And findes monge Skraggy Mountaines borne
More brightnesse than ere Shined in Court
More Sweetnesse then ere Nimph Adorned.
Hee now beginns to think the fire
That burnes in's brest, a Pleasant Thinge,
And with many a broken Sigh
He Fanns and raises it still highere.

Shee farr above Cry Affectation,
And not unverst in Gallantrye
With soft replyes and Gentler Lookes
Flatters Artfully his Passion.

He more and more Inflamed, and growne
Bolder by those sparks of favour
Curses th' Intermedlinge Grate
That keepes him from more Solid Ones.

And beggs against his next returne
Love may Soe good Orders Settle
That twixt devotes, their may be found
Admission free not barrs of Metall
Wast not Strange that such a Lover
In full Current of his Passion
Should reflect on Separation
From a beauty Soe Propitiouse.

But duty and honor then conjoined
A suddaine disengagement prest.
And though his heart were broke asunder
Whilst with Love they both Contest,
Hee must away and now those Eyes
Were meetinge, Seemed the Spheare of fire
Mutual Conflagration dartinge
Fountaines growe of teares at Paretinge.

Soe wee have Seene a Summers Sunn
Surprizingly producinge Showers
By Excesse of former heate,
Water and Enamell Flowers.
At takinge Leave a kisse of Hand
Was not denyed by griefe. And soe
His Soule all Flowinge to his Lipps
Hee seemed Expired, In Driven Snowe.
Struck with such Prodigiouse whitenesse,
The Clowded Monarck stood Intranc'd.
Imagine then a Subjects Pleasure
By Envye of a Kinge Enhanc'd.

Reference Sources.

British Library:

Additional Manuscripts (Add. Ms).
Bedford Manuscripts: Fourth Earl's Miscellaneous Papers.
Braye Manuscripts.
Calendar of State Papers – Domestic (CSPD):
Calendar of State Papers – Venetian (CPSV):
Carte Manuscripts.
Carte: Collection of Original Letters.
Catalogue of Royal and Noble Authors.
Clarendon State Papers
Commons Journal (CJ).
Egerton Manuscripts.
Firth Manuscripts.
Hamilton Manuscripts.
Harleian Manuscripts.
Historical Manuscripts Collection (HMC): Finch
De Lisle and Dudley.
Fox Ormond
VII Report.
10th Edition.
Portland Manuscripts.
Bath.
Lismore Papers.
Lord Digby's Cabinet Opened.
Mercurius Politicus.
Nicholas Papers.
Reliquiae Baxterianae.
Rushworth Historical Collection

Sumner, Ann: The Political Career of Lord George Digby (Doctoral Thesis, Cambridge University, 1985).
Thomason Tracts (TT).
Thurloe State Papers.
Verney Papers.
Victorian County History (VCH).

Bodleian Library:
Clarendon Manuscripts.

Leeds University:
Brotherton Collection.

Sherborne Castle Archives.

Dorset Record Office:
Digby Papers.

Yale University (Beinicke Library):
Osborne Manuscripts.

University of Minnesota Library:
Parliamentary Diary of Sir Thomas Peyton.

Institute of Historical Research:
Camden Miscellany: A Secret Negotiation with Charles I.
Royal Ordinance Papers.
Letters of Charles the First to Henrietta Maria; ed. J. Bruce.

Public Record Office (PRO):
Digby Transcripts (SP31/8/198).

Victoria and Albert Museum
Forster Collection.

Bibliography.

- Ashley, Maurice: Rupert of the Rhine. UK.PBS 1976.
- Ashton, Robert: English Civil War. Weidenfeld 1978.
- Aubrey, John: Brief Lives. Cresset Press 1944.
- Aylmer Gerald E.: Rebellion and Revolution. OUP 1986.
- Barbour, Violet: Henry Bennet, Earl of Arlington. OUP 1915.
- Birkenhead, Earl of: Strafford. Hutchinson 1938.
- Bruce, J. (ed.): Charles I in 1646. Camden Soc. 1855.
- Bryant, Arthur : King Charles II. Longmans 1931.
- Carte, Thomas: Life of James, Duke of Ormond. Oxford 1851.
- Carlton, Charles: Charles I – The Personal Monarch. Routledge 1983/95.
- Chapman, Hester W.: The Tragedy of Charles II J. Cape 1964.
- Clarendon, Earl of: Four Portraits. Clarendon 1989.
- Clarendon, Earl of: History of the Rebellion. Clarendon 1888.
- Clarendon, Earl of: Life. Clarendon 1661.
- Clark, Sir George: The Later Stuarts. Clarendon 1934.
- Clarke, J.S.: The Life of James II. 1816.
- Day, W. Editor of the Pythouse Papers London 1879.

- Digby, H.M. Kenelm Digby and George Digby: Digby, Long & Co 1912.
- Edwards, Peter: Dealing in Death. Sutton 2000.
- Evelyn, John: Diary, edited by William Bray. Warne 1818.
- Fletcher, Anthony: The Outbreak of the Civil War. Edward Arnold 1981.
- Gardiner, S.R.: History of the Great Civil War. 1893.
- Green, M.A.E.: Letters of Henrietta Maria. London 1857.
- Gregg: Charles I. London 1981.
- Gumble, T: Life of General Monck, Duke of Albemarle. London 1761.
- Hibbert, Christopher: Cavaliers and Roundheads: BCA 1993.
- Hirst, Derek: Authority and Conflict: England 1603-1658. OUP 1986.
- Hutton, Ronald: Charles the Second. Clarendon 1989.
- Hutton, Ronald: The Restoration. Oxford Press 1985.
- Jarrold, Clare: The Fair Ladies of Hampden Court. J. Long 1911.
- Kishlansky, Mark: A Monarchy Transformed. Cambridge
- Kitson, Frank: Prince Rupert. Constable 1998.
- Longueville, Thomas: The Life of Sir Kenelm Digby.......Longmans 1896.
- Manning, Brian: The English People & the English Revolution. Penguin 1976.

- Morrah, Patrick: Prince Rupert of the Rhine. Constable 1976.
- Nicholas, Donald: Mr Secretary Nicholas. Bodley Head 1955.
- Ollard, Richard: Clarendon and his Friends. Atheneum 1988.
- Oman, Carola: Henrietta Maria. London 1936.
- Palmer, J.: CharlesII: Portrait of an Age. 1979.
- Pepys, Samuel: Diaries.
- Petrie, Sir Charles: Letters of King Charles I. Cassell 1935.
- Rogers, H.C.B.: Battles & Generals of the Civil War. 1968.
- Russell, Conrad The Fall of the British Monarchies 1637-1642. OUP 1991.
- Scott, Eva : The King in Exile. Constable 1904.
- Scott, Eva: Travels of the King. London 1907.
- Stone, Lawrence: Crisis of the Aristocracy. London 1965.
- Symonds, Richard: Diary of the Marches of the Royal Army. CUP 1998.
- Townshend, Dorothea: George Digby, 2nd Earl of Bristol. Fisher Unwin 1924.
- Trevelyan, Charles: England Under the Stuarts. London 1946.
- Walker, E: Historical Discourses. London 1705.
- Warburton, Eliot: Memoirs of Prince Rupert. Richard Bentley 1849.
- Warner, G.F.: Edited: The Nicholas Papers. Camden Society 1886.
- Warwick, Sir P. Memoirs of the Reign of K.C.I. Ballantyne 1813.

- Wedgwood, C.V.: The King's Peace. Collins 1955.
- Wedgwood, C.V.: The King's War. Collins 1958.
- Whitcombe, D.T.: Charles II & the Cavalier House of Commons. MUP. 1966.
- Wilson, Derek: The King and the Gentlemen. Hutchison 1999.
- Wood, Anthony: History and Antiquities of Oxford. Oxford 1792.

Notes.

1. Catalogue of Royal and Noble Authors iii P191-2.
2. P. Morrah: Rupert of the Rhine, P101.
3. The King and the Gentleman, Derek Wilson: P338.
4. CSPV 1640-2 P184.
5. Longueville P82.
6. Letters of King Charles I P34.
7. Petition of George Digby to the House of Commons from Articles dated May 1, 1626. HMC Finch Vol. 1 P51.
8. A True Relation of the Unfortunate and Untimely Deaths… pamphlet in Sherborne Castle Archives.
9. Ibid.
10. Sherborne Castle Archives E136/8.
11. Egerton MS 2978 f.18.
12. Dr R. Darwall-Smith, Fellow of Magdalene College, Oxford.
13. Clarendon State Papers III Supplement P51.
14. Mark Kishlansky: A Monarchy Transformed pp34-40.
15. CSPD 1634-5 P81.
16. Ibid P129.
17. Memoirs of the House of Russell P127.
18. Egerton MS 2646 f.21.
19. Letters concerning Religion P118.
20. England under the Stuarts; Trevelyan P186.
21. The King's Peace; Wedgwood P265.
22. Northumberland to Leicester: HMC De Lisle & Dudley VI P201.
23. CSPD 1638-9 P637.
24. Birkenhead: Strafford P212.
25. Dorset Record Office D53 P30.
26. Ibid Vol. I ff298 & 302.
27. Add. Ms 6411 f60b.
28. Ibid.
29. Ann Sumner P37.
30. Bedford Mss, Fourth Earl Miscellaneous Papers.
31. Edwards: Dealing in Death P19.

32. CSPD 1640-1 P104-6.
33. Brian Manning: The English People & the English Revolution P13
34. George Digby; Townshend P17.
35. Clarendon's Four Portraits P13.
36. Osborn MSS File B no. 1760; Yale University Beinicke Library.
37. Thomason Tract E196(6).
38. Commons Journal II P25.
39. Ibid.
40. Rushworth IV P146.
41. The Speeches of the Lord Digby in the High Court of Parliament; Brotherton Collectionat Leeds University LT30, pp1-9.
42. Ibid. pp11-25; Jan. 19, 1641.
43. Ibid; also Rushworth III P170 and TT E196 (6).
44. Rushworth Vol. III pp154/5.
45. Townshend P20.
46. Manning P16.
47. The Third Speech of Lord George Digby to the House of Commons (1641); TT E196 (30).
48. Trevelyan P206.
49. Rushworth Part 2 Vol. 2 P1347.
50. Manning P20.
51. Rushworth IV P226.
52. Strafford P274.
53. Add. MS 14, 828 f.7.
54. Lismore Papers Second Series P134.
55. Hamilton MS M9/119.
56. Conrad Russell: The Fall of the British Monarchies P266.
57. Strafford P276 and Appendix A.
58. The Trial of Strafford; Rushworth P541.
59. The Lord Digby's last speech against the Earle of Strafford… TT E198 (1).
60. Diary of Bulstrode Whitelocke P127
61. Conrad Russell P290.
62. The Outbreak of the English Civil War: Fletcher P12.
63. Verney Papers, ed. Bruce P49.

64. The Lord Digby's last speech against the Earle of Strafford, April 21, 1641.TT E198 (1).
65. Ibid.
66. Conrad Russell P290.
67. Mozley Essays P78.
68. Rushworth III Vol. 1 P56.
69. Strafford P317.
70. The King's Peace P386.
71. Fletcher P14.
72. Ibid. P16.
73. Rushworth III Vol. 1 P348.
74. Clarendon State Papers Vol. III Suppl.; Clarendon History Vol. IV P127.
75. CSPV 1640-2 P272.
76. Fletcher P31.
77. Reliquiae Baxterianae P25.
78. The King's Peace P404.
79. Trevelyan P215.
80. CSPV 1640-2 P184.
81. CSPD 1641-3 P81.
82. Parliamentary Diary of Sir Thomas Peyton, University of Minnesota Library .
83. Conrad Russell P220.
84. Diary of John Evelyn IV P121.
85. The King's War P22.
86. Bodleian MS Clarendon Vol. 21 1634 f125.
87. Manning P62.
88. Fletcher P150.
89. Clarendon History Vol.I P451.
90. Ibid. P88.
91. Ibid. P89.
92. CSPD 1641-3 P192.
93. Clarendon History Vol. I P451.
94. Ibid. P455.
95. Fletcher P168.
96. Conrad Russell P439.
97. A Terrible Plot against London and Westminster Discovered; TT E131.
98. Cavaliers and Roundheads: Hill P30.

99. Manning P88.
100. Fletcher P171.
101. The Lord Digbie's Apologie for himself, Oxford January 4, 1643: TT E84 (32) P6.
102. English Civil War: Robert Ashton P146 and Authority and Conflict: Derek Hirst P215.
103. Sumner P114.
104. Gregg: Charles I P342.
105. Aylmer: Rebellion and Revolution P40.
106. Fletcher P172.
107. CSPD 1641-3 P217.
108. Manning P94.
109. Manning P102.
110. Clarendon History IV P155 and G. van Prinsterer Archives III P496.
111. CSPV 1640-2 P285.
112. Clarendon History IV P155.
113. Conrad Russell P406.
114. Mr Secretary Nicholas P154 and Hutton: The Restoration P167.
115. Clarendon P67.
116. Law Journal Vol. IV P501.
117. Manning P106.
118. Trevelyan P221;and History of Eighteenth Century Thought P160.
119. Nicholas Papers edited by G.F.Warner I P62.
120. Egerton MS 2546 f20.
121. Trevelyan P222.
122. Hibbert: Quoted in Cavaliers and Roundheads, P31.
123. Trevelyan P222.
124. Clarendon History IV P155.
125. Manning P110.
126. CSPD 1641-3 Pp241-243.
127. The King's War P61.
128. Clarendon and his Friends P67.
129. Clarendon History IV P125.
130. The King's War P62.
131. The Late Hurliburly at Kingston upon Thames; TT E131.
132. Rushworth P502/3 dated January 26, 1641.

133. Commons Journal II P433 and Sumner P135.
134. Apologie.
135. Commons Journal II P45; State Trials IV P138.
136. HMC 10th Appendix vi P145; Historical Memorials Part 3 I P555.
137. Edwards P197.
138. CSPV 1640-2 P289.
139. Townshend P31.
140. TT E138 (10).
141. CSPD 1642 dated January 21, 1642 P263.
142. Ibid P286: Robert Fox to Pennington.
143. TT E135 (6).
144. State Trials IV P133.
145. Apologie.
146. The King's War P73; Acts and Ordinances I pp1-5.
147. Nicholas Papers P162.
148. HMC Report VII P441.
149. Parliamentary Speech by the Earl of Bristol: Sumner P147.
150. Hull's Managing of the Kingdom's Cause P5 and King's Pamphlets No. 161; London June 18, 1644.
151. TT E154 (26).
152. Sumner P154.
153. Clarendon History V pp432/3.
154. Ibid pp436/7.
155. Clarendon VI pp388-390.
156. Fletcher P329.
157. Sumner P159.
158. TT E116 (48).
159. HMC Vol. 4; Stephen Charlton to Richard Levesen.
160. Braye Mss pp147/8.
161. Warburton Vol. I P368.
162. Morrah P70.
163. Cavaliers and Roundheads P55.
164. Clarendon II P365.
165. Edgehill 1642. The Campaign and the Battle P211/12.
166. History & Antiquities of Oxford: Wood P452.
167. Warburton P140.
168. Prince Rupert Vol. I: Warburton P465/6.
169. The King's War P141.

170. Add. Ms 18980 f6).
171. Ibid.
172. Marlborough Miseries TT E245(8).
173. The King's War P153.
174. Marlborough Miseries P7.
175. Clarendon History VI P158.
176. Royal Ordinance Papers I: Ian Roy P188.
177. Rushworth V P165.
178. Ibid. P266.
179. The King's War P184.
180. Edwards P197.
181. Warburton Vol. II P225.
182. The King's War P247.
183. A True and Impartiall Relation to the Battaile betwixt his Majesties Army…TT E69 (10).
184. Clarendon VII P208.
185. Gardiner War I P214/5.
186. Selections from Clarendon P58.
187. Aubrey's Lives II P245.
188. Selections from Clarendon P60.
189. Clarendon Life I P204.
190. Ibid. P85.
191. Gardiner P246.
192. Warwick Memoirs P279.
193. Royal Ordinance Papers Part 2 P502 n.
194. Gardiner P260.
195. Clarendon's History P190.
196. Collection of Original Letters Vol. I: Carte P46.
197. Add. Ms 18981 f130.
198. Daly: Implications of Royalist Politics P747.
199. A Secret Negotiation with Charles I, Camden Miscellany.
200. Hutton: Structure of the Royalist Party P565.
201. Ormond V pp520/1.
202. Gardiner Vol. I P275.
203. M. Ashley: Rupert of the Rhine.
204. Pythouse Paper, ed. Day: Richmond to Rupert on November 9, 1643; P17.
205. Gumble: Life of Monck: Pp17/18.
206. CSPV Vol. 27 P64.

207. Edwards P205/6.
208. Ibid. P177.
209. Ibid. P208.
210. Ormond VI P118.
211. Cavaliers and Roundheads P163.
212. Add. Ms 18981 f32.
213. Ibid. ff99-102.
214. Ormond VI P87.
215. Warburton II pp416-419; Worcester June 8, 1644.
216. Ibid. P417.
217. PRO SP/16/502 No. 16.
218. Ormond VI P87.
219. V&A Forster Collection; Warburton Vol. II pp437-9.
220. Clarendon's History III P378.
221. Add. Ms 18981 ff 203-5.
222. Ibid. ff208-9.
223. Warwick Memoirs P279.
224. Ibid. P272.
225. HMC I pp5/6.
226. Add. Ms 5460 f375.
227. Royalist Ordinance Papers P84.
228. Clarendon History VIII P96.
229. Ormond VI: P190.
230. Ibid.
231. Add Ms 18981 f218.
232. Carte Ms 12 ff427-8; October 3, 1644.
233. Royal Ordinance Papers P84.
234. Add. Ms 18981 f264.
235. The King's War P360.
236. Ormond VI P199; September 13, 1644.
237. Ibid.
238. Gardiner Vol. II P38.
239. Ormond III P325.
240. Warburton III P28; Rupert to Legge from Bristol, Oct. 16, 1644.
241. Add Ms 18981 f297.
242. Ibid ff303-4.
243. Firth Ms C7 f217.
244. J.S.Clarke: The Life of James II, pp24-5.

245. Ormond III P77; March 29, 1644.
246. Ibid. P119.
247. Ibid. P164; Ormond to George July 17, 1644.
248. Ormond VI P194; Aug. 13, 1644.
249. The King's War P317.
250. Gardiner P158.
251. The King's War P317/8.
252. Ibid.
253. Ormond VI P41.
254. Ormond V P529.
255. Ormond VI P77.
256. Ibid. P39.
257. Clarendon Life I P217.
258. Add. Ms 546I: Sabran's Despatches.
259. The Lord Digbies Designe to Betray Abingdon TT E268 (7).
260. Ibid.
261. Ormond VI P262; letter dated March 4, 1645 from Oxford.
262. Clarendon Life I P217.
263. Ibid P182.
264. Ibid. P217.
265. TT E329 (15).
266. The King's War P409.
267. Clarendon's History II P831.
268. Quoted in Gardiner Vol. 2 P184.
269. Carte Original Letters I P90.
270. The King's War P436.
271. Ormond VI P287.
272. Mr Secretary Nicholas P209: Nicholas to the king.
273. The King's War P442.
274. HMC Portland Mss 1 pp224-225.
275. Carloa Oman: Henrietta Maria P95.
276. Clarendon Life I P220.
277. Ibid. P217.
278. Gardiner Vol. 2 P231.
279. Ibid. P232.
280. CSPD 1644-5 P521.
281. Walker Historical Discourses P129.
282. Clarendon Life I P269.
283. Ormond VI pp301-2; June 19, 1645.

284. Warburton III P125; letter to Legge dated June 30.
285. Royal Ordinance Papers
286. CSPD 1645-7 P12.
287. Warburton III pp142-4.
288. Richard Symonds's Diary of the Marches of the Royal Army.
289. Clarendon History IX P68.
290. Add Ms 33596 f9.
291. Warburton III P161.
292. Add Ms 33596 f10.
293. Warburton III P165.
294. Lord Digby's Cabinet Opened: George Digby to Jermyn from Ascot, August 7.
295. Ibid.
296. CSPD 1645-7; P39 Aug. 1, 1645.
297. Clarendon History IX P72.
298. CSPV Vol. 27 P220.
299. Gardiner Vol. 2 P291.
300. Leeds University: Letter to Jermyn August 7, 1645; Sherborne letters P52.
301. CSPD 1645-7 pp58/9, 72/3.
302. Warburton III P170-2.
303. CSPD 1645; Sept 16, 1645.
304. Gardiner Vol. 2 P303.
305. Warburton Vol. III P156.
306. Clarendon Life P257.
307. Clarendon History X P90.
308. CSPD 1645-7 pp111-112.
309. Ibid. P121.
310. Egerton Ms 2533 ff339-400.
311. CSPD 1645-7 P141.
312. Clarendon History IX P90.
313. The Diplomatic Correspondence of Jean de Montreuil, Scottish Historical Society 1898-91 P10.
314. Add Ms 33596 P17.
315. HMC Report VIII Appendix P212b.
316. Gardiner Vol. 2 P342.
317. Ibid. P347.
318. Ibid. P345.

319. Rushworth IV P130; and Digby's Cabinet Opened P52, Aug. 27, 1645.
320. TT W298 (31).
321. Ormond VI P219.
322. Ibid. P301.
323. Sumner P374.
324. Clarendon State Papers II P199.
325. The Bloody Treatie; TT E311; Symond's Diary in Townshend P85.
326. A Great Victory obtained by General Poyntz and Col. Copley; TT E305 (14).
327. Cabinet Opened TTE329 (15).
328. Rushworth IV Vol. 1 P130.
329. CSPD 1645-7 P12; July 10, 1645 from Raglan.
330. Gardiner II P371.
331. Charles 1 in 1646; ed. J. Bruce, Camden Society 1855 P52.
332. Harleian Mss 6988 f121; Charles to Glamorgan April 6, 1646.
333. The King's War P282.
334. Clarendon SP III Suppl. Lvii.
335. Ibid.
336. Townshend P112.
337. Letters of King Charles I P160; January 30, 1646.
338. Ibid; October 20, 1645.
339. Rushworth IV Vol. 1 P241.
340. Gardiner Vol. III P47.
341. Ibid. P48.
342. CSPD January 1646.
343. Clarendon SP II P199.
344. TT E329.
345. Townshend P118.
346. H.M.Digby P237.
347. Townshend P122.
348. Ormond VI P371.
349. TT E329 (12).
350. The King's War P564/5.
351. Clarendon SP III Suppl. Lvii
352. Clarendon History X P13.
353. Clarendon SP III Suppl. Lviii.

354. Ormond VI P394.
355. Clarendon SP II pp230, 239.
356. Ormond VI P394; Letter to Ormond, June 17.
357. Townshend P127.
358. Gardiner III P13.
359. Ollard P126.
360. M.A.E.Green: Letters of Henrietta Maria P326.
361. Charles Carlton: Charles I: The Personal Monarch P206.
362. Letters of King Charles P175; March 22, 1646.
363. Clarendon SP II P330.
364. Clarendon Life Vol. I P197.
365. Ibid.
366. Ormond VI P530.
367. Townshend P148.
368. Ibid. P149.
369. Clarendon SP2626; October 17, 1647.
370. Townshend P150.
371. Clarendon SP2470.
372. HMC Vol. 4.
373. Morrah P218.
374. Carte: A Selection of Original Letters and Papers Vol. I P153.
375. Morrah P220.
376. Carte Letters P155.
377. Kitson: Prince Rupert: P33.
378. Carte Letters P158.
379. Roy P89; Carte Letters P158.
380. Clarendon SP III f71/2.
381. Ibid. P84.
382. Townshend P155.
383. Trevelyan P286.
384. Clarendon State Papers III: Suppl. Lxi.
385. Ibid.
386. Nicholas Papers Vol. I P92.
387. Clarendon History XII P60.
388. Clarendon SP II P5.
389. Townshend P156.
390. Nicholas Papers P130.
391. Clarendon SP III P174.
392. Mercurius Politicus No. "8.

393. Digby Papers: Sherborne, Vol. 2 f9.
394. HMC Bath ii P106: Letter from Sir George Radcliffe to Colonel Holles at Bologne on August 23, 1652.
395. Clarendon SP II P127.
396. Clarendon SP III Suppl. Lxiv.
397. Townshend P158.
398. Clarendon SP III P173.
399. Nicholas Papers P230.
400. Clarendon SP III Suppl. Lxiii
401. Clarendon History Vol.XIV P96.
402. Sherborne Papers Vol. 2 f56.
403. Mercurius Politicus No. 157 P2510.
404. Digby Transcripts P649.
405. Ibid. P669.
406. Ibid. P705.
407. Ibid. P805.
408. Thurloe State Papers Vol. II P646.
409. Digby Transcripts P805.
410. Ibid. P849.
411. Clarendon History Vol. VI P48.
412. Clarendon SP III P194.
413. Ibid. P200.
414. Clarendon Ms 53 f38.
415. Clarendon Mss Vol. 1 part iii f35; letter from George to Hyde Nov. 18, 1656. Also Clarendon SP III P200.
416. Travels of the King: Eva Scott; P292.
417. Eva Scott P292.
418. Townshend P167/8.
419. Eva Scott P292.
420. Charles II P324.
421. Eva Scott P281.
422. Clarendon SP III P321/2.
423. Ibid. P359; George to Ormond.
424. Ibid. P320; George to Hyde, Jan. 14, 1658.
425. Ibid. P321.
426. Ibid. P401/2; George to Hyde Apr. 26, 1658.
427. CSPD Interregnum Vol. 180; HMC Fox to Nicholas March 24, 1658 P340.
428. Clarendon SP III Suppl. Lxix.

429. Ibid. Lxx.
430. Ibid.
431. Ormond III P690.
432. Clarendon SP III Suppl. Lxxi.
433. Ibid IV P96.
434. Ibid. P105.
435. Bryant P65.
436. The Restoration: Hutton P59.
437. CSPD 1659-60 P59.
438. Clarendon SP III P594; Hyde to Ormond Nov. 1, 1659.
439. Charles II P352/3.
440. Ormond III P689.
441. CSPV Vol. 32 P212.
442. Clarendon Mss 120.
443. R.A., 68, IV.v.
444. Quoted in Bryant P67/8.
445. Clarendon P168.
446. Hutton P91.
447. Clarendon SP IV P614.
448. Ibid. P627.
449. Ibid. P643.
450. Ibid. P648.
451. Ibid. P680.
452. Clarendon Life II P5.
453. Clarendon SP IV P680.
454. Whitelocke Diary P613.
455. Barbour P50.
456. Quoted in Townshend P211.
457. CSPD Sept 1660.
458. VCH Herts 3, P449 citing CSPD 1660/1, pp289, 523; CSPD 1663/4 P502.
459. HMC 8th Report Appendix 1, P219a.
460. Dorset Record Office Digby papers Vol. II f193; Letter to John Digby January 17, 1661.
461. Clarendon Life Vol. II P395.
462. Sherborne folio 209.
463. Ibid. folio 203.
464. Ibid.
465. Townshend P217.

466. Ibid.
467. Clarendon Life Vol. II P149.
468. Ibid. P161.
469. Ibid.
470. CSPV Vol. 29 P293; May 20, 1661.
471. Clarendon SP V P97.
472. HMC Finch P120: Anthony Isaacson to the Earl of Winchilsea, May 19, 1661.
473. Evelyn Diaries Vol. I P363.
474. Clarendon State Papers III Appendix xxi.
475. Townshend P216.
476. HMC Vol. 7(1) in the PRO: Kenelm to George August 7, 1662.
477. Hutton P191.
478. Clarendon Life Vol. II P263/4.
479. CSPV Vol. 32 P282.
480. Hutton P197.
481. Barbour P60.
482. Hutton P202.
483. Sherborne folio 236.
484. Parliamentary History IV; Cobbett P278.
485. Clarendon and his Friends P226.
486. CSPV Vol. 29 P259.
487. Clarendon's Life Vol. II P397.
488. Ibid. P396..
489. The Later Stuarts: Clark P71.
490. CSPV Vol. 34 P2.
491. Pepys P354; Feb. 22 1664.
492. Ibid.
493. County and Court P158.
494. HMC Finch P274: Sir William Morice to the Earl of Winchilsea.
495. Clarendon Life Vol. II P400.
496. Carte Mss V pp36, 290.
497. CSPV Vol.33 P283.
498. HMC Ormond III P141.
499. Clarendon SP V P382.
500. Ibid.
501. Ibid. P383.

502. Verney Manuscripts: W. Denton to Sir Ralph Verney October 20, 1670 P488.
503. CSPD 1663-4; September 21, 1663; P264.
504. Ibid. P263.
505. Ibid. P264.
506. Lawrence Stone: Crisis of the Aristocracy P58.
507. Sacharissa by Ady P175.
508. Evelyn's Diary Vol. 1 P519.
509. Sherborne folio 296.
510. Clare Jarrold: The Fair Ladies of Hampton Court Pp163/4: Athenaeum II : Wood P826.
511. Quoted in Townshend P237.
512. Clarendon SP III Suppl. Lxxiii.
513. Sherborne folio 184: "A Narrative of the Kings and the Earl of Bristols Adventure with the beautiful Nunn of Hiscea of the Pyrenees."

INDEX.

A

Acton, Sir William 31
Alonsi, Don 222
Antrim, Lord; Randall McDonnell 145
Arlington, Earl of; Henry Bennet 290
Arundel, Lord; Earl Marshal of England 21
Ashburnham, Colonel William 85
Astley, Sir Jacob 98, 125
Aston, Sir Arthur 99, 104

B

Balfour, Sir William 64, 99
Bamfield, Colonel Joseph 227
Bath, Earl of 57
Bedford, Duke of; John Russell 17, 18, 232, 247
Bellasis, Lord John 155
Bennet, Henry 228, 229, 261, 266, 290
Berkeley, Charles 228
Berkeley, Sir John 227
Birkenhead, John 106
Bond, Maximilian 64
Booth, Sir George 237, 238
Boucher, George 108

Brereton, Sir William 192
Bridgeman, Orlando 51
Brooke, Sir Basil 119
Brown, Sir John 180
Browne, Major-General Sir Richard 126
Butler, James; Earl of Ormond 122
Byron, Sir John 66, 72

C

Calderon, Maria 223
Cambiac, Abbé 216
Campbell, Archibald; Earl of Argyll 21
Capell, Sir Arthur 139
Carlisle, Lady 68
Carr, Robert; Earl of Somerset 10
Carteret, Sir Philip 197
Cavendish, Lady Arabella 273
Charles I x, 211, 237, 252, 253, 254, 277, 280, 281, 289, 290, 291, 292, 294, 297, 299, 303, 304
Charles II ix, 122, 249, 290, 293, 305, 306, 319
Christian IV, King of Denmark 83

Churchill, Lady Anne 273
Clanricarde, Earl of 200
Clare, Earl of; John Holles 111, 291, 308
Clarendon, Earl of; Edward Hyde ix, 279
Cockram, Colonel 84
Con, George, Papal Nuncio 41
Condé, Prince of 196, 210, 216, 232
Conway, Viscount Edward 28, 29, 192
Cooper, Anthony Ashley 260
Copley, Colonel 178
Cork, Earl of 143
Cornwallis, Sir Frederick 205
Cottington, Lord Francis 30, 116, 208
Crofts, Will 16
Cromwell, Oliver 61, 212, 220, 254
Cromwell, Richard 245
Culpeper, John 32, 128, 135

D

Denby, Earl of: Basil Feilding 84
Denham, Sir John 274
Derby, Lord and Lady 181
Deveruex, Robert; Earl of Essex 52, 56, 67, 68, 82, 95, 97, 135
De Braganza, Catherine 255, 256
De Montmorency, Isabelle-Angelique 216
De Ruyter, Admiral Michael 275
De Witt, Admiral 275
Digby, Anne; Countess of Sutherland 234
Digby, Anne; Duchess of Bristol 92, 204, 247
Digby, Beatrix (nee Dyve) 3
Digby, Diana, Baroness Moll 217, 232, 233, 253, 271
Digby, Everard 2, 4
Digby, Everard, Sheriff of Rutland 2
Digby, Francis 34, 208, 232, 253, 271, 273, 278
Digby, George: son of Kenelm Digby 4, 18, 23, 32, 91, 185, 186, 204, 257, 258, 291
Digby, John, brother of George 1, 2, 5, 6, 10, 14, 91, 206, 306
Digby, John, First Earl of Bristol 5, 201
Digby, Kenelm 4, 18, 23, 32, 91, 185, 186, 204, 257, 258, 291
Digby, Sir George of Coleshill 2

Dorset, Earl of; Edward
    Sackville 10, 63
Dunsmore, Lord 57
Dyve, Lewis 3, 11, 16, 55,
    75, 77, 84, 96, 139,
    166, 214, 217, 218,
    221, 222
Dyve, Sir John 3

E

Earle, Sir Walter 25, 34
Elector Palatine, Charles
    Louis 6, 71, 77, 83,
    84, 138, 141, 165,
    169
Elector Palatine, Frederick
    V 77
Elizabeth, Queen 2, 10
Elizabeth Stuart 1, 2, 10,
    77, 83, 96, 101, 255
Elliot, Thomas 79
Essex, Charles 92
Essex, Earl of: Robert Devereux 52, 56, 67, 68,
    82, 95, 97, 135
Evelyn, John 252, 272, 296
Eythin, Lord; James King
    129

F

Fairfax, Lord Ferdinando
    82, 89
Fairfax, Thomas 231
Falkland, Viscount; Lucius
    Cary 19

Fanshawe, Sir Richard 250
Farrel, Colonel 226
Fawkes, Guy 1
Felton, John 14
Fleetwood, Charles 167
Forth, Lord; Patrick Ruthven
    125, 126, 138
Fowke, John 69

G

Gage, Sir Henry 147
Gardiner, Thomas 31
Gassion, Field-Marshal 205
Gerard, Sir Charles 176,
    205
Glamorgan, Earl of, Edward
    Somerset 85
Goffe, Dr Stephen 179
Goring, Colonel George 81,
    91, 127, 128, 131,
    136, 137, 139, 149,
    152, 153, 154, 155,
    159, 160, 166, 167,
    168, 171, 227, 281
Grenville, Sir John 248
Grenville, Sir Richard 137

H

Hampden, John 72
Harcourt, Comte de 115
Harrington, Lord 1
Haselrig, Sir Arthur 47
Henningham, Abigail 2
Henrietta Maria 14, 15, 23,
    41, 55, 78, 83, 94,

115, 159, 194, 196, 198, 207, 210, 211, 214, 215, 227, 228, 237, 249, 251, 252, 256, 289, 291, 292, 301, 304
Henrietta Stuart 14, 15, 23, 41, 55, 78, 83, 94, 115, 133, 159, 194, 196, 198, 207, 208, 210, 211, 214, 215, 227, 228, 237, 241, 249, 251, 252, 256, 289, 291, 292, 301, 304
Henry, Prince of Wales 2
Henry IV of France 14
Henry Stuart 1, 2, 3, 10, 14, 21, 45, 49, 78, 94, 99, 101, 114, 133, 139, 144, 147, 172, 196, 228, 229, 254, 261, 266, 290
Herbert, Edward 69
Hertford, Earl of 29, 91, 92
Heselrigge, Sir Arthur 69
Heylyn, Peter 12
Holborne, Robert 51
Holles, Denzil 92, 93, 102
Holt, Sir Thomas 97
Hopton, Sir Ralph 61, 91
Hotham, John 65, 83
Hotham, Sir John 83
Hudson, Michael 182
Hungerford, Sir Edward 104
Hyde, Anne; Duchess of York 272
Hyde, Edward, Earl of Clarendon ix, 12, 32, 55, 85, 143, 152, 162, 175, 187, 190, 197, 209, 212, 279

I

Inchiquin, Earl of; Murrough C'Brein 146, 190
Infanta Anna of Spain 2, 3
Innocent X, Pope 185
Ireton, Henry 254

J

James, Duke of York 227, 250, 273, 277
James Graham, 5th Earl and Montrose 28
James I 2
Jermyn, Henry 94, 114, 133, 172, 196
Jones, Lieutenant-General 201
Juan, Don 223, 224, 225, 226, 228, 236, 240, 242, 243

K

Knatchbull, Abbess Mary 234, 243

L

Lambert, General 237, 245, 246, 252
Lane, George 225
Langdale, Sir Marmaduke 151, 172
Laud, William 12, 20
Legge, Colonel William 164
Leicester, Earl of; Robert Sidney 58
Lennox, Duke of 58
Lenthall, William 31
Leslie, Alexander; Lord Leven 21, 28
Leven, Lord; Alexander Leslie 124, 163, 171
Lichfield, Earl of 109, 153, 157, 160, 174, 192
Lindsey, Earl of 88, 89, 94, 98
Lockhart 240
Lord D'Aubigny 101
Lord Grandison 105
Lorraine, Duke of 161, 179
Louis XIII, King of France 115
Louis XIV, King of France 206, 207, 255
Lucius Cary, Viscount Falkland 32
Luis, Don 239, 240, 241, 242, 243, 244
Lunsford, Colonel Thomas 64

M

Mainwaring, Randall 64, 69
Manchester, Earl of; Edward Montague 69, 121, 125, 129, 139, 140
Mancini, Hortense 241
Mandeville, Viscount, Lord Kimbolton 68
Margaret, Russell 274
Marlborough, Duke of 273
Massey, Colonel Edward 150
Matthew, Toby 43
Maurice, Prince 84, 85, 95, 96, 114, 131, 150, 174, 290
Mazarin, Cardinal 161, 194, 206, 207, 214, 215, 240
McDonnell, Randall; Lord Antrim 145
Meldrum, Sir John 88, 123
Moll, Baron 233
Monck, Colonel George 122, 245, 246, 247, 248, 251, 254, 291, 299
Montague, Wat 23
Montreuil, Jean de 302
Morland, Samuel 237
Moseley, Lieutenant-Colonel 119
Muskerry, Lord 191

N

Nicholas, Edward 57, 211, 212, 261, 266
Northampton, Earl of 5

O

O'Neill, Daniel 137, 145, 204, 239
O'Neill, Owen 199
O'Neill, Owen Roe 145, 190
O'Neill, Philem 60
Ogle, Thomas 119
Orange, William, Prince of 77, 78, 79, 159, 178, 179, 213
Ormond, Earl of; James Butler 122
Overbury, Thomas 10

P

Packer, Major William 251
Palmer, Barbara, Countess Castlemaine 257, 258
Parma, Princess of 256, 257
Pellam, John 75
Pembroke, Earl of; Philip Herbert 82, 101
Pennington, Isaac 38, 71
Pennington, Sir John 74, 77
Percy, Harry 118, 121, 135
Philip II of Spain 3
Philip IV, King of Spain 223
Pickering, Colonel John 166
Pollard, Hugh 85
Poole, Sir Neville 104
Portland, Earl of; Jerome Weston 146, 164, 166, 288, 301
Poyntz, General Sydenham 162
Preston, Thomas 191, 200
Pym, John 26, 38, 45

R

Rich, Henry, First Earl of Holland 21
Richelieu, Cardinal 43
Richmond, Duke of 58, 95, 121, 148, 160
Riley, Thomas 119
Rinuccini, Archbishop Giovanni 184
Robartes, Lord 260, 262
Rogers, Richard 25
Rossiter, Colonel 154, 168
Rupert, Prince x, 77, 94, 97, 107, 126, 128, 131, 137, 141, 155, 158, 159, 160, 162, 164, 165, 167–169, 170, 171, 174, 176, 177, 205, 206, 250, 279, 291, 292, 298, 304
Russell, Edward 274
Russell, Lady Anne 17
Russell, Lord William 17, 34
Russell, Penelope 274

Ruthven, Patrick; Lord Forth 95, 126, 138

S

Sabran, Marquis de 133
Saye and Sele, Lord 100, 120
Schomberg, General 225
Selden, John 51
Seymour, Lord 57
Shaftesbury, Lord 167, 278
Sheldon, Archbishop 260
Skippon, General Philip 74
Slingsby, Sir Henry 247
Somerset, Edward, Earl of Glamorgan 85
Southampton, Earl of; Thomas Wriothesley 148
Spencer, Charles 273
Spencer, Robert; Earl of Sutherland 272, 273
Stapleton, Sir Philip 74
Stradling, Sir Edward 86
Strangeways, Sir John 11, 63
Strode, William 69
Sutherland, Earl of; Robert Spencer 234
Sydney, Sir Phillip 169

T

Taafe, Viscount Theobald 203
Talbot, Father 230
Temple, Sir Richard 263
Tradescant, John 252
Trevor, Arthur 118, 126, 150
Tromp, Maerten 108
Tuam, Archbishop of 186
Turenne, Marshal Henri 213, 227, 229

V

Vane, Henry 45, 49, 139
Vane, Sir Harry 46
Venn, Captain 63
Verney, Sir Edmund 101, 289, 295, 308
Villiers, George, Duke of Buckingham 5, 208, 277

W

Walcot, Charles 3
Waller, Edmund 101, 146
Walsingham, Edward 164, 179, 190
Warwick, Earl of 29
Wentworth, Thomas, Earl of Strafford 23
Weston, Thomas 116
Whitelocke, Bulstrode 46, 295
Williams, Archbishop John 66
Willis, Sir Richard 176, 237
Wilmot, Lord Henry 99
Windebank, Francis 34

Wintour, John 43
Wollaston, Sir John 119
Wright, Edmund 31

Y

Yeamans, Richard 108

About The Author.

Roy Digby Thomas is an indirect descendant of George Digby, and author of Digby: The Gunpowder Plotter's Legacy, a biography of George Digby's cousin, Kenelm.

He spent four years researching this book, and has uncovered fresh information about George Digby. This has enabled him to reappraise the life of this famous statesman, and set the record straight. He also throws new light on the important part played by George's wife, Anne, in the restoration of King Charles II.

Printed in the United Kingdom
by Lightning Source UK Ltd.
108892UKS00001B/30